P9-DMY-100

Collective Action and
the Civil Rights Movement

AMERICAN POLITICS AND POLITICAL ECONOMY SERIES
Edited by Benjamin I. Page

Dennis Chong

Collective Action and the Civil Rights Movement

The University of Chicago Press
Chicago and London

The University of Chicago Press, Chicago 60637
The University of Chicago Press, Ltd., London
© 1991 by The University of Chicago
All rights reserved. Published 1991
Printed in the United States of America
09 08 07 06 05 04 03 02 01 00   4 5 6 7 8

Library of Congress Cataloging in Publications Data
Chong, Dennis.
    Collective action and the civil rights movement / Dennis Chong.
        p.   cm. —(American politics and political economy series)
    Includes bibliographical references and index.
    ISBN 0-226-10440-0 (alk. paper). —ISBN 0-226-10441-9 (pbk.)
    1. Public goods.   2. Social choice.   3. Civil rights movements—
United States.   I. Title.   II. Series: American politics and political
economy.
HB846.5.C48   1991
323.1'196073—dc20   90-48848
                                                                    CIP

⊗ The paper used in this publication meets the minimum requirements
of the American National Standard for Information Sciences—Perma-
nence of Paper for Printed Library Materials, ANSI Z39.48–1992.

For M & G, J & B

Contents

Figures

Acknowledgments

There is a famous paradox of Zeno's in which Achilles races a tortoise. Since the tortoise is much slower than Achilles, it is given a big lead at the start of the race. Achilles tries to make up this handicap once the race begins, but in the time that it takes him to cover the initial distance separating them, the tortoise is able to crawl ahead to keep its lead. Alas, though the tortoise is slow, every time that Achilles catches up to where it used to be, it manages in the meantime to move beyond his reach. It seems that Achilles can never catch the tortoise.

I have felt occasionally that writing a book is a bit like being trapped in Zeno's paradox. Through countless drafts and revisions, one inches towards the elusive goal of finishing. But it seems that the completion of one task merely leads to another, and that the end is always somewhere on the horizon. In the meantime, family and friends grow increasingly skeptical about this supposedly forthcoming book.

Fortunately, there is an end to the process just as there is a limit to how long the tortoise can maintain its lead over Achilles. And just as Achilles eventually overtakes the tortoise, authors ultimately complete their books.

My completion of this book, however, has benefited from the assistance of a number of people. I want to thank Herbert McClosky in particular for supporting the project from beginning to end. He shared his research resources with me and gave me invaluable advice throughout the period in which I wrote this book. It is my hope that some of his high standards of research and writing have rubbed off on me. More important, I want to thank him for the generosity and kindness he showed me throughout my years at the University of California in Berkeley. He has been a teacher, a colleague, and a friend to me, and I have profited greatly from our relationship.

I also wish to thank Christopher Achen, Carol Cantor, Jay Casper, Jack Citrin, Marissa Martino Golden, Russell Hardin, Herbert Jacob, Jim Johnson, Jenny Mansbridge, Benjamin Page, Greg Pollock, Neil Smelser, and Michael Taylor for reading part or all of the manuscript in its various stages and offering both important suggestions and encouragement for the enterprise. I owe a special debt to Barry Preisler for enduring countless hours of conversation during which I tried out new ideas on him; his reactions to these trial balloons were invariably on the mark.

I want to thank my colleagues at Northwestern University for providing me with an extremely hospitable environment in which to complete the book. The Department of Political Science and the University provided grants in the late stages of research and writing; in this regard, I would like to thank especially Jay Casper, Jerry Goldman, and Benjamin Page. I also wish to thank Samantha Luks for providing very capable research assistance at Northwestern.

I greatly appreciate the care with which the University of Chicago Press, and especially editor John Tryneski, has supported this project.

Jacob Lawrence and the Seattle Art Museum generously granted permission to use his drawing *Struggle No. 2* on the cover of the book.

Lastly I am grateful to Terri Garland for giving me support of a more general kind.

Dennis Chong

Evanston, Illinois
November 1990

1 | Public-Spirited Collective Action

*Well, in a way everyone's self interested, aren't they? But you must
admit there are degrees of it.*

Kingsley Amis, *Lucky Jim*

This is a study of the dynamics of public-spirited collective action.
By "public-spirited collective action" I am referring to large-scale political activism that is motivated by such public concerns as the environment, peace, civil rights, women's rights, and other moral and
ideological issues. I will address two major questions: (1) how do "rational" individuals decide whether or not to participate in such social
movements? and (2) how do these individual decisions translate into
collective outcomes? In short, what is the relationship between—to use
Thomas Schelling's (1978) phrase—"micromotives and macrobehavior"?

Although I will develop a general model of collective action, most
of the examples I will cite to illustrate my study are drawn from the
postwar civil rights movement in the United States. The modern civil
rights movement is probably the quintessential example of public-
spirited collective action in our time. Not only did it spark radical
changes in American society, it also served in subsequent years as the
inspiration and model for a host of new public concerns. The student
movement, the peace movement, the women's movement, the homosexual rights movement, and other social movements are all to a significant extent riding on the coattails of the civil rights movement.
Moreover, from the standpoint of research, the civil rights movement
constitutes an excellent case to use in the testing of hypotheses about
collective action because it has been so thoroughly documented. Detailed histories have been written, as well as memoirs and biographies;
consequently, we are confident about the facts of this case, a claim that
cannot always be made about other episodes of political activism.

The major premise in this study is that people are rational actors
whose decisions are guided by rational calculations. A rational person
is assumed to be driven by the pursuit of goals. In and of itself, this

assumption would not provide us with any leverage to account for individual behavior, since with no great difficulty we could infer the presence of *some* goal orientation in *every* action. What gives the rationality premise some explanatory power is the corollary assumption that only goals that are private in nature have any intrinsic value to an individual. Only private goals, in other words, are pursued for their own sake.[1]

Private goals are differentiated from socially defined goals in that the former do not require the consideration of other individuals for their contemplation and enjoyment. On the other hand, socially defined goals such as fame, honor, and power derive their meaning and value only in the context of a social collectivity, since notoriety and esteem necessitate the adulation or respect of an audience, and power requires that there be subjects to be persuaded, influenced, ruled over, · or dominated. Fame, honor, power, and other socially defined goals cannot be contemplated without reference to more than a single individual.

Socially defined goals, under the assumptions of the rational choice model, have value only to the extent that they are instrumentally valuable for the attainment of intrinsic goals. In other words, a rational individual never seeks socially defined goals for their own sake but only insofar as they can be used as stepping-stones to private goals.

At first glance, it would seem to follow straightforwardly why a rational individual would participate in a movement. If he valued the goal of the movement more than the cost of his participation, then it would be in his interest to become involved. On the other hand, if the cost of participation was excessive, he would refrain.

But this simple interest-based explanation turns out to be flawed for two reasons. First, it misconceives the nature of the goods that are sought by participants in social movements; and second, it misunderstands how these goods must be produced.

Goals such as civil rights, women's rights, peace, and the like are public rather than private goods. As public goods, they are distinguished by three qualities: (1) they are "jointly supplied"; (2) noncontributors to the production of these goods cannot be excluded from their benefits; and (3) the benefits from these goods are not susceptible to "crowding."

---

1. See Laver (1981), Elster (1986, 1989), and Taylor (1988) for excellent discussions of the assumptions underlying rational choice theory.

Consider each of these features in turn. First, private and public goods vary in the extent to which their benefits can be partitioned and shared equally among members of a group. Pure public goods are jointly supplied, meaning that whenever the good is produced, all members of a group benefiting from its production do so to an equal degree. In contrast, the benefits of a pure private good can be divided up in any number of ways among the beneficiaries. Every member of the group can receive an equal share; one person can monopolize the entire good; or any intermediate outcome can be instituted. The proverbial pie, for instance, is a private good; it can be cut into any number of equal or unequal slices and distributed, or it can be given whole to one person. On the other hand, the public goods that were pursued over the course of the civil rights movement were close to being pure public goods in this respect. The removal of Jim Crow barriers, the passage of national legislation expanding the rights of blacks, the curtailment of racial prejudice, and other goals achieved by the civil rights movement are all public goods that bring similar benefits to all blacks.

A second difference between private and public goods is the extent to which noncontributors to the production of these goods can be excluded from receiving any benefits. In the case of private goods, noncontributors can be barred entirely from consuming the good. The pie has to be bought from the market before it can be eaten; those who do not pay the price of the private good are denied access to it. Noncontributors to public goods, on the other hand, nonetheless cannot be restricted from consuming them. Whether or not a person participated in the civil rights movement had no bearing on whether he would reap the benefits generated by those who did. The social and legislative changes produced by the movement, in other words, are not enjoyed exclusively by those who made the effort but by all those sympathetic to the cause, including those who did not participate.

A third contrast between private and public goods is the extent to which each is susceptible to crowding. When a person consumes a private good, he uses up the utility or benefit available from that good as he consumes it. His enjoyment of the good "crowds out" the potential enjoyment that others would receive from it. Once the pie is eaten, the benefits of the pie are no longer available to others. Public goods are different. In the pure case, the benefits of a public good are not susceptible to crowding. My use of a public good does not subtract from your enjoyment of it. The accomplishments of the civil rights movement, for example, are not susceptible to crowding. One person's enjoyment of the right to vote, the right to attend desegregated schools, and the right to equal access to public accommodations does not detract from another person's enjoyment of the same freedoms.

Civil rights, women's rights, peace, and other collective goals, moreover, are public goods that can be produced only if large numbers of people work to achieve them. This points to the second weakness in a simple interest-based explanation. Blacks, women, students, and antiwar protesters had to marshal their collective resources to make their demands felt in the political system. No individual could supply the public good for the benefit of the entire group, and, more importantly, no average contributor could significantly affect the likelihood that the public good would be produced; rather, a collective effort was necessary to obtain a group objective.

A COLLECTIVE ACTION PROBLEM

It turns out that rational individuals often will have difficulty producing public goods that depend upon collective contributions. Since these goods, if supplied, can be enjoyed equally by everyone, including those who have not contributed their share of the cost, there will be a strong temptation for everyone to let other people pay for them. Small groups sometimes have the ability to overcome this problem. When the group of individuals seeking a public good is sufficiently small that individual decisions to contribute or not contribute are contingent on the willingness of everyone else to contribute (I will contribute if everyone else does, but not otherwise) then each individual will have a determinant impact on whether the public good is produced. Each individual knows that if he refuses to contribute, everyone else will do likewise, and the good will not materialize. Under these circumstances, each individual in deciding whether to contribute only has to ascertain if the value of the public good to him exceeds his share of its cost; if it does, then it is economical for him to contribute.

For many public goods, however, the contribution or noncontribution of any single individual is irrelevant to whether the public good is provided. The question with these goods is not whether any individual contributes but whether enough people overall contribute. Any individual contribution will not make the difference in whether or not the good is generated. Rather, if enough people in the group contribute, the public good will be provided. On the other hand, if not enough members of the group contribute, then the public good will go wanting. From the standpoint of any individual, therefore, it is not what he does that counts; it is what the *other* members of the group do that will determine the outcome of the process.

In a national oil shortage, for instance, my decision to cut back on the use of my automobile will not prevent a national crisis from developing; such a crisis can be averted only if there is an adequate amount of conservation being practised by the rest of the population. Whether a serious fuel shortage will be averted depends on the behavior of other people and not my behavior alone.

Under these circumstances, what incentive do I have to act as a responsible citizen? My behavior does not matter, so why should I inconvenience myself? If everyone else works to conserve fuel in the public interest, then the crisis will be averted. But if everyone acts only for himself, there will surely be a crisis. Since in the first scenario there is no crisis, I should feel free to drive to my heart's content. In the second scenario there is a crisis, and any attempt I might make to prevent it would be wasted, for I alone cannot change anything; therefore I should still go ahead and drive to my heart's content.

The same logic applies to social movements that seek public goods. The goals sought by the civil rights movement required the wholesale participation of large numbers of concerned citizens. Any average activist could not have any significant impact on the outcome of the movement, yet he would be eligible to share in any of the benefits that resulted from its efforts. For any rational individual in these situations, the temptation will be to save on the cost of contributing to the public good. If others come through and produce the good, he will share in its benefits without having shared in its cost. If the other members of the group do not produce the good, then his single contribution would not have made any difference.

A collective action problem arises when individuals, acting out of pure self-interest, are unable to coordinate their efforts to produce and consume certain public goods they find desirable. Each individual, figuring that he can enjoy with impunity the fruits of the public good without contributing, tries to get a free ride on the efforts of others. Unfortunately, since everyone thinks alike, no public good is produced, and everyone is worse off than he would have been had each contributed his fair share and the public good been provided.

Collective Action as a Prisoner's Dilemma

The collective action problem, as I have characterized it above, can be simply recast in the game-theoretic terminology of a "prisoner's dilemma" game (Hardin 1971). (See figure 1.1.) Not all collective action problems in the provision of public goods, it should be noted, have the preference structure of a prisoner's dilemma. In general, a collective action problem arises whenever individuals arrive at strictly Pareto-inferior outcomes in the pursuit of their self-interest (Taylor 1987, 19). Depending on the case being studied, then, some collective action problems might be more accurately modeled by alternative games such as "chicken" or "assurance," two other staple games in the literature (see Taylor 1987; Taylor and Ward 1982; Hardin 1982; and Hampton 1987). Moreover, different types of collective action problems arising in the course of the same case may call for more than one game structure, or even hybrid game structures. Indeed, I will argue later that public-spirited collective action, when placed in the context of ongoing community interaction, is often transformed from a prisoner's dilemma into an assurance game.

In the original parable of the prisoner's dilemma, two apprehended suspects to a serious crime are detained incommunicado and faced with the following choice: each has been given the opportunity to turn state's witness for the purpose of convicting the other; if one prisoner agrees to confess while the other keeps silent, the confessor will get off scot-free while the other prisoner will be convicted and sentenced to ten years in prison. If neither prisoner confesses, both will escape prosecution for the serious crime, but will nevertheless be prosecuted and convicted for a minor crime that carries a one-year prison term. Finally—and herein lies the dilemma—if both prisoners elect to confess to the authorities, both will end up being convicted for the crime, although they will receive a slightly reduced sentence (e.g., five years) for having cooperated with the police.

Suspect 2

	Stay Mum	Confess
Stay Mum	1, 1	10, 0
Confess	0, 10	5, 5

Suspect 1

FIGURE 1.1. The Prisoner's Dilemma. The first entry in each cell is the payoff to the row player (i.e., suspect 1), while the second entry is the payoff to the column player (i.e., suspect 2) for that particular combination of choices. In this case, the payoffs are penalties (years in prison); therefore smaller numbers are preferred.

From the point of view of either prisoner, it turns out that it is better to confess to the police no matter what the other prisoner does. Each reasons that if the other confesses, he would be wise to confess as well, since under this contingency, a confession would amount to a five-year term, whereas holding out would result in a sentence twice as long. Moreover, it is still better for each to confess even if the other stays mum, since that will lead to freedom (i.e., the dropping of all charges) as opposed to a one-year stay in prison for keeping quiet.

Unfortunately, what is reasonable and desirable at the individual level turns out to be collectively disastrous; matched confessions by the prisoners reward them with identical five-year prison terms, a much worse outcome than if they had both refused to cooperate with the authorities.

Mutatis mutandis, political activists face the same collective action problem in contemplating whether or not to participate in a cause (see figure 1.2). Assume that each individual is engaged in a game against all other potential participants in the collective endeavor. Each individual is faced with the choice of either participating or not participating—i.e., cooperating (C) with the group or defecting (D) from it. Similarly, the rest of the group, taken as a whole, can choose either to participate or to abstain. If the rest of the group does not contribute, the public good will not be obtained, and the individual would be wise to conserve his resources. If, on the other hand, the rest of the group does contribute, the public good will be obtained *whether or not* the individual contributes, so he may as well refrain from contributing under this contingency also. Therefore no matter what the rest of the group decides to do, the individual should not contribute to collective action. But if every individual decides not to contribute, the public good goes unprovided, which is clearly suboptimal, since the lot of every person can be improved if all contribute.

In sum, when collective action is formulated as a prisoner's dilemma, it appears that plans to initiate mass political action are doomed from the start; rational individuals will prefer to be free riders rather than participants in collective efforts to obtain public goods.

Synopsis

The first half of this book explores various ways out of this collective action problem. I consider both "internal" solutions that do not involve changing the payoff structure of the prisoner's dilemma (PD) and "external" solutions that entail changes in individual preferences and expectations (Taylor 1987, 22). One solution, explored in chapter 2,

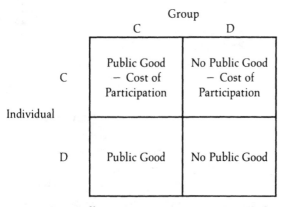

FIGURE 1.2. Collective Action as a Prisoner's Dilemma. Entries are payoffs to the individual.

builds on the principle that small groups are more likely to cooperate than large groups. As I suggested above, when the group is small, each member of the group may have a pivotal impact on whether or not the public good is produced. This would be the case, for example, if everyone decided to cooperate only if he could see that every other group member was cooperating. If the group operates with perfect information—everyone knows the nature of the collective good and the critical role that everyone plays in producing it—then every member will contribute with the confidence that the others will follow suit.

Small groups can turn collective action problems into such all-or-nothing situations because group members can monitor each other's decisions and make their own choices contingent. Cooperation in small groups may also be the product of social pressure. Large groups, on the other hand, will have more difficulty creating such artificial strictures to compel participation. For this reason, large groups are more likely to be victimized by the collective action problem than small groups.

Large groups of political activists nonetheless sometimes pursue goals that are of the all-or-nothing variety. I will show, for example, that there were occasions during the civil rights movement when the goal being sought required the support of virtually all activists or members of the black community in order to be sustained. In these instances, cooperation among group members was facilitated.

In chapter 3 I consider the material and social incentives that people receive for participating in collective action. These rewards constitute "selective incentives" that are distributed only to those who cooperate. People who would normally abstain might be enticed to participate by the value of these selective incentives. Material incentives, I argue, have only a minor role in stimulating public-spirited collective action. For this reason, I concentrate in this chapter on the social pressures to participate that arise in the normal course of affairs when group members interact on a regular basis.

When an individual is part of a community, his interactions with other group members are better modeled as an "iterated prisoner's dilemma" rather than as a prisoner's dilemma that is played only once. Individual calculations in an iterated game have been shown to contrast with decision making in the one-shot prisoner's dilemma. When the game has both a history and a future, cooperation in both small and large groups is possible under certain conditions. These conditions, however, become more stringent in principle and more difficult to satisfy in practice as the size of the group increases. I maintain that with respect to the types of public action I am studying, cooperation tends to be possible only if the incentives generated by the iterated game are supplemented by additional social incentives such as the desire to gain or sustain friendships, maintain one's social standing, and avoid ridicule and ostracism. These gains may outweigh any economic or material benefit that would result from being a free rider.

In particular, I argue that reputational concerns often underlie participation in public-spirited collective action. To refuse to contribute to a cause may cast doubt on one's character, reliability, and dependability. If a person fancies himself an advocate of such values as freedom, equality, peace, and justice, then active involvement in collective efforts aimed at furthering those ends is the most effective way to prove such convictions. Private declarations of one's dedication to these ideals are vacuous and hypocritical if they are not reinforced by appropriate action when the opportunity arises in the political arena. A person who does not live up to his reputation when the chips are down will reduce his credibility in all of his affairs.

A number of examples from the civil rights movement highlight the importance of reputational considerations in people's decisions to participate in various campaigns. I also emphasize, however, that such personal commitments were typically augmented by sincere concern, sympathy, and affection for others. Social interaction, I argue, promotes not only the development of mutual obligations and commitments but also the formation of other-regarding interests.

In chapter 4 I assess the expressive or participatory benefits behind political activism. These are psychological benefits (feelings of efficacy, empowerment, righteousness, etc.) that people derived from contributing to a group effort, taking part in a historic event, voicing concerns in a public forum, and striving for a noble cause. While political activism is a means to an end, it is also an exciting and uplifting experience in and of itself. This collateral aspect of collective action may be sufficient to repay the cost of participation and eliminate the temptation to free ride.

However, any resort to expressive or participatory benefits to solve the collective action problem has continually troubled analysts for two reasons. First, the concept of expressive benefits implies that participation is a noninstrumental activity. People participate because participation is intrinsically valuable. This is close to saying that people participate because they *want* to participate, which resolves nothing. It only raises the additional question: why do they want to participate? A rational choice explanation of an action cannot be based on the essential value of the act itself. Rather, an action must be accounted for by the results that it is expected to produce (Benn 1979, 298; Elster 1983).

Second, expressive benefits can be invoked arbitrarily to explain any outcome. There would seem to be no way to measure the worth of participation in the historical events of one's lifetime or the value of the experience of voicing one's political concerns. The danger, then, is that we can always rely on the strength of expressive benefits to explain collective action or, alternatively, their weakness to account for the failure to organize collective action. Therefore what was originally a vexing and difficult collective action problem gets "solved" in an ad hoc and trivial fashion.

With regard to the place of expressive benefits in rational choice theory, I am of two minds. While critics of the use of this concept have made cogent arguments, I still believe that expressive benefits are among the enticements of collective action and must be considered in any analysis of the collective action problem. How else to explain the enthusiasm of participants in public-spirited collective action? Therefore instead of abandoning the concept of expressive benefits, I suggest ways to specify its role and characteristics more carefully so that not too much collective action is predicted by the theory. Much that passes for expressive activity, I show, is actually socially instrumental in nature, valuable not for its own sake but because it serves other goals. Also, I argue that expressive activity frequently serves personal goals and in this regard cannot be distinguished from other narrowly rational behavior. Lastly, even expressive activity that is clearly noninstrumental tends to be pursued not unconditionally but only under restricted conditions.

In chapter 5 I elaborate on the circumstances under which these social and psychological incentives affect participation in collective action. Members of a group, I argue, are enthusiastic about contributing to collective action or are pressured to do so, only when such collective action has a realistic opportunity to achieve the desired public good. When collective action is widely regarded as futile, or as an ineffective symbolic protest at best, these social and psychological incentives vanish.

Therefore prior to the development of effective organizations and an ethos of protest, group members will see collective action as being unproductive—an empty, symbolic gesture that would not help the group and could well work to its detriment, especially if protest begets spiteful retribution from a more powerful opposition. On the other hand, there will be strong incentives for individuals to participate when collective action is carefully planned and executed and has the power to improve the lot of the group. Moral prescriptions will hold more sway over the individual, since there is now a reason to do one's duty; and psychological incentives to participate will also increase when one has the opportunity to be a member of a successful collective effort.

As I show in chapter 6, when social and psychological incentives are operative, they have the potential to transform the prisoner's dilemma facing prospective activists into a type of coordination problem known as an "assurance game." Whereas in the prisoner's dilemma each individual prefers free riding to participating, in the assurance game participation is preferred to inactivity *under the right condition*—the condition being that "enough others" also participate to make collective action successful. Assurance games still present many collective action problems to political activists, but they are of a different kind than those posed by the prisoner's dilemma.

In an assurance game, collective action may be frustrated because everyone wants to follow the lead of others. Until the movement becomes viable, the social pressures and incentives to participate remain latent. Therefore unless there are some leaders who are willing to pay the heavy start-up costs of collective action in the absence of these incentives, mass coordination will not occur. By thinking about collective action as an assurance game, we also gain a number of important insights into the dynamics of social movements. Bandwagon and contagion effects, in particular, are better understood within the framework of an assurance game than that of a prisoner's dilemma.

After discussing the calculations that an individual makes before electing to participate in collective action, I develop in the second part of the book a formal supply-and-demand model of how these individual choices translate into collective outcomes. For this part of the analysis, I move from game-theoretic models to a simple dynamic model using difference equations. In this model I explicitly incorporate the role that leadership, community, obligations, resilience, success, government responsiveness, and opposition play in efforts to mobilize a group. Although the model contains only a small number of parameters, it provides a general explanation for a number of previously diverse observations about collective action. In chapter 7 I introduce the model, enumerate a number of deductions from it regarding the dynamics of collective action, and use the model to analyze the origins of the civil rights movement. In chapter 8 I make several additional deductions from the model about the strategies that are likely to be employed by the government and by proponents and opponents of collective action.

In chapter 9 I discuss the reasons behind the collapse of collective action. Invariably, public-spirited collective action loses its momentum and winds down. Any explanation of this process must be consistent with explanations of the emergence of collective action. Again, I emphasize how individual calculations of the value of collective action change over time depending on the success or failure of such efforts. Both success and failure, I show, reduce the value of cooperation in the assurance game. The civil rights movement declined because it succeeded so well in accomplishing its immediate agenda.

A summary is provided in chapter 10.

2 | *All-Or-Nothing Public Goods*

All for one and one for all!
The Three Musketeers

In *The Logic of Collective Action,* Olson (1971, 43–65) suggested that small groups would more easily cooperate than large groups in supplying themselves with public goods. Large groups are more difficult and costly to organize. Individual decisions are less likely to have an impact on the outcome of collective action, and each member receives a smaller share of the total benefits of the collective good. Small groups, on the other hand, are more likely to be "privileged," that is, to contain one individual who benefits sufficiently from the provision of the collective good that he is willing to bear its entire cost. Decision making in small groups is also easier to coordinate and more likely to be interdependent and subject to monitoring. A defector can be identified and pressured to do his part by the rest of the group. Group members can more readily convey their intentions to each other and arrive at a mutually beneficial cooperative agreement.[1]

In general, the creation of interdependence among individual actors plays a critical role in favorably resolving the prisoner's dilemma for the group as a whole. In chapter 3 I discuss how regular social interaction creates interdependence and mutual obligations among group members so that each person makes decisions contingent on the decisions of others. In this chapter I will examine a special type of public good whose features ensure that group members will act on a contingent basis. After describing the characteristics of this public good, I will argue that certain campaigns during the civil rights movement, such as boycotts and nonviolent demonstrations, were facilitated by the pursuit of such goods.

This special kind of public good, known as an "all-or-nothing" good, requires unanimous support to be produced (Laver 1981). Since

---

1. See Hardin (1982, chap. 3) for a general discussion of the controversies surrounding the relationship between group size and collective action.

collective goods of this sort will be destroyed by a single defection, it is in the self-interest of each person to pay his share of the total cost: to opt for a free ride under the circumstances would make not only the others worse off but himself as well.

Such goods no longer present a prisoner's dilemma to the group; instead, as figure 2.1 illustrates, each individual is best served if he coordinates his actions with the actions of others. Moreover, between total defection and total cooperation, everyone prefers CC to DD, since the value of the public good exceeds anyone's share of its cost. More importantly, given the all-or-nothing characteristic of the public good, no one has an incentive to free ride. For these reasons, group members ought to be able to coordinate their actions to produce the best outcome.

All-or-nothing goods enjoy a property known as "pure jointness of production": they depend on the cooperation of everyone. Most of the public goods we are concerned about here do not have this all-or-nothing characteristic; typically, individual contributions not only are not pivotal, they have no discernible effect. Nevertheless, we should find that where pure jointness of production pertains, the public good will be more easily generated. Furthermore, collective action problems may sometimes be solved using measures that create pure jointness of production. Popkin (1988) points out, for example, that revolutionary entrepreneurs in Vietnam shrewdly reframed the objectives of the movement so that individual participation was critical. Successful leaders encouraged cooperation "by breaking up a large goal into many steps with critical thresholds. If a large goal can be broken into many small independent pieces, all of which are necessary to the larger goal, the free-rider problem can be overcome, for if each person has a mo-

		Group	
		C	D
Individual	C	Public Good − Cost	No Public Good − Cost
	D	No Public Good	No Public Good

FIGURE 2.1. The All-Or-Nothing Game. Entries are payoffs to the individual.

nopoly on a necessary factor for the final goal, all contributions are essential" (21).

It will not always be apparent to group members that they are pursuing an all-or-nothing good. For this reason, effective leadership and organization often will still be critical to the success of collective action, but the task of deterring free ridership will be eased in such cases. The successful production of certain public goods, therefore, will depend on whether or not people *think* the good must be jointly produced. How an audience member reacts to a cry of "fire" in a crowded theater, for example, will depend on the impact he believes he will have on the preservation of the collective good—public safety—which is at stake in that situation. A tragic outcome may actually be the unintended product of quite rational behavior by individuals who discount (or disregard) their personal influence on the behavior of others.

Psychologist Roger Brown (1965, 739–43) offers the following game-theoretic analysis of the audience's reaction. At the shout of "fire," each patron is faced with the choice of either proceeding calmly or running to the exit. If he chooses to walk calmly out of the theatre and the rest of the audience does likewise, there is a good chance that all will emerge safely. He can, however, improve upon his chance of surviving by running to the exit while everyone else walks, since it is possible that he will be engulfed by the flames even during an orderly evacuation. The worst outcome for him would be if everyone else in the audience raced to the exit while he took his time, since this would probably leave him either trampled or trapped in the theatre in the ensuing mayhem and confusion. Lastly, if he runs while everyone else runs, he stands a better chance than if he alone walks, although his likelihood of surviving is much less than if everyone, including him, keeps his head.

As is probably apparent by now, each member of the audience finds himself caught in the grips of the familiar prisoner's dilemma. Each individual calculates that he is better off running than walking to the exit, no matter what the rest of the audience does. Hence, running is always (i.e., unconditionally) superior to walking. So he makes a mad dash for the exit. Unfortunately, since every audience member faces the same situation and makes the same calculation, everyone else also ends up running to the exit. And panic and tragedy ensue.

Why then do people sometimes cooperate in these panicky situations? The answer, I believe, goes back to the nature of the collective good that is at stake. This good—a safe and orderly exit—in many instances can be enjoyed either by nearly all of the theater patrons or none of them. We cannot say all-or-none, because clearly those sitting nearest the exit doors are likely to escape with their lives whether panic or calm prevails. But the important point is that a single person who tries to capitalize on the good behavior of others by pushing his way through the crowd can rest assured that he will instigate a chain reaction. A panicky individual therefore has the potential to spoil the collective good for everyone—not, however, by his actions alone but by the reaction he is able to trigger by his imprudent behavior. Hence the collective good in this case is not strictly speaking ruined by a sole individual but by the collectivity itself as those within it react to each other's uncooperative choices.

Because an attempt to free ride produces a suboptimal outcome, a "walk don't run" dictum has been developed to guide behavior in these perilous situations. One might ask why an explicit norm is necessary at all when rational calculation alone would lead to cooperation. The answer of course is that panicky situations are by definition those in which an individual is prone to act in a reflexive, careless, and *irrational* manner. The norm therefore offers an intelligent guide to action when one is least likely to be able to conduct one's own careful, studied analysis of the situation. The existence of a group norm in these situations also informs each individual of the likely behavior of other individuals. One's own impulse to behave irrationally is tempered by the norm, and, equally important, one is reassured (to the extent he believes others share the group norm) that other people are unlikely to behave irrationally either (cf. Elster 1989).

A norm that encourages calm and cooperation will also produce *tolerance* for a limited amount of deviant (in this case, panicky) behavior. Such tolerance can be critical in keeping the situation under control. For example, should one person start to push and shove his way to the exit, others will probably try to restrain him or reassure him that there's no reason to panic; but barring that, they may simply let him go, in essence conceding to him a free ride. As long as only one person or a few individuals lose their heads, others are likely to tolerate the defections and, in so doing, stem a chain reaction and prevent a tragic outcome. Once again the group norm has a settling influence on the crowd and puts a check on impulsive actions.

Alternatively, Michael Taylor (1976) outlines certain special circumstances under which a group, without relying on norms, might still be able to produce a collective good when maximum support is not a condition. According to Taylor, the tide running toward free ridership will be stemmed at the point where an additional free rider would render impossible the production of the commodity by all remaining individuals. In other words, individuals will try to get something for nothing only so long as that something will continue to be provided in spite of one's noncontribution.

Everyone cannot be a free rider, however, if cooperation among a minimum number of individuals is necessary for the collective endeavor to remain viable (i.e., profitable for the cooperators). Therefore defection will be preferable only until the size of the cooperative group is whittled down to the minimum number needed to support the good, at which point the good is being purely jointly produced (e.g., after some theater patrons start to run, the rest of the audience may keep in check, knowing that any more running will create a panic). The collective good is still profitable for the remaining cooperators to provide, so they are better off subsidizing the rest of the group than defecting themselves. Any individual in the surviving group who defects under these circumstances would have to hurt himself in order to punish the noncontributors.

Cascading defections, for example, is a problem that confronts doctors in the United States who wish to protect a woman's right to an abortion. Many doctors who support a woman's right to an abortion nevertheless prefer not to perform abortions themselves (Kolata 1990). A 1985 survey of the American College of Obstetricians and Gynecologists revealed that while 84 percent of the membership supported a woman's right to an abortion, only one-third of the supporters actually performed abortions. Furthermore, two-thirds of the practitioners indicated that they performed abortions infrequently. Doctors are stigmatized if they perform abortions, and the fear of stigma both reduces the propensity to perform abortions and of course further stigmatizes the small number who do perform them. Consequently more and more doctors have been capitulating to social pressure, leaving an increasingly small number of especially committed physicians who bear the stigma and perform abortions because they believe, "in most instances correctly, that if they don't provide the service, no one will" (11). The emphasis on "no one" is not farfetched, since many women in small communities or rural towns are discovering that they now have to travel to a nearby city in order to obtain an abortion.

One has the impression, however, that these remaining doctors are sufficiently zealous that they would perform abortions even if this service were widely available. In other words, not all doctors appear eager to shift the burden onto other doctors; rather, some doctors seem willing to provide this collective good for everyone, and in this sense the group is privileged. If, on the other hand, it were the case that everyone preferred to free ride and looked for opportunities to do so, it is difficult to calculate whether defection would be halted. A problem with the Taylor scenario in such cases is that we have to assume there are some individuals who are for one reason or another too slow to realize the benefits of free riding (Laver 1981, 54–57). As a consequence of their leadfootedness, they are left holding the bag. It is, however, more than a little paradoxical that a group of individuals who are alert enough to know how many people are needed to sustain the public good can also be so dim-witted that they cannot see when others are playing them for suckers. More than likely, under the assumption of mutually rational individuals, everyone will scramble to become a free rider. It would seem that only a norm providing information about the most prudent behavior in this circumstance would be able to stem total defection.[2]

How Boycotts Can Be Sustained

Local boycotts organized during the civil rights movement also shared some of the features of all-or-nothing collective goods. In these boycotts, blacks wished to present a united front in order to dispel criticisms that they lacked determination or that they were being coerced by a small faction within the group. For this reason, any individual who broke the boycott against the group's wishes sent an encouraging signal to the opposition and harmed the interests of the group.

Strictly speaking, no single defection in a boycott can destroy the public good for the whole group; but as in the burning theater example, a limited number of defections can induce a chain reaction that has that effect. Limited defections give merchants hope that they can outlast the boycotters, and such optimism on their part reduces their willingness to negotiate. In the absence of negotiations, more boycotters will become unwilling to make sacrifices for a goal that does not appear attainable. These additional defections further inspire the store owners and make them even more reluctant to make concessions, which in turn causes more people to break the boycott, and so on, until the boycott is ultimately destroyed. In light of this scenario, supporters of the movement have a strong incentive to support the boycott and avoid free rides, since any attempt to escape the personal costs of the

2. On the other hand, the mass defection envisioned by Laver cannot be confirmed or rejected purely on the basis of the model, because the model says nothing about how people commit themselves to particular strategies (Taylor 1987, 93).

boycott (such as the inconvenience of traveling to distant stores to do one's shopping) would detract from its likely impact.

These dynamics also characterize strikes. During the 1987 professional football players' strike, for example, union leaders were dismayed that individual players broke ranks and trickled back into camp a few at a time over a number of days. When veteran linebacker Reggie Williams of the Cincinnati Bengals crossed the picket line, teammate Cris Collinsworth lamented, "I wanted him to cross right away. Then it would have been clear he wasn't with us from the start. This makes it look like our union is cracking under pressure, and that could encourage the owners to mistakenly think they can completely break us." A second teammate, Turk Schonert, was more blunt when he suggested that it would be "a long year—a quiet year" for Williams, but "maybe Reggie is happy with that and doesn't need any friends on the team" (*Chicago Tribune* 1987).

Because small numbers of individuals can destroy the united front of the protesting group and at the same time give sustenance to the opposition, there is a strong incentive on the part of individuals within the group to punish defectors—by, for instance, blocking their path to a business or verbally abusing and harassing them. A cooperator who must choose between either disciplining or ignoring a defector can either act to preserve the boycott or allow it to be broken. If he is in a better position than others to mete out punishment, he may not be able to shift responsibility for sanctions onto someone else; in such instances, it is in his interest to pay the cost of punishment in order to protect the collective good.

In Tuskegee, Alabama, in 1957, blacks boycotted white businesses to protest a plan to redraw the town boundaries that would effectively exclude all but a handful of blacks from the voter rolls. The boycott was successful immediately since there was almost unanimous cooperation among blacks in town. Most blacks, it appears, gladly honored the boycott by shopping in local black stores and by taking their business to stores in the neighboring communities. For those reluctant to cooperate, social pressures to join usually proved compelling:

A black observed shopping in a downtown Tuskegee store was made the object of ridicule. . . . Black maids whose duties included buying groceries for their white employers began wearing their aprons to the food stores to signal that they were not willingly breaking the boycott. (Norrell 1985, 98)

Moreover, merchants should not have chortled when the boycott suffered from defection. Rural blacks who initially broke the Tuskegee boycott delighted white merchants who saw this development as a portent of things to come. One store owner told a reporter that he was unconcerned about the boycott because "country nigger customers" still bought from his business, a remark which promptly caused the withdrawal of their patronage (ibid., 96).

Alabama officials struck back by accusing blacks of violating the state's antiboycott law, which made it illegal to sustain a boycott by force; but in order to prosecute they had to obtain convincing evidence that there was an organized coercive campaign underway. Although a court order subsequently enjoined the black organization at the head of the boycott from pressuring blacks to avoid white stores, ultimately no coercion could be demonstrated. For the most part, blacks did not need to be pressured to join the boycott, since they were already sold on the effectiveness of such action (ibid., 98–99).

Nonviolent Protest

The same factor that explains panicky or sensible crowds and offers insights into the successfulness of boycotts—whether or not the collective good enjoys (or is perceived to enjoy) pure jointness of production—also helps us to understand why the strategy of nonviolence was such an effective tactic during the civil rights movement. First let me review how nonviolence was supposed to work; then I will provide two alternative explanations of why nonviolence succeeded—one which relies on irrational behavior and a second which does not.

In an article written shortly after the Selma campaign, King (1965, 16–17, 57) summarized the strategy of "aggressive nonviolence." Ideally a campaign would consist of four acts. First, the demonstrators would attempt, in a lawful manner, to exercise their constitutional rights. Second, in so doing they would be attacked, without legitimate provocation, by their racist opponents. Third, media coverage of this senseless violence would leave a deep impression about the conditions of the South that would shock and outrage the American public and bring forth their sympathy and support for the goals of the civil rights movement. And fourth, the federal government would be compelled by the weight of public pressure to intervene and correct the problems with appropriate legislation.

Nonviolence therefore operated on the principle that the crowd's or audience's reaction to a conflict between two parties will significantly affect its course. As Schattschneider (1960) observed, "it must be assumed that every change in the number of participants is about something, that the newcomers have sympathies or antipathies that make it possible to involve them. By definition, the intervening bystanders are not neutral. Thus, in political conflict every change in scope changes the equation" (4–5).

Like the latter-day civil rights movement, abolitionism relied on this principle in trying to make northern audiences aware of the South's callous treatment of slaves. Abolitionists resorted to writings, speeches, lectures, polemical tracts, eyewitness accounts, and testimonials by fugitive slaves to expose the inhumanity of the slave system. While these hair-raising tales and testimonials shocked and repulsed readers and listeners, most northerners nevertheless did not accede to the accompanying call to action. As horrible as the problem of slavery clearly was, northerners continued to regard it as a southern problem that was remote from their immediate lives.

Ultimately southern repression of the abolitionists was required to convince many northerners that the conflict over slavery affected their own rights and liberties. The extreme actions taken by southern authorities to prevent distribution of abolitionist literature and to disrupt abolitionist meetings and rallies demonstrated to northerners that the South not only violated the rights of blacks but also threatened, in the course of defending slavery, to undermine the democratic values of the republic. Thus, while the religious and moral precepts preached by abolitionists were by themselves insufficient to stimulate widespread northern activism, the South's hostile response effectively transformed the dimensions of the conflict in a manner that redounded to the benefit of abolitionism (Dillon 1974).

The best way that civil rights activists could enlarge the scope of the conflict in the United States was to draw the attention of white northern liberals to the plight of blacks in the South and to escalate the conflict to a point where the federal government could no longer maintain a hands-off approach. Both goals called for dramatic campaigns that attracted widespread (and favorable) media attention. The media was crucial to this strategy because it had the ability to transform local skirmishes into events of national importance. Public opinion could be mobilized against the southern status quo only if the conflict intensified and became salient to the general public. Likewise, federal government officials were typically moved to action only when events appeared to be getting out of hand; in particular, when violence erupted, the government could no longer avoid responsibility in the eyes of the public nor could it delegate responsibility to other parties, such as local authorities.[3]

In the 1960s, the prospect of adverse international publicity also affected the Kennedy administration's civil rights policy. For example, shortly before a summit meeting with the Soviet Union, the administration was acutely aware of its image abroad when it decided what to do about the freedom riders:

> It was bad enough that Kennedy had to prepare for these fateful talks weakened by the Bay of Pigs. To face Khrushchev against the backdrop of racial strife within the bosom of the free world, while commanding troops against his own people, would open Kennedy to ridicule from the Soviet leader. Clearly, the Army option threatened multiple disaster and was a dreaded last resort. Calling out the national guard, Kennedy's next choice down the military scale, was not much better. By far the most palatable alternative was to protect the Freedom Riders' bus with a force of U.S. marshals and other civilians within the federal service. (Branch 1988, 434)

THE PUBLIC RELATIONS (PR) GAME

It is useful to examine the strategy of nonviolent protest in terms of a game between the protesters and the local authorities. Both the protesters and the authorities have a choice between two courses of action. The protesters can be orderly or they can be violent; the authorities can exercise self-control or they can employ unnecessary force. Thus, there are four possible outcomes to the confrontation.

From the protesters' perspective, it is obvious that their best outcome is realized when they choose nonviolence while the authorities use unjustified force. A nonviolent strategy works only if the protesters are seen as blameless victims. Since the protesters' overwhelming concern is to maintain self-control, I assume that their second prefer-

---

3. Consequently nonviolence is almost certain to be ineffective if it is not able to find support among third parties to the conflict. In South Africa, for example, the state has not been subjected to the same domestic pressures and constraints on the use of violence against blacks as American authorities were during the 1950s and 1960s. For fear of a public outcry, evidence of police brutality in the United States was often concealed or denied, whereas it has had little impact among the white South African population. South African officials for this reason have been more concerned about keeping the truth of their regime from the international audience (Lelyveld 1985, 201), and so it is to that audience that black activists have been increasingly aiming their appeals in hopes of changing the nature of the conflict.

ence is for both parties to be orderly. On the other hand, the worst fear of the protesters is that they will be the ones to perpetrate violence while the authorities behave in a lawful, responsible fashion. This outcome would lend credibility to charges from white supremacists that the activists are "professional agitators" intent on stirring up trouble in a heretofore peaceful community. Only slightly less undesirable is an outbreak of violence between the two parties, since the protesters likely would be routed and yet would be seen to be at least partially responsible for the bloodshed.

Assumptions about the preference order of the authorities are more difficult to make. One possibility is that the authorities prefer to use force no matter how the protesters behave. If this were so, the (rather uninteresting) solution to the game would have the police using unjustifiable force against the peaceful protesters, with both sides being pleased with the outcome—the demonstrators will have scored a public relations coup and the police will have relished the opportunity to vent their contempt and hatred for the "rabble-rousers."

There is, however, evidence that local authorities during the civil rights movement tried to avoid incurring the wrath of a morally outraged public. Calmer heads among them realized that the civil rights activists were trying to bait them into taking rash action. Police Chief Laurie Pritchett, a "farsighted police officer" (Branch 1988, 527), successfully dashed the Albany desegregation campaign by adhering (more or less) to standard police procedure in dealing with the activists and conscientiously avoiding the use of excessive force. Similarly, during the Selma voter registration drive, Alabama officials were privy to Martin Luther King, Jr.'s, plan to provoke a violent response from Sheriff Jim Clark and his posse. Consequently, Wilson Baker, Selma's director of public safety made every effort to keep Clark and his posse away from the demonstrators: "We were determined not to give 'em [the activists] what they wanted and succeeded for two days that first week they marched in here. We would try to set him [Clark] down and talk with him. . . . [T]he members of his posse . . . were real anxious for action, and we had persuaded him to keep 'em in the courthouse: 'Let 'em march. Don't arrest. Meet nonviolence with nonviolence!'" (Raines 1977, 198).

When news of the Selma-to-Montgomery march first reached Governor George Wallace, he was inclined to go along with the recommendation of his press secretary, Bill Jones, to let the marchers go rather than block them. Jones also suggested that the highway along which the marchers would be traveling be closed off to all support vehicles because he calculated it would be impossible for them to cover the entire distance without supplies: "I did not believe—nor did any of us who were present—that King and his fellow travelers could march the 50 miles to Montgomery. I firmly believed my plan could make them the laughing stock of the nation and win for us a propaganda battle" (Garrow 1978, 68).

Therefore although the local authorities might relish a bloody confrontation with the demonstrators more than any other outcome (especially since most of the blood spilled would surely come from their foes), they also realize that it would be strategically unwise to bash heads without provocation. Orderly protesters should be left alone—this outcome is the second most preferred because it denies the protesters the opportunity to win sympathy and support as a result of police brutality. The third best outcome from the standpoint of the authorities happens when the protesters alone act violently. This scenario is not as attractive as the one in which everyone is peaceful because, although the authorities still win a public relations victory, some of them are liable to be injured in the process. All this is moot, however, because this outcome will not occur in practice: since the authorities prefer more than anything a head-to-head confrontation, they would immediately shift to a violent strategy if it became apparent that the protesters were using violence.

The worst outcome for the authorities occurs when they lose control and forcefully put down peaceful and orderly protests. This plays into the hands of the activists, who are willing to suffer personal injury in order to publicize their grievances and expedite social reform.

In sum, the preferences of the authorities and the activists are represented by the game matrix in figure 2.2. The activists have a dominant strategy; they want to be orderly at any cost, whether the authorities are combative or accommodating. On the other hand, the authorities' preference is contingent on the disposition of the protesters—if the protesters get rowdy, the authorities will crack down on them; but if they are well-behaved, the authorities will be lighthanded. In other words, the authorities will use a tit-for-tat decision rule.

What makes the public relations game interesting is that if both sides act in their best interests, the outcome—an orderly, uneventful demonstration—is suboptimal for each party. The protesters would rather see the authorities act rashly, while the authorities would like to see the protesters step out of line, thereby giving them a reason to use force. This stalemate leads to some interesting strategic maneuvers.

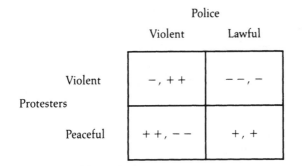

FIGURE 2.2. The Public Relations (PR) Game

Southern police forces, for example, often satisfied both their interest in good public relations and their desire to beat up the protesters by allowing surrogates to act in their stead. Probably the most famous instance of this tactic occurred in Montgomery when Police Commissioner L. B. Sullivan allowed local hoodlums ten to fifteen minutes to savagely pummel an incoming busload of freedom riders before sending police officials to restore order (Garrow 1986, 157).

On the other hand, we can expect the activists to try to provoke the policemen into using violence. Specifically, the activists will do everything they can to be disruptive without actually crossing the threshold into disorderly behavior. This might entail violating a local parade law, defying a court injunction against a march, or employing some other assertive tactic. The trick is for the activists to *tempt* the policemen into shifting to a combative response by appearing to be combative themselves. At the same time, since blameworthiness is critical in determining how the public will react to the conflict, the demonstrators have to avoid appearing as if they are surreptitiously trying to provoke the police into using violence. As Garrow's (1978) meticulous analysis of press reporting and congressional statements on the Birmingham and Selma campaigns shows, even small amounts of unruliness in Birmingham hurt the public relations impact of the demonstrations. What the demonstrators must do, then, is incite the police while seemingly going about their business exercising rights that, at least in theory, all citizens enjoy.

One of the most provocative options available to demonstrators was to march at night. Under cover of darkness, a violent response by the police or by local vigilantes was almost assured. When civil rights activists conducted a night march in Marion, state troopers attacked and beat them after the street lamps were intentionally blacked out. Reporters attempting to cover the event were also clubbed, and the lenses of their cameras were sprayed with black paint.

Because of the darkness and confusion, however, and because of the difficulty reporters had carrying out their jobs, this attempt by the protesters to escalate the campaign almost backfired. Local officials tried to pass the story that there was very little violence and that what violence occurred was instigated by the demonstrators. Jimmie Lee Jackson, a black youth who died as a result of injuries suffered during the march, was said to have first attacked a state trooper.

Out-of-town reporters, including John Herbers of the *New York Times,* initially conveyed the official line that the police were merely responding to lawless behavior by the demonstrators; it was only in their follow-up stories that they dismissed the official version of events and reported that the state troopers had conducted an unprovoked assault against the marchers. Even the *Alabama Journal* joined the chorus of critics when it lambasted the "stupidity and brutality" of the state police during the episode (Fairclough 1987, 240).

On Police Brutality

Why did the activists so often succeed in suckering the police? One (extremely plausible) reason is that the authorities are seeking a pretext or rationalization for responding aggressively, so they can be counted on to construe most of the protesters' tactics as being of a disorderly nature. In his study of police violence, Rodney Stark (1972) concludes that

> unnecessary use of force by the police is a relatively routine occurrence. The case seems conclusive. The police advocate illegal use of force. . . . This being the case, it is easy to understand why the police are likely to resort to unjustified force in situations when they are admittedly under extra stress: during confrontations with mass demonstrations and protests or during riots. Hitting people is the customary police tactic for dealing with trouble. (83)

Moreover, the deep-seated desire of many policemen to bully and brutalize the protesters makes them susceptible to poor or irrational judgments. Even though Sheriff Clark knew that the civil rights activists in Selma were trying to goad him into arresting them, and that it was not in his interest to do so—in fact, they were about to quit the campaign and leave town if he would not jail them—he nevertheless could not restrain himself. Charles Fager (1974) notes that "there was something obsessive about Clark's response to the sight of a line of black faces ringing his green marble courthouse; he may have thought he was acting for some calculated end, but he looked and carried on like he couldn't stop himself from striking out at them" (34). According to Wilson Baker, when Clark realized how much he had helped his adversaries by his actions, he would reproach himself, but to no avail: "He'd scream bloody murder that he'd never do it again, he wouldn't fall into that trap again and go out the next day and do the same thing" (Raines 1977, 200). For his inadvertent contribution to the cause, civil rights activists facetiously voted Clark an honorary member of their organizations.

The Bloody Sunday incident in Selma typified how the local authorities could be driven to irrational behavior by their desire to seek a pretext for violence. If we are to believe Alabama authorities, law enforcement officials received strict instructions from the governor not to use violence against the protesters. However, at the Edmund Pettus Bridge, when the marchers refused to turn back, the state troopers and Clark's posse formed a wedge and proceeded to run over them. A moment later tear gas was shot into the crowd of marchers, causing them to disperse. As Baker explains, this justified even greater brutality: "Once the gas cannister explodes, and the gas goes, they [the marchers] go to running and running over state troopers, and the state troopers take that *as an excuse* to fight back, and all hell broke loose" (ibid., 202; italics mine).

But there is another way to explain why nonviolence worked for the protesters but not for the police that does not rely on the irrationality of the authorities. Both the civil rights activists and the local authorities were parties to separate conventions that served the interests of each group. The activists were committed to a convention of nonviolence which they had been trained to uphold regardless of their treatment at the hands of the police. The police were instructed to keep to a convention of lawful procedure in order to avoid accusations of brutality by the media and other observers. In Albany, Chief of Police Pritchett had spent months instructing his officers to conduct themselves lawfully. He revealed subsequently that "the Albany Police Department was indoctrinated to this plan of nonviolence. . . . At each roll call (they) were lectured and shown films on how to conduct themselves in this non-violence operation" (Fairclough 1987, 101).

Yet in practice the local authorities were more likely than the activists to harm their collective interest by departing from their convention. For their transgressions, they often elicited the wrath of the press and the public. I believe the reason for this difference stems from the relative incentives that activists and authorities had for honoring their commitment to the group norm.

In the case of the activists, the strategy of nonviolence worked only as long as every activist adhered to it. Nonviolence, therefore, is an all-or-nothing collective good. A single departure from nonviolence by an undisciplined activist justified the harshest crackdown by the police; the slightest appearance of lawlessness from the demonstrators "legitimized" (in terms of the standards then prevailing) police brutality. Therefore an individual who strikes out at a policeman can count on experiencing a momentary visceral pleasure, but he also realizes that this gain will be quickly canceled by the vicious retaliation meted out by the police. One punch will assuredly be rewarded with a dozen clubs. But not only will the individual perpetrator of violence be punished by the police, so will his colleagues suffer for his imprudence. Once order is destroyed, the police can claim they were provoked by the demonstrators, and this excuses all sorts of mayhem on their part, including attacks on innocent third parties. A single violation of the group convention therefore destroys the collective good (a peaceful and politically successful demonstration) for everyone.

Although nonviolence required amazing *individual* discipline and restraint, it was at heart a *social* pact founded on the commitments of each individual to uphold a collective agreement. James Forman ([1972] 1985) was reluctant to subscribe to a nonviolent strategy because he knew, given his constitution, that "it would be a terrible test of my nerves to submit to this type of group discipline" (149). On a picket line protesting the hiring practices of a grocery store, Forman and his fellow demonstrators were beset by a group of thugs who heckled them and sprayed them with soft drinks. It took all of Forman's resolve not to retaliate:

> Each time I walked the line and found those five or six hecklers, I
> had to steel myself. I didn't want to break the discipline of the
> group by striking back. I had agreed to engage in this nonviolent
> demonstration and I wanted to keep group discipline. It was my be-
> lief in collective discipline, more than anything else, that kept me in
> the nonviolent group at those moments. (ibid.)

While the police are adhering to their own convention, the individual incentive to abide by the group norm in their ranks is not nearly as persuasive as it is in the case of the activists. The local authorities want to play by the rules in order to mollify their critics; more precisely, they want to give the "appearance" of executing the laws in a proper fashion. The appearance of lawfulness, however, allows for the occasional exception to the rule. An officer who loses his temper harms the image of the police and thereby detracts from the collective good, but it does not bring forth a general condemnation of the police force. Just because an officer or two strays from the norm of proper police procedure, this does not warrant a sweeping accusation of police brutality. The argument can be made (and usually sustained) that an individual or two lost his temper, and that this is only human in a tense situation.

For example, Albany Police Chief Pritchett selectively followed a policy of nonviolence.

> Police brutality and violence to whites or Negroes, drunks, prostitutes, thieves, demonstrators, peacewalkers, he condemns and seeks to minimize in public and the jail. Negroes report cruel *exception* to this policy and believe that Pritchett holds it, when he does, only to present a "good image" to the public and create the impression that he is a responsible, progressive law-enforcement official. (Little 1968, 213; italics mine)

A police officer within the ranks therefore can satisfy his desire to beat up the odd activist without fearing that the collective good (a lawful police force) will be appreciably damaged; since each individual policeman can indulge his aggressive impulses without feeling personally responsible for destroying the group's goal, he will probably do so. The problem from the vantage point of the authorities, however, is that if too many officers take advantage of their "free shot" at the demonstrators (as they are prone to do in the absence of appropriate countermeasures), accusations of police brutality will indeed be appropriate and the police will have been outmaneuvered by the demonstrators in the public relations game they are playing.

On the other hand, where the convention of nonviolence was weakly maintained among the protesters, the police gained the upper hand. Such was the case during an unorganized spontaneous march originating from Albany's Harlem which collected bystanders and onlookers who were not trained in the discipline of nonviolence. The march turned rowdy as some of the black bystanders heaved bottles and rocks at the police despite furious attempts by veteran activists and leaders to keep them under control. Laurie Pritchett capitalized on this turn of events by ordering his police force to regain control of the streets without resorting to weapons except in self-defence. Pritchett made sure that reporters noted the police's exemplary control in contrast to the actions of the protesters: "There was no violence on our part," he boasted at a news conference; "the officers never took their nightsticks from their belts" (Branch 1988, 618). King in contrast declared a day of penance for his side.

Summary

The all-or-nothing feature of boycotts and nonviolent protests discussed in this chapter helps explain how these public goods were sustained during the civil rights movement. Boycotts were easier to sustain because limited defections from them created serious doubts in the minds of the opposition about the steadfastness of the movement and the degree of support behind it. Similarly, participants in nonviolent demonstrations were more likely to uphold the group philosophy because of the devastating consequences of a single deviation from it. The police, on the other hand, experienced great difficulty maintaining their nonviolent convention because individual acts of violence were countenanced.

However, we have to recognize that, while the all-or-nothing nature of nonviolent protest helps to explain why nonviolence was such an effective strategy, it does not explain why the participants in these demonstrations chose to participate in the first place—only why they upheld the group norm *after* already having decided to contribute. Organizing a demonstration is still a standard collective action problem. Everyone has an incentive to allow others to do the demonstrating for him; and everyone will prefer to be among the free riders who suffer no inconvenience but still enjoy whatever benefit is created by the demonstration.

By the same token, if boycotts can withstand significant numbers of defectors, they too are susceptible to the collective action problem. Each individual will reason that he can violate the boycott without affecting its eventual success or failure; if enough people behave in this "rational" manner, everyone will suffer in the end.

3 | Selective Social Incentives and Reputational Concerns

Without friends, no one would choose to live.

Aristotle

From a practical standpoint, we ended chapter 2 only slightly better off than when we began. All-or-nothing public goods were shown to circumvent the collective action problem because individual contributions to such goods have a pivotal impact on whether or not they are produced; but applications of this principle to public-spirited collective action appear to be limited. In the course of the civil rights movement, boycotts were aided by this quality, and nonviolent demonstrations could be more effectively executed because nonviolence was an all-or-nothing good.

We were not able, however, to account for the emergence of such demonstrations in the first place. Demonstrations are a prime example of the type of collective action that is hard to initiate because they require large numbers of contributors, any one of whom is insignificant to the overall effort. Boycotts will also be difficult to mount if they can weather a certain degree of free riding.

As I explain in this chapter, in order to coax an individual to cooperate under these more difficult conditions, it is necessary to provide him with an added inducement to participate over and above the benefits he will receive from the public good itself. Since he will receive the benefits of that good whether he contributes to it or not, a so-called selective incentive may elicit his share of the cost. Selective incentives are private benefits that can be enjoyed only by those who cooperate; therefore cooperators are rewarded with these additional benefits, whereas noncooperators are denied them. Members of professional organizations, for example, often receive trade publications and journals, reduced-fare travel packages, subsidized health insurance programs, and other products or services. In the civil rights movement, membership in the NAACP (National Association for the Advancement of Colored People) during its formative years brought solidary and financial rewards. Association meetings gave middle-class blacks an opportunity to socialize and provided a convenient forum in which black professionals could advertise their services to prospective clients (Wilson 1973, 174). The association therefore helped its members in much the same way that the American Medical Association fosters a patient referral system among physicians in the organization (Hardin 1982, 192). Clearly if the value of these incentives exceeds the cost of membership, then it is in the self-interest of the rational individual to join.

Selective incentives can be material, social, or psychological in nature. Because material rewards are the most easily identified and the most accurately measured, they are usually the first incentives we look for when trying to find the motivation behind political participation. Olson (1971, 60–63) recognized the significance of social incentives but held that their effectiveness would be limited to small group interaction. He regarded moral and psychological incentives as simply subclasses of the broad category of selective incentives, but he refused to incorporate them into his explanation of collective action because he believed that "it is not possible to get empirical proof of the motivation behind any person's actions; it is not possible definitely to say whether a given individual acted for moral reasons or for other reasons in some particular case. A reliance on moral explanations could thus make the theory untestable" (61).

We would be hard-pressed, however, to account for much public-spirited collective action by tracing it to the material incentives supplied to participants. Even a cursory examination of the reasons behind participation in political causes reveals that selective material incentives are seldom of sufficient value to constitute the primary motivating factor. For the average participant in causes such as the women's movement, the civil rights movement, and the student movement, the material inducements offered were slim.

Perhaps those at the forefront of a movement will be in a position to cash in on their contributions. The leaders of collective action may win full-time institutional positions as a reward for their efforts. This would hold for revolutionary movements aimed at overthrowing a government, but it can apply just as well (if not better, because of the lower risk) to social activists who are subsequently given administrative positions on watchdog panels, advisory boards, investigatory commissions, and the like after successfully winning recognition of the plight of a particular group in society. Oberschall (1973) even suggests that the prospects faced by many fledgling revolutionaries are often better than is usually imagined: "It is true that for every Fidel Castro there are a Che Guevara and several other unsuccessful Latin American revolutionaries, but in the case of the African nationalists of the post–World War II period the success rate was strikingly high" (116). But again, such payoffs to successful leaders are typically beyond the reach of the rank and file, and the leadership usually has no way to provide alternative compensation to them. Even "obvious" material incentives given to supporters of a cause are not, upon closer scrutiny, always what they seem. For example, in Mississippi, Student Nonviolent Coordinating Committee (SNCC) workers went from door to door offering to help residents with their daily chores (washing cars, picking cotton, cutting wood, etc.) not so much to "buy" their participation as to win their confidence and trust (Carson 1981, 79–80).

Moreover, we cannot explain, by pointing to selective material incentives, why people who do not support the goals of collective action typically do not enlist. In principle, a material selective incentive should carry the same attraction for those who see the goal of collective action as a collective "bad" as for those who regard it as a collective good. Since rational individuals of either persuasion dismiss, in their decision calculus, the value of the collective goal, because their contribution will not affect whether or not it will be produced, the only relevant factor is the benefit of the private goods being offered. If the value of these goods exceeds the cost of participation, then it is rational for an individual—whether he's a supporter or opponent of the cause—to pay the entry fee (DeNardo 1985, 52–57).

But this is where the analogy between economic and political behavior separates. The individual sells his labor in the marketplace and usually does so without respect to the product that is being manufactured by the firm. The only issue in the worker's mind is whether the wage offered by the firm compensates him adequately for his time and effort. The prospective activist, however, will not indiscriminately deliver his services for money. On the contrary, consistency between the goals promoted by the cause and his own values is likely to be the sine qua non of his participation. While other conditions would undoubtedly have to be fulfilled before he felt compelled to participate in collective action, these considerations would in all likelihood be moot if he were unsympathetic to the cause. As the sociologists Fireman and Gamson (1979) put it, "Whether one's taste for chocolate affects one's propensity to take a job in a chocolate factory, surely one's taste for civil rights affects one's propensity to join in a civil rights movement" (14).[1]

Social and psychological incentives, on the other hand, are often linked inextricably to the goals of collective action. I do not seek the friendship and esteem of just anyone but only of those I care about, and I will tend to care more about those who share my views and my concerns than about those who do not. By the same token, if I cooperate to protect my reputation in the eyes of others, then I must cooperate in ventures that are consistent with my reputation. I cannot, for example, be someone who is known to defend the rights of the disadvantaged in our society if I refuse to join protests on behalf of blacks, women, and the poor. Likewise, any psychological incentive to participate will usually be inseparable from the goal of collective action. Unless I enjoy rabble-rousing of any sort, I will get no pleasure from lending my energies to a movement that seeks social changes which I oppose.

Social incentives (to be discussed in this chapter) and psychological incentives (to be discussed in chapter 4) reduce the temptation to free ride and increase the attraction of cooperation in collective action. In this chapter I discuss how social pressures to cooperate arise in the course of regular social interaction. Ongoing social interaction is more accurately modeled as an iterated prisoner's dilemma than as a single-play game. Several authors have shown that under limited conditions, spontaneous cooperation is possible in the iterated game without the introduction of extragame considerations. A limitation of this "internal solution," however, is that cooperation in large groups is likely to occur only under fairly stringent conditions. I will argue that for large groups to cooperate, these internal incentives typically have to be supplemented by various social incentives and pressures arising from membership in a community. Along these lines, I explore how our interest in developing a good reputation affects our willingness to contribute to collective action, and finally, how commitments and obligations formed for narrowly rational reasons can nonetheless inspire sympathetic behavior that is unselfish and other-regarding.

SOCIAL INCENTIVES

The desires to gain or sustain friendships, to maintain one's social standing, and to avoid ridicule and ostracism are all social goals that

---

1. Of course this oversimplifies. For example, conscientious individuals take their politics into the marketplace when they refuse to work for a firm that has ties to

constitute selective incentives for individuals to participate in collective action. Such social gains might outweigh any strictly economic or material benefits that would result from becoming a free rider. At the least, social pressures will tend to make the malingerer or slacker attempt to conceal his true nature and create the *illusion* that he is contributing his fair share to the collective enterprise.

Social ties and concerns of course can also *inhibit* people from participating in a cause that is considered unpopular in their community. Southern white men and women active in the civil rights movement, for example, often found themselves caught in the middle of a tug-of-war between their personal ideals and the social norms of their families and friends. It was common for their parents to be ashamed of their actions and to try to make them feel guilty for bringing dishonor to the family name. Some parents accused their children of hurting their businesses and making it more difficult for them to do their jobs (Evans 1979, 43).[2]

It seems self-evident that social pressures will be both more salient and subject to more effective enforcement in small, tightly knit groups than in large, impersonal collectivities in which members are protected by the cloak of anonymity. Hence, small groups have an advantage over large groups in the production of collective goods. Large groups nevertheless can take advantage of the selective incentives provided by social pressures if they in turn comprise a network of much smaller organizational units. At these lower levels, friendship and familial, religious, and professional relationships create an array of *ongoing* exchanges, obligations, and expectations that individual members have considerable incentive to uphold.

Preexisting social networks play a central role in the emergence of collective action. If we make a close examination of various forms of collective action, from the mob or crowd to the social reform movement to the full-scale revolutionary movement, we find that at all levels,

---

the defense industry. On the other side, mercenaries will go to war if the price is right.

2. Variations in community conflicts appear to explain why post-*Roe* v. *Wade* antiabortion activists are more single-mindedly opposed to abortion than pre-*Roe* v. *Wade* activists. Pre-*Roe* v. *Wade* activists had broader social and professional ties that subjected them to conflicting social pressures and influences; these cross-pressures had a tempering effect on their antiabortion politics. By contrast, the newer activists tend to live in more homogeneous environments in which their friends and associates share their views; this gives license to a more zealous and uncompromising approach to their political activism (Luker 1984, 146).

collective action invariably involves the confederation of smaller organized units rather than the aggregation of previously isolated, atomized individuals.[3] (See Taylor 1976, 1982, 1987, 1988, on the general importance of community.)

For instance, the Free Speech Movement on the Berkeley campus was at its core a coalition of highly politicized student organizations, all of which felt similarly threatened and harmed by the decision of the administration to limit soliciting, organizing, and fund-raising on the main campus mall. The women's suffrage movement was facilitated by a large network of women's clubs, organizations, and professional associations (Degler 1980, 324). The Union League movement during Reconstruction capitalized on existing black fraternal, educational, religious, and relief groups (Fitzgerald 1989, 30).

Similarly, the civil rights movement in the South relied heavily on the ability of black church leaders to mobilize their congregations to contribute to organizational activities, participate in economic boycotts, join in public rallies and meetings, and the like (Oberschall 1973; McAdam 1982; Morris 1984). The abolitionist cause consisted of an elaborate network of national, regional, state, civic, and collegiate organizations (Aptheker 1989). Abolitionism was also strengthened by the development of Negro mutual aid or self-help societies. Mutual aid societies were designed to assist the poor as well as to educate and inform, but they quickly took on political connotations. "The close affinity between abolitionism and Negro improvement was illustrated by an interracial group in Boone County, Indiana, which organized a society for the moral and literary advancement of the Negro, and then proceeded to organize an antislavery society, thus becoming two societies with an identical membership" (Quarles 1969, 102).

Indeed, a common tactic of organizers is to piggyback political groups onto organizations centered around social activities. For example, early organizers of the farmers' unions and clubs in the late 1800s recognized that the appeal of these groups would be strengthened if they served a social as well as economic purpose. Meetings were

3. In contrast, Le Bon's ([1895] 1960) classic work views collective behavior as unruly, spontaneous, unregulated mob action. Le Bon argued that individual self-restraint was lost in crowds, and that crowds consequently were driven by a debased group mind. Normally civil and well-behaved individuals can either indulge their basest impulses or zealously pursue noble ideals, depending on how their energies are channeled by the leader of the crowd. In the safety and anonymity of the multitudes, each participant is susceptible to reckless behavior.

organized to promote friendship, recreational activities, and mutual aid, as well as to share information about politics, prices, and farming practices. The meetings themselves were meant to be entertaining and enjoyable. Organizers emphasized that women and children should be brought along, and that good music should be provided. Anyone interested in holding a meeting was instructed to corral a neighbor or friend, and the two were then to ask two more, and so forth. Early arrivers at the meeting were urged to light the house and to provide it with heat so that passersby would see that there was activity in the building (McNall 1988, 190–93).

Even the deadly serious American Communist Party came to realize in the 1930s that people often join organizations in part to socialize and enjoy the company of others. In order to broaden its appeal, the Party held picnics, dances, and other social events. But despite such efforts, Party life more commonly violated this rule by remaining overwhelmingly tedious. Endless meetings and speeches, esoteric terminology, burdensome and excessive party chores and duties, constant dues collections, exploitation of new Party members, and other disincentives weakened the commitment of individual members and discouraged many Communist sympathizers from joining the Party (Klehr 1984, 154).

The Iterated Prisoner's Dilemma

The collective action problem takes on new features when potential contributors to the public good have ongoing social ties. Ongoing social interaction is much better modeled by a serial or iterated prisoner's dilemma game than by a single-play game. The single-play game is both ahistorical and futureless. The players carry no reputations for being cooperative or recalcitrant; their choices have no bearing on future transactions; and their interaction is limited to a single exchange, after which their "association" is terminated.

By contrast, real social exchange occurs within social networks and involves regular and repeated interactions (not all of which need to be prisoner's dilemmas). How a person conducts business with his associates today will affect the tenor of his future transactions with them. For this reason, an individual's frame of reference in any transaction includes not only the transaction at hand but the much broader matrix of exchanges that he is or will be party to, all of which may be contingent upon the current transaction.

Under these circumstances, one's rational strategy is less apparent than in the single-play prisoner's dilemma. If there is only one play (or one exchange), each player is better off defecting no matter what course of action is pursued by his opponent, since defection is a "dominant" strategy in the game. While the outcome in the case of mutual defection, ironically, is not Pareto-optimal or "collectively rational," this does not make each player's strategy any less individually rational. Only when the game is iterated does each player have an incentive and an opportunity to reach a more profitable collective solution.

People who distrust each other therefore can promote cooperation by committing themselves to multiple exchanges. During the 1960 presidential election campaign, for example, the Kennedy camp, after having lost the endorsement of Jackie Robinson to Nixon, sought the support of the next most influential black, Adam Clayton Powell. Powell made it known that his endorsement was available only for cash, first demanding three hundred thousand dollars but eventually settling for fifty thousand dollars in return for ten endorsement speeches. There was a small problem, however: Powell did not trust the Kennedy camp to pay if the speeches were delivered first, and the Kennedy camp did not trust Powell to deliver the speeches if he were paid in advance. The solution? Kennedy turned the money over to an intermediary, who would pay it out in five-thousand-dollar installments following each endorsement speech (Branch 1988, 343). (But what incentive did Kennedy have to make the final payment?)

Taylor (1976, 1987; see also Axelrod 1981, 1984) has shown that in the two-person iterated prisoner's dilemma (or PD supergame), mutual tit-for-tat strategies (in which each player cooperates on the first play and thereafter mimics the other player's preceding move) can constitute an equilibrium if the players do not overly discount future payoffs. In simple terms, each player will stick to his strategy and not be tempted by a one-time gain from suckering his opponent if he values sufficiently the future benefits he will receive from mutual cooperation as opposed to mutual defection.

Hardin (1982)[4] uses a different tack in discussing the possibility that cooperative conventions will form when the prisoner's dilemma is played an indefinite number of times. In principle, the indeterminacy of the number of iterations is critical, since this means that the players are unaware of when the last game will be played. Conversely, if the exact number of plays were known to the players, they would approach

---

4. All citations of Hardin in this section and the next refer to this book.

the last game in the same way they would approach any single-play prisoner's dilemma; contingent strategies (which assume future encounters) would be abandoned, and both players would treat each play as if it were the last.

When the game is played a determinate number of times, each player can no longer assume that his present choice will affect the choices of his opponent in future games. This will be true if the game is played twice or two thousand times. Consider the general case in which n plays are stipulated: if the play of the nth or last game is determined at the outset, then there is also no reason to consider contingent strategies in the nth $-$ 1 game; each player knows beforehand that the other will defect on the nth play, so the nth $-$ 1 play should be approached in the manner of a single prisoner's dilemma game. But if the nth and nth $-$ 1 plays are predetermined, then it would be foolish to adopt a contingent strategy on the nth $-$ 2 play. Thus the nth $-$ 2 play will be approached as a single-play prisoner's dilemma, and both players will defect. Of course this logic is relentless. Reasoning backwards like this leads ultimately to the conclusion that both players will defect on every play of the game (Luce and Raiffa 1957, 97–102).[5]

As impeccable as this logic is, most people find it bizarre. They suspect, as I do, that in practice the players would not be so obdurate as to stumble through an unbroken string of mutual defections. More likely the players would, by way of contingent choosing (such as tit for tat), work themselves into a superior pattern of cooperation at least until they approached the end of the game, when each player might be tempted to add a few sucker payoffs to his total, knowing that if trust broke down at this point, the losses would be inconsequential. Unless sucker payoffs are substantially greater than payoffs for cooperation, the early defector who takes his opponent for a fool will be worse off in the long run. (For discussions of experimental game results, see Rapoport and Chammah 1970 and Dawes 1980.)

But these cooperators in a fixed-play prisoner's dilemma would be behaving practically rather than rationally in the strict sense. The

5. Kreps et al. (1982) show that if players in a finitely repeated two-person PD believe there is a possibility that they are dealing with an irrational tit for tatter, then we can expect mutual cooperation to persist for some portion of the game (up to a threshold) before defection eventually takes over. With the introduction of uncertainty, rational players have an interest in developing a reputation for being a cooperator. Under these assumptions, unconditional defection is no longer inevitable in a finite two-person PD. See also Kreps and Wilson (1982).

question remains whether such rational players can reach a cooperative outcome. Hardin (1982, 165–66) argues that in the open-ended iterated prisoner's dilemma, the players can attain a "coordination equilibrium" in which there is mutual cooperation. A strategy produces a coordination equilibrium if a switch in strategy by either player will not improve anyone's outcome. In a two-person prisoner's dilemma, a tit-for-tat strategy results in a coordination equilibrium because no one will benefit from a change in strategy by either player.[6] Noncontingent strategies such as CCC . . . (unconditional cooperation) or DDD . . . (unconditional defection) do not generate coordination equilibria; in the case of unconditional mutual cooperation, each player has an incentive to switch to a defection strategy; conversely, if they are both defecting unconditionally, each player can make the other better off by cooperating.

Examples of tit for tat between two players abound and often arise in the most peculiar circumstances. A favorite illustration of mine involves the pugilist "Iron" Mike Tyson who, despite his fearsome reputation, actually displayed a considerable amount of cooperation in the ring with his opponents. Tyson developed a habit of allowing himself to be held in a clinch by his opponents when he needed a rest. Most of his foes welcomed any opportunity for a breather from Tyson's relentless onslaught, so they rested when he did and allowed him to dictate the pace of the bout. Such mutual cooperation was a regular feature of Tyson's fights until he got into the ring with James "Buster" Douglas, who broke with convention and refused to play Tyson's game. When Tyson rested, Douglas punched, upsetting Tyson's rhythm so much that he eventually knocked him out in the tenth round of their championship bout (Berger 1990).

We should bear in mind that the two-player PD can consist of two individuals or two teams or organizations of actors pursuing unified strategies. Axelrod's (1984) example of the live-and-let-live system of trench warfare in World War I shows how two opposing groups can act in concert to produce a less deadly cooperative outcome. Both sides deliberately avoided inflicting too much harm on the other side so as not to instigate a destructive chain reaction. The students and the police in South Korea appear to have developed similar cooperative rules of engagement. Neither side carries lethal weapons: "For all the ferocity of street fighting, the weapons have been the same for years: stu-

---

6. As Taylor (1987, 72) points out, mutual tit for tat will be a coordination equilibrium only if future payoffs are not excessively discounted.

dents throw rocks and gasoline bombs at the police, and the officers fire canisters of tear gas so powerful that it causes adults to gasp and children to scream in pain" (Haberman 1987, 12). It is in the interests of both sides to be bound to temperate strategies. The students have an obvious stake in self-preservation against the vastly more powerful state security apparatus, while the government seeks to avoid a repeat of the massacre that took place in Kwangju in 1980, when soldiers gunned down hundreds of civilians. The conventional wisdom in Korea is that a repeat episode would bring down the regime.

The conditions for cooperation in large groups are more difficult to satisfy. As in the two-person case, individuals must not discount the future too heavily, but there must also be ways to monitor and deter defectors. If these conditions are met, cooperation is possible if each member of the group elects to cooperate as long as everyone else cooperates, but defects otherwise—even if there is only one defector. Alternatively, if there are some unconditional defectors in the group, cooperation by the remaining individuals is still possible if the cooperation of some members of this subgroup depends on the continued cooperation of all of its members. Taylor (1987, 104–5) argues therefore that some level of cooperation is possible in the n-person supergame, but he is less certain that mutual cooperation will occur in practice. The major practical obstacle to cooperation is that conditional cooperation requires monitoring, and the more people there are, the more difficult it becomes for anyone to see if others are upholding their end of the agreement.

Hardin arrives at similar conclusions in his analysis of coordination equilibria in the n-person PD supergame. One possible coordination equilibrium would obtain if each player initially chose to cooperate and continued to cooperate so long as *everyone else* cooperated. For Hardin, "a coordination equilibrium . . . has great appeal over the Prisoner's Dilemma equilibrium of total defection. The appeal is that the coordination equilibrium can result from convention, in which event it is supported by a double incentive to each player. Each player has an interest in his or her own conforming and an interest in others' conforming" (171).

Two conditions, according to Hardin (173–87), must be fulfilled before such conventions will arise. First, each party to a convention has to know something about the knowledge and preferences held by the others. Each individual would seek assurance that the others were aware that they were party to a collective action problem and that they approached the situation with a common preference ordering. Everyone does not have to have information about everyone else; it would be sufficient if the total collectivity broke down into a number of smaller cliques within which the members were familiar with each other.[7]

Second, the parties to a convention would have to possess sanctions in order to punish recalcitrant individuals. The force of the convention is sustained only insofar as no one has an interest in defecting. In the smallest group of two persons, the player who violates the convention makes the other player worse off than if he (the other player) also decided to break the convention; thus, in a two-person game, we would expect defection by one player to prompt defection by the other player. The predictability of this reaction should keep both players in line (co-operating). When the group, however, is large enough that a certain amount of defection will only marginally reduce the profits of the remaining cooperators, the cooperators will have to endure a loss in order to punish violators.

By expanding the prisoner's dilemma to include just one more player, we can see immediately how threats have less credibility in the n-person game ($n > 2$) than in the two-person PD. As usual, assume that in the three-person PD the reward for defection is directly related to the number of cooperators, but that if all defect, the payoff to each player is worse than it would have been had all cooperated. Figure 3.1 enumerates the possibilities.

As in the two-person PD, each player's dominant strategy is to defect, which collectively generates a suboptimal outcome (a payoff of -1 apiece). Consider what happens, however, if two of the three players manage to forge a coalition in order to improve their position. Should either or both shift to a cooperative strategy, they would (collectively) be better off irrespective of the choice of the third player.

However, assuming that payoffs are not transferable, the only viable coalition is one that is mutually cooperative, which would increase the payoff of each player from -1 to at least 0 (if the third player defects) and possibly $+1$ (if the third player cooperates). But since the third player receives a higher payoff by defecting ($+3$) than by cooperating ($+1$), he will defect and reap the maximum payoff through free ridership. The question is whether this third member of the group can be persuaded to change his ways by the coalition.

---

7. Dawes and Orbell (1982) tested the hypothesis that thinking per se will bring various moral and ethical considerations to bear on the PD problem and will consequently foster higher levels of cooperation. However, their results showed that mere contemplation did not increase the incidence of cooperation.

Collective Outcome	Individual Payoff for C	Individual Payoff for D
All C	+1	
2 Cooperate 1 Defects	0	+3
1 Cooperates 2 Defect	−2	+2
All D		−1

FIGURE 3.1. Payoffs in the Three-Person Prisoner's Dilemma

Clearly, reforming a recalcitrant individual is more difficult in the three-person PD than in the two-person PD. The two players in the coalition can punish the defector only by simultaneously punishing themselves (by returning to the defect strategy). Contrast this predicament with that found by the two members of the coalition themselves. We can think of these two players as being engaged in their own private prisoner's dilemma; the difference in their case is that if one player is played for a sucker by the other, he can and will carry out his threat to punish his partner; doing so not only establishes the credibility of his threats but also improves his payoff, since the payoff for mutual defection is greater than the sucker's payoff.

In the three-person PD, the coalition's threat to disband may be scoffed at by the free rider. The free rider's enviable position turns out to be a powerful incentive for each player to avoid forming a coalition with any other. At the same time, given universal defection, there will be a contrary pressure for any two players or all three players to improve matters by forming a coalition. Under these circumstances, it is not difficult to imagine a shrewd and wily player cultivating a reputation for niggardliness in order to convince the remaining players that their only hope for improving their payoffs is to form a cooperative coalition. Unfortunately, if there is an abundance of shrewdness in the group, total defection results. One final pessimistic note: even if the group forms a cooperative coalition of three, the coalition is likely to be unstable, since each individual will be tempted to break the pact and play the other two for suckers. Also, each will want to be the first to defect, since the remaining coalition of two does not possess a credible punishment and may well be resigned to subsidizing the lone free rider. (See Rapoport 1970, 79–83).

As this example shows, if the group has a problem imposing sanctions—because the group is too large and scattered or because penalties hurt the whole group as well as the loafer—it will have difficulty sustaining the convention (cf. Hechter 1987).

In order for "contract by convention" to work, the parties to the agreement must believe that the long-run costs of free riding outweigh any short-run benefits. No altruism is required. People cooperate only because they figure it is in their interests to get along with those whom they expect to depend on in the future. Many social conventions, Hardin observes, "may be of such character that whether one conforms to them partly determines whether one can associate pleasurably with a relevant group" (174–75). But this of course does not mean that people will not *try* to take advantage of their colleagues, or that cooperators do not *wish* they could free ride with impunity. The desire to free ride is neither diminished nor extinguished by conventions but only made less attractive by the countervailing threat of sanctions.

However, if a group can punish a free rider only by discontinuing production of the collective good, it will probably choose to ignore the violator rather than sacrifice the benefits of continued cooperation. The problem here is that by tolerating a single free rider, the group may unintentionally encourage others to try to free ride with impunity. Consequently, in order to maintain its credibility, the group will probably have to occasionally make good on its threat to punish loafers, even if this means diminishing its own well-being.[8] Unfortunately, even if the group makes good on its threat to punish loafers by defecting en masse, it still will not rehabilitate those who disregard social pressures and never do their fair share. These loners are a lost cause to the group and will be excluded from its calculations; no attempt will be made to bring them into the fold.

Once again, however, any such leniency leaves the door open to further defection. Other group members will draw the lesson that "for me to free ride without serious expectation of sanctions may require that I have already established a pattern of iconoclastic free riding" (Hardin 1982, 182). The number of people who will actually cultivate

8. Axelrod's (1981, 1984) "evolutionary" solution to the collective action problem suffers from this problem. Axelrod addresses only iterated two-person interactions and concludes that conditional cooperation (a tit-for-tat strategy) does better than a variety of alternative strategies in a round-robin tournament. Again, it is unclear or even doubtful that this result can be generalized to n-person interactions. Conditional cooperation is effective in two-person prisoner's dilemma games because noncooperation can be directly sanctioned.

a bad reputation in practice will no doubt vary according to the circumstances of the particular convention; suffice it to say that we all know people who manage to be excused from their duties and responsibilities because they are notoriously poor at these tasks (e.g., sitting on committees). "That there are many perhaps rationally determined cantankerous people," Hardin similarly offers, "is event from experience. That it could be easy to establish a pattern of obstinate free riding while escaping some conceivable sanctions is suggested by commonplace arguments that one can establish a reputation for almost anything, including self-serving irrationality" (182).

SMALL-SCALE AND LARGE-SCALE CONVENTIONS

Hardin argues, nonetheless, that large-scale conventions can be fabricated out of the building blocks of dyadic or other small-group interactions. One who is party to a large-scale convention is also party to a multitude of small-scale conventions whose maintenance may depend on how he behaves in the larger context.

According to Hardin:

> My failure to conform to the implicit contractual obligation of our large-number convention may call into doubt my reliability in our small-number convention. My violation need have no perceptible impact on you—it is merely the generalization of such behavior to our other interactions that would affect you. . . . [Y]our failure to sanction me for a violation of a convention that covers a very large group to which we belong may seem to involve costs to you. Even though you will not perceptibly benefit from my conformance to our large-group convention, your failure to sanction might reduce the credibility of your sanctioning me in much smaller-group conventions under which you would perceptibly benefit from my conformance. One cannot easily separate sanctions under one convention from those under another. Hence the interweaving of dyadic and small-number conventions with large-number conventions may make it possible to enforce the latter. (Hardin 1982, 196–97)

While this is a plausible account of how large-number conventions can be maintained, it does not describe how narrowly rational individuals would behave. A rational individual would try to avoid participating in the large-scale convention, since any threats brandished by the rest of the group to disband because of a single defector could be safely discounted. In lieu of group punishment, a party to a small-group, e.g., dyadic, convention with this defector, in Hardin's view, would punish this individual even though doing so is costly; he would carry out the punishment in order to maintain the credibility of his threats in the small-number convention.

But Hardin slips on two points here: first, he does not explain why the dyadic partner of the defector has not also defected in the large-scale convention; everyone should defect, not just a few devious individuals, leaving no one available to mete out punishment. Second, granting that there are some cooperators, he does not explain why any of them should make a generalization about how a person will behave in a small-number convention based on observations of his behavior in a large-number convention. Even if the rational defector from a large-number convention is not sanctioned (as he expects—indeed, he decides not to cooperate on the basis of this expectation), he will nonetheless continue to adhere to the small-number convention, for in that context the threats of his partner *are credible.*

On the other hand, the partner who has cooperated in the large-scale convention would be justified in becoming *wary* of the dependability of someone who has taken advantage of others in another context; but as long as the free rider continued to honor his commitment to the small-number convention, it would be in the interest of his partner to reciprocate and reap the benefits of their agreement. The moment the large-scale free rider gets greedy and becomes a small-scale free rider, his partner can at that point sever the cooperative pact, since it is clearly contrary to his self-interest to continue cooperating with the defector.

Unfortunately, instituting a system of social incentives to sustain large-scale conventions, consisting of punishments for noncooperation and honor and praise for cooperation, is itself a collective action problem. Recalcitrant individuals will have to be disciplined by the community at large, and the attendant costs will have to be borne by the members of the community. Similarly, if cooperators are given social rewards that can be ultimately "cashed in" for private goods, the rest of the community must be willing to bear the costs of those goods. Collective rewards therefore pose the same problem as collective threats and punishments: both constitute public goods that cannot be sustained without significant costs to members of the community. For each individual, there will be a temptation to avoid his or her share of the costs and to free ride on the contributions of others.[9]

9. The only consolation here is that the inclination to free ride may be weaker in the case of these second-order public goods. Michael Laver (1981) suggests, for ex-

Hume ([1739–40] 1969) offered a possible reason why people enforce conventions even when their interests are unaffected. His explanation rests on the idea that people develop secondary sentiments in favor of general moral rules when they experience the advantage of such rules in their own dealings. In Hume's analysis, people first honor their agreements because it is prudent for them to do so. Men and women quickly realize that as individuals, they are not sufficiently endowed to provide all their requirements for living; if everyone behaves selfishly and seeks to maximize only his own welfare, then each reaps less than he would have by cooperating with others. But in order for cooperation to occur and to continue, people must behave justly—that is, they must bargain in good faith, live up to their promises and commitments, and be honest. The rule of justice therefore is a convention which is upheld because it promotes the well-being of those who abide by it. Or as Hume says, "tis only from the selfishness and confin'd generosity of men, along with the scanty provision nature has made for his wants, that justice derives its origin" (547).

However, while this explains why pairs of individuals or small groups are likely to develop and sustain conventions which are in their mutual interest, we still must wonder how large groups can remain cooperative. In large groups, the occasional violator of the convention will benefit not only in the short run but also in the long run. Therefore an individual is without a "natural" (i.e., self-interested) obligation to obey the convention. Hume suggests the following explanation: men learn through experience that exercising restraint on their passions furthers their own goals. For this reason, "they are naturally induc'd to lay themselves under the restraint of such rules, as may render their commerce more safe and commodious" (550). What begins out of expedience, however, (viz., the observance of rules) eventually becomes a matter of deep commitment. Out of *sympathy* with

---

ample (although I believe he overstates his case), that both punishments and honors can be effective only if they are endorsed by virtually all members of the society. Once an individual realizes that he will destroy the public good for everyone, including himself, if he refuses to support it, the incentive to free ride will be effectively removed. No longer is there an opportunity to benefit from the public good while not paying for it: "If you refuse to sell me goods I want because I am a coward or a liar, then the sanction has no effect if my friend, who has not been excluded, may purchase these goods on my behalf. The only way to enact this sanction will be to exclude my friend too, so that the remaining members of the group are unanimously refusing to deal with me. Exclusion, therefore, involves the unanimous cooperation of group members" (68).

our fellow human beings, we approve of acts of justice and frown upon acts of injustice even when our own interests remain undisturbed: "Nay when the injustice is so distant from us, as no way to affect our interest, it still displeases us; because we consider it as prejudicial to human society" (550). Moreover, "an esteem for justice, and an abhorrence of injustice" are encouraged by politicians who regard such sentiments as contributing to the peace and good government of society. The education system and our parents further reinforce these values because honor in a man is thought to be beneficial both to himself and to society (551–52).

By this development, justice comes to be regarded as a virtue and injustice as a vice. To the natural self-interested obligation to conform to the rule of justice we add a broader *moral* obligation. "The *general rule* reaches beyond those instances from which it arose. . . . Thus self-interest is the original motive to the *establishment* of justice; but a *sympathy* with public interest is the source of the *moral approbation*, which attends that virtue" (551).

REPUTATIONAL CONCERNS

But there is another way to understand how a system of rewards and punishments is sustained which in some sense is more coldly calculating (although I suggest later that it need not be) and which also helps to resolve new or second-order collective action problems. Although one may choose not to punish a defector directly by breaking off a dyadic or small-number convention, one is likely nonetheless to behave differently toward the defector in ways which, if contemplated originally by the would-be defector, might prove to be incentive enough for him to honor his commitment to the large-number convention.

In particular, a person tagged with an untrustworthy reputation will not be tolerated for violating small-number conventions even if the violation was made inadvertently. For example, if I suspect, because of your bad-faith behavior elsewhere, that you cannot be trusted to uphold your end of a bargain, then as soon as I think you are reneging on the agreement, I will break off our agreement. In other words, tit for tat will be played ruthlessly to the letter of the strategy. On the other hand, if you instead had a history of playing fair, I will probably be much more forgiving and give you a chance to redeem yourself. I will try to preserve our mutually beneficial convention by playing tit for two tats, or some such lenient strategy.

In addition to losing the benefit of the doubt in existing relationships, a defector will also be a less attractive partner in new cooperative ventures. It's obvious that I will prefer an honest person over a person with a shady past when I choose a partner. Moreover, it is in my interest to do so.

While the damage done by being caught in the occasional lie or deception may be repaired with a string of good behavior—although this may only result in a spotty reputation—there are circumstances in which one's choice will constitute a litmus test of one's character. According to Goffman (1967, 216), the properties of one's character ultimately can be displayed only under duress or, as he puts it, in "perceived fateful circumstances." The only question in these situations is whether one is able to maintain self-control and to perform well under stress.

In the extreme case, a single outstanding action in such contexts will mark one's character for life. One is reminded of Graham Greene's (1985) novel *The Tenth Man*, in which thirty men held hostage in a Gestapo prison in France during the Second World War are forced to choose three among them to face the firing squad. Charlot, a rich lawyer, has the misfortune to draw one of the marked ballots. In a state of horror and panic, he offers his money and house to any man who will take his place. A poor man, to everyone's astonishment, comes forth and accepts the offer—his life in exchange for Charlot's fortune, which he bequeaths to his dear mother and sister.

Following his release from prison, Charlot returns home to the house he once owned, now occupied by the dead man's mother and sister. Using an assumed name, he pretends that he was one of the prisoners, that he knew Charlot and witnessed the infamous transaction. At one point, he tries in vain to defend himself to the dead man's sister by suggesting that Charlot's actions were not that extraordinary, but only slightly beyond the pale: "He acted like a coward, of course, but, after all, anybody's liable to play the coward once. Most of us do and forget about it. It was just that the once in his case proved—well, so spectacular" (96).

But she would hear none of his excuses. In her eyes, Charlot's willingness to sacrifice another man's life for his own revealed that he *was* a coward, not merely that he was capable of a cowardly act. What happened in prison therefore was not any ordinary incident that could be swept aside or explained away but a choice that betrayed Charlot's character.

Our notions of reputation and character stem from our belief that people have consistent personalities and traits. Either they are a certain way (e.g., honest, fair, selfish, etc.) or they are not. We also think that certain combinations of traits go together. We suppose honest people to be generous and to possess other positive traits and bad people to be bad through and through. "Courage is the first of human qualities," Churchill wrote, "because it is the quality that guarantees all others." Goffman (1963) observed that we assume that people have only a single biography. Furthermore, we assume that there is coherence to the entries in this biography; the pieces presumably combine into a consistent whole.

> Anything and everything an individual has done and can actually do is understood to be containable within his biography, as the Jekyll-Hyde theme illustrates, even if we have to hire a biography specialist, a private detective, to fill in the missing facts and connect the discovered ones for us. No matter how big a scoundrel a man is, no matter how false, secretive, or disjointed his existence, or how governed by fits, starts, and reversals, the true facts of his activity cannot be contradictory or unconnected with each other. (Goffman 1963, 62)

Actually, it is more realistic to believe that each of us behaves differently with different people. I might lie to someone who is a stranger while being completely forthright to a friend. This would account for the discrepant reports and evaluations we receive about particular individuals from those who are on different terms with them and have had different experiences and relationships with them. I may have always known my friend Joe to be generous but someone who knows him less well may opine that he is self-serving. Perhaps he is both, in the sense that he has *behaved* both munificently and selfishly in different contexts in the past.

Our impulse nevertheless is to label a person in some consistent fashion across situations; and since people expect consistency from us, we tend to oblige by forging and living up to our reputations. Our biographies therefore constrain the actions that we can take in our lives. For every social identity, certain activities are deemed unconventional or even unacceptable. We might say that society coaxes us to be consistent to the point of irrationality. Instead of following rules selectively and allowing for frequent exceptions to the rule when it serves our interest, we adhere to general rules and in so doing protect our reputations at all times. "Every one," Hume admonished, "who has any regard to his character, or who intends to live on good terms with mankind, must fix an inviolable law to himself, never, by any temptation, to be induc'd to violate those principles, which are essential to a man of probity and honour" ([1739–40] 1969, 552).

It so happens, Goffman (1971) observed, that the social norms which guide our behavior are typically general rules that are applied to classes of events. Consequently we tend to infer that an individual who breaks a rule in any particular circumstance will also do so in other circumstances that are part of the larger class. Similarly, compliance with the rule on a particular occasion creates the impression that one will abide by the general rule whenever it is applicable. Individual actions are therefore believed to be symptomatic of "the actor's general relation to a rule and, by extension, his relation to the system of rules of which the one in question is a part. And, of course, such information often is taken as relevant for an appraisal of the actor's moral character" (97).

A person who violates a social norm is subject to sanctions, either from the party that has suffered directly as a result of this violation or, as Hume suggested, from a third party that executes punishment out of sympathy for the party that has been wronged. It is important to recognize that the same reputational concerns that can motivate compliance to the norms can also provide the motivation behind their enforcement. Compliance with the norms reveals that we are willing to operate according to the generally acknowledged rules of social interaction; we indicate by our actions that we wish to be a member of the community which is governed by those rules. Both our willingness to reward those who abide by the rules and our willingness to punish those who violate them reflect our identification with the system of rules. My refusal to sanction a delinquent, in other words, may be taken as a sign of my disrespect for the norms and raise questions about my moral character almost as if I had committed the violation myself.

ON REPUTATION AND COOPERATION

A concern for one's reputation can also contribute to the development of other-regarding interests. As Socrates advised, the easiest way for a person to maintain a good reputation—a reputation for honesty, trustworthiness, and fair play—is to become the person he wants others to think he is. Reputations therefore can be considered general commitment devices, rationally conceived but relatively unconsciously or habitually followed. People take their cues from their environments about the most profitable or successful courses of action, and they follow them as a general rule rather than rethink their strategies for every decision that needs to be made. Reputations are like roles in the sense that, as Dixon explained in *Lucky Jim,* "the longer you played it, the better chance you had of playing it again" (Amis 1953, 146).

Sometimes it will be in our interest also to have an emotional commitment to these roles. If it is in my long-term interest to be a cooperative person, but there are short-term temptations to be selfish, then it will be easier to cooperate if it makes me feel good to do so. Moreover, in public action, the participant who "throws himself" into the fray or "immerses himself" in the action will receive more praise and social esteem than the person who appears to respond only out of a sense of duty or obligation or only to satisfy personal needs that may or may not be associated with the goals of the movement. Political activists, even if instrumental in their choices, therefore still reap greater dividends over the long haul if they neither behave instrumentally nor even reflect the emotions of a person behaving for ulterior reasons. In short, it can be rational to appear to act for "irrational" (i.e., unselfish) reasons. (Contrast this to the rational reputation for irresponsibility discussed above.)

Why are the *intentions* behind one's actions so important to others? "One reason," according to Krebs (1982):

> surely relates to the fact that the intentions behind an act may supply a better basis for predicting subsequent behavior than the act itself. Another reason relates to the credit and blame observers seek to attribute to the people who perform the helping acts. It is not as much behavior that observers are interested in as the (internal) personality or character of the people who initiate it. In general, people tend to assume that people who behave altruistically are good, and that people who behave egoistically are bad. (450)

For this reason it may be in my self-interest to develop genuine (or not consciously calculating) concern for the welfare of others. In this way I perform my duty as a general rule without being concerned that in any particular instance my personal sacrifice may not be recouped in either the short term or the long term. Sometimes my investment will not be repaid nor my generosity returned, but precisely by not viewing my actions as investments, I will be more likely to behave in a consistently moral fashion and to establish an admirable reputation.

On the other hand, if I am a calculating individual I will have more difficulty developing a good reputation. I will have to expend much more mental energy working out the probable consequences of my actions. The temptation to best another, especially a stranger, when there are no repercussions, combined with the desire to act morally toward another when this pays dividends leaves me with an endless series of complex calculations. Will I see or retain the services of this person again? Does this person have the resources or the goodwill to return my favor? If this person is a stranger, does he know people who know me? Are there witnesses to my transaction with this person?

Given the uncertainty entailed in each of these judgments, I am likely to err occasionally. Should I err on the side of morality, I may suffer a loss in a particular exchange; however, if I act selfishly when I should have been fair-minded, my reputation as an honorable person may be irreparably damaged, and this can have serious repercussions in my future dealings.

I may rationally choose not to take this risk to my reputation. A reputation is too valuable and too fragile a commodity to be endangered for the prospect of a one-shot gain that would result from exploiting the good faith of another. As Cicero (1971) wrote about reputation: "First you must acquire it, and then you have to invest what you have acquired" (142). This attitude might allow others to take advantage of me occasionally, but I am willing to absorb these small losses in order to protect against a much greater loss to my reputation that a moment of selfishness could produce. I even have reason to hope that when others capitalize on my generosity, my reputation for goodwill and trustworthiness will be further enhanced even though my immediate self-interest is harmed.

Unconditional trust may even elicit the trustworthiness of one's opponent. Gandhi, for example, in the spirit of *satyagraha*, taught that continued trust will ultimately elevate one's opponent to the point where he will respond in good faith, even if he does not reciprocate immediately. The patience of the *satyagrahi*, Gandhi explained, is nurtured by his belief in the efficacy of this process: "He is never afraid of trusting the opponent. Even if the opponent plays him false twenty times, the Satyagrahi is ready to trust him for the twenty-first time" (Schechter 1963, 68).[10]

10. It was in this spirit of *satyagraha* that Gandhi exorted his countrymen to follow him in complying with South Africa's Black Act. The South African minister of finance and defense, Jan Christiaan Smuts, had offered a compromise to Gandhi: if the Indian population would register themselves in compliance with the act, he would make every effort subsequently to repeal the law. Gandhi's decision to accept this proposal caused great consternation among his followers because they doubted Smuts's sincerity. Some opposed vigorously—Gandhi himself was severely beaten by dissenters within his ranks as he made his way to register—but most Indians were persuaded

I do not wish to carry this argument too far. A sincere and unselfish individual who allows himself to be taken time and again cannot under normal circumstances be considered rational. In order to be effective, therefore, an emotional commitment to unselfish behavior has to be balanced by a realistic assessment of whether others are taking advantage of one's generosity. The emotions, if permitted to hold sway over conscious strategic considerations, have the potential to undermine both short-term and long-term interests. For this reason, I hesitate to assign a more general rational basis for the emotions along the lines developed recently by Robert Frank (1988). Frank's thesis is that the emotions commit us to actions that although irrational at the moment of execution, benefit us in the long run. For example, a person who threatens to retaliate against anyone who attacks him will, when challenged, sometimes have to make good his threat or else it will lose its deterrent value, even though the cost of retaliation may be excessive. If he is by nature a mean-spirited individual or given to rage, he will have the wherewithal to do what is in his interests; on the other hand, a more deliberate calculator might shy away from retaliation and ultimately harm his interests. Although I agree that the emotions are often effective enforcers of commitments, I do not think that they can be shown in any general sense to be consistently rational. Anger and vengeance, for example, are most effective when tempered and used judiciously—as in the tit-for-tat strategy, which is retaliatory but not unforgiving. An unadulterated commitment to retaliation such as that displayed in the intergenerational blood feud between the Hatfields and the McCoys (which Frank himself cites) highlights the disastrous consequences of emotional commitments that operate indiscriminately.

I prefer instead to think of rationality as a delicate combination of thinking as well as feeling. One may enter into social exchange with an emotional commitment to goodwill and fair play, thereby increasing one's credibility as a desirable partner, but this should not mean that a person will allow himself to be repeatedly played for a sucker. Similarly, to provide an effective deterrent it may be necessary for you to be *seen* as a mad dog, but if you *are* a mad dog then you are likely to throw yourself into more fights than make sense in terms of your interests. Therefore the "presentation of self" as a mad dog is likely to be a

---

by Gandhi's appeal and voluntarily registered. Despite wholesale compliance, Smuts, as many suspected he would, neglected to fulfill his part of the compromise. The Indian population, outraged over the double-cross, promptly collected their registration papers and burned them in a public act of defiance (Schechter 1963, 68–69).

superior strategy insofar as tough talk is balanced by strong self-control. If necessary, some artificial means of binding oneself to take resolute action may be employed to ensure against expediency (Schelling 1980; Elster 1979).

REPUTATION AND CIVIL RIGHTS ACTIVISM

Reputational concerns therefore may counteract the temptation to take advantage of the efforts of others in the provision of collective goods. We refuse one-time gains through free riding in order to retain the esteem, respect, and continued goodwill of those we care about. The selective incentives to participate are the accumulated future benefits that we will reap as a reward for cooperation in the current collective endeavor. Cooperators will shun defectors and instead seek out other cooperators to participate with them in mutually profitable joint ventures. As Taylor (1988) points out, these are relatively costless sanctions (as long as alternative partners for social interchange are available) which only slightly—if that is possible—contradict expectations of individual behavior derived from a thin theory of rationality (see also Hardin 1985). By my account, even these sanctions can be rational if their enforcement contributes favorably to one's standing in the community. In any event, the threat of such sanctions may be sufficient to keep in check temptations to free ride. Our social identities are closely tied to the social identities of the people we associate with, because those who witness our associations will use such information to draw inferences about us. Reputation building is in this respect based on being with the right people rather than on doing something in a more active vein (Goffman 1963, 47).

But unless we have heeded Socrates' advice and become the morally upstanding person we want others to think we are, the impulse to free ride will remain. We will defend our reputations vigorously when it is at risk and be more self-serving when reasonably assured that no one is looking. The temptation to free ride will be especially great when the cost of upholding one's reputation (as a person who does his part) is significant, as it is in the risky types of collective action being considered here. Under such circumstances, we should expect a certain amount of surreptitious free riding even among people who are normally inclined to do the honorable thing. People will attempt to free ride without being detected or to have an excuse for free riding that will exempt them from (public) shame. In practice it will be easier to drop out with impunity if the group is large and impersonal and there is considerable anonymity within it. In small groups, any individual defector will be easily detected and subjected to considerable social pressure.

Reputational considerations were often the deciding factor in determining participation in various campaigns of the civil rights movement. The experience of the freedom riders, for example, demonstrates that even among those with an extraordinary moral commitment to a cause, social pressure may be the added selective incentive needed to motivate participation.

In 1961, a small band of thirteen freedom riders braved frightful mob violence as they wound their way through southern bus stations. Angry mobs in South Carolina and Alabama smashed, burned, and bombed their buses and viciously beat the freedom riders, leaving one elderly white activist with permanent brain damage. Local police officials were of little assistance to the freedom riders. Electing a hands-off policy, they occasionally intervened only to arrest those black activists who broke the color line and sought service at the stations. The depth of the freedom riders' moral convictions is attested by the fact that, after such brutality, they actually *debated* whether or not to continue on their journey, concluding that they should not succumb to the violence (Meier and Rudwick 1975, 137–38).

After the freedom riders had been routed in Alabama, recently elected Congress on Racial Equality (CORE) leader Jim Farmer tried to sneak out of the next leg of the journey through dangerous Mississippi. Fortuitously, Farmer missed the earlier clashes between the freedom riders and mobs in Birmingham and Montgomery when he had to return home to attend to the funeral of his father. Farmer reflects on that occasion: "I must confess that while I felt guilty at leaving, there was also a sense of relief at missing this leg of the trip, because all of us were scared" (Raines 1977, 112). In his unusually candid autobiography, Farmer (1985, 2) recounts how he felt he had too much to lose by going on the freedom rides ("Who would expect me to risk being cut down so early in the promise of a leadership career?"). Nor did he believe he would attain much fame and honor in martyrdom ("And how could I let myself be wiped out now, before anyone outside the inner circle of the movement even knew I was there? Not now, maybe later.").

As the freedom riders boarded the two Trailways and Greyhound buses, Farmer wished them well, shook their hands, gave them the thumbs-up sign, and waved good-bye to them. One of the freedom riders, however, a pretty teenage girl, could not understand what Farmer was doing when he shook her hand through the open bus window and told her to "have a safe trip" and that his prayers were with her. In a shocked voice, she pleaded desperately, "You're coming with us, aren't you, Jim?" Farmer, anticipating this awkward moment, "went through my prearranged litany of excuses: I'd been away from the office for four weeks; my desk was piled high with papers. People would be angry with CORE if they got no timely response to their letters, and would not contribute money. . . . All of us want to be where the action is, but no such luck. Some of us are stuck with the dull jobs, the supportive ones. I could not be there in person, but she knew I'd be there in spirit" (3).

Of course none of these excuses rang true to the girl; when she continued her pleading, Farmer realized that he would never be able to face himself or his friends and colleagues in the movement if he bailed out on a pretext and then something terrible happened to the freedom riders. Thus shamed, Farmer gathered his luggage and joined the trip, quite certain that it would be his last.

Martin Luther King, Jr., also declined the freedom riders' invitation to join them as they resumed their campaign in Montgomery. King was on probation in Georgia, and if he was arrested again, he risked going to prison at what he thought a very inopportune time. It is noteworthy that King's reasoning, like Farmer's, was rejected as disingenuous by the freedom riders, many of whom were also on probation. One freedom rider expressed his disappointment that King did not simply admit that he would not go because he was afraid. The whole episode illustrates the extreme relativity of our notions of courage and cowardice (Oates 1982, 174–75; Raines 1977, 123).

In general, the sincerity of those in the movement was often doubted by their fellow activists unless they could prove that they had paid a price for their involvement. Mary King (1987) recalls that SNCC worker Ivanhoe Donaldson passed this test because he had joined the organization "after 'dropping out' of Michigan State University—a badge of honor to us because it signified that he had put his future on the line for his beliefs" (98). She also points out some of the consequences of this martyr complex: "Competition and bragging were frequent in the movement as to who had been jailed or beaten the most. It was acknowledged to require courage" (117).

When James Farmer gave up the freedom ride the first time on account of the death of his father, he had a "good" excuse for leaving, and others could not take umbrage toward him; but he provided a much less convincing account of his behavior when he tried to persuade the freedom riders on the second leg of the journey that he could not join them because he had paperwork to catch up on. Whereas the first explanation excused him from participating in the freedom ride by leaving him no choice but to go home, the second explanation was a transparent excuse for not fulfilling his commitment to the other participants. The difference between good and bad accounts for one's delinquency has been captured by Goffman (1971), who explains that "the more an actor can argue mitigating circumstances successfully, the more he can establish that the act is not to be taken as an expression of his moral character; contrarily, the more he is held responsible for his act, the more fully it will define him for others" (112).

When we say that others see through our excuses, we mean that they do not accept our ostensible explanation but are aware of the underlying truth, which reflects poorly on us. Seeing through someone also has a more literal meaning in that it is related to visible stigmata—such as physical deformities. When someone sees through us, it is almost as if he sees the stigma that we bear. We feel naked or exposed to the scrutiny of such a skeptic.

As King's experience with the freedom riders shows, however, the criteria for a good excuse can become severe as people become increasingly committed to a cause. On another occasion, King was invited by Atlanta students to participate in a sit-in protest that was expected to result in arrests. Again he was ambivalent about participating and delayed his decision. On this occasion, King created what he believed to be a foolproof excuse to avoid the protest by agreeing to a meeting with John Kennedy in Miami just prior to the 1960 election: "The students would be angry, but they would have to accept a meeting with one or both of the presidential candidates as a legitimate reason for missing a demonstration" (Branch 1988, 349). The meeting fell through, however, when Kennedy would not agree to inviting Richard Nixon, and King was left to participate in the Atlanta demonstration.

Any excuse for nonparticipation will therefore be regarded with suspicion. With total commitment, the valuation of the cause surpasses virtually every possible alternative consideration, so that it becomes almost inconceivable that an obligation to something other than the cause can have a higher priority.[11]

Among people who are totally committed to a cause, excuses are

---

11. Former University of Miami football coach Howard Schnellenberger made this distinction between a commitment and a total commitment. In the creation of ham and eggs, he explained, the hen that provided the eggs gave of itself, but the pig that provided the ham made a total commitment.

sometimes sought where none are needed. Following a Marion, Alabama, night march in which the demonstrators were trounced by state troopers, a sympathy march was quickly organized by SCLC in nearby Selma. A speech delivered by march leader Hosea Williams "whipped" the crowd "to a fever pitch" before it departed from Brown Chapel (Fager 1974, 76).

Outside, however, Wilson Baker and his policemen blocked the path of the marchers. Baker was determined to stop the march, because it was certain to cause more bloodshed, especially since the Marion incident had attracted racists from all over the area who were raring for a fight. He first appealed to Williams to lead the marchers back into the chapel, but when Williams refused, Baker moved quickly to place him under arrest. Baker then turned to the other leaders of the march and told them that he would release Williams if they would take the people back into the church. The situation seemed hopeless to the marchers. The path was blocked by a solid phalanx of policemen, and in the distance the state police served as reinforcements. Therefore they reluctantly accepted Baker's offer and retreated, whereupon Williams was set free.

Despite having little choice under the circumstances, Williams was unhappy with Baker's ploy. It made him look bad. He called it "dirty pool" and suggested to Baker, "If you're going to arrest me, take me down to the jail, don't hold me here and then let me out. It don't look right" (77). What he meant is that if the police were intent on stopping the march, he wanted the option of resisting to be taken from him completely so that he would no longer have any choice over the outcome. The removal of choice thus would have ensured removal of his personal responsibility.

Shame is an effective motivator when delinquents can be identified and singled out for derision. But there must still be someone or some group of individuals who are themselves sufficiently motivated to take the initiative by indicating their willingness to participate. In so doing, they exert pressure on those among them who are recalcitrant. Farmer's embarrassment stemmed from the dedication of the other freedom riders, without whom there would have been little threat to his self-image and reputation.

During the Montgomery bus boycott, a number of participants were asked to use their cars to provide transportation for those who normally commuted to work by bus. Car ownership was a major status symbol for blacks and served to distinguish those in the middle class from their lower-class counterparts. Many of those with automobiles were afraid their cars would be damaged and therefore were reluctant to comply with this request. In order to persuade them, it was necessary for some of the preachers at the head of the movement to assure them that they were going to lend their own automobiles to the car pool. This initiative, combined with the rapid consent of some other supporters of the boycott, undoubtedly created pressure on those car owners who were less responsive to the idea. Ultimately such peer pressure made noncooperation sufficiently unattractive for the hold-outs that a number of them were persuaded to do what in effect was more than their fair share (Williams 1987, 78).

In Albany, SNCC activists targeted the high school students, who were thought to be more receptive than adults to political activism. They befriended the students, participated in everyday activities with them, and in so doing became familiar and accepted members of the community. All along, SNCC's strategy was to mobilize the students on the theory that they would then place pressure on adults to participate either out of concern for the students or embarrassment over having allowed youngsters to lead the way (Morris 1984, 240). The same dynamics were evident during the 1960 Nashville sit-in when student activists chose to remain in jail rather than pay a fine. "Outside the courtroom, many Negroes were shocked at the news that their city, forced to choose, had imprisoned some of the finest students in the area instead of the white hoodlums who had attacked them. Some also felt shame at remaining aloof from the protests while such treatment was being meted out to the nonviolent students" (Branch 1988, 279).

To give another example, in Selma, as elsewhere in the South, black schoolteachers were notorious for their reluctance to risk their livelihood for the cause. In fact, many blacks in the movement became full-time participants only after they had been expelled from their schools for earlier activities by black administrators who gave in to pressure from the white community. Therefore few civil rights workers in Selma had reason to believe that the schoolteachers would lend a hand in the campaign to register voters. That they did participate, contrary to expectations, was due largely to the efforts of the Reverend Frederick D. Reese, a local leader who shamed the teachers for relinquishing their citizenship by not registering to vote.

The teachers, appropriately embarrassed, decided to conduct their own march to the courthouse. They gathered in an elementary school auditorium where roll was called by the march's organizer. "Only a few were permitted to indulge their fears and stay behind: the very aged, the seriously infirm, and one member of a couple if both spouses were teachers and there were young children at home" (Fager 1974, 37). Thus, the initiator of the march not only shamed the teachers into committing themselves to participate, but by taking attendance he devised an obvious method to ensure that people lived up to their promises. Those who backed out without possessing a legitimate excuse (of which there were but a few) were easily identified.

The key role played by the organizer in this case was to discredit the rationales then popular among the schoolteachers for their nonparticipation in the movement. By forcing the teachers to confront their reasons for not contributing, and to recognize them for what they were—excuses—the Reverend Mr. Reese probably made it uncomfortable for the teachers not only to face him but to save face among one another. It is as if a comfortable myth shared by the teachers that their behavior was defensible was suddenly dispelled; now they would have to be either responsible citizens or not-so-admirable free riders. Therefore sometimes people shame each other into participating.

Similar "reciprocal" reputational pressures also contributed to the decisions of the four Greensboro students to demand their right to be served at the Woolworth's lunch counter. They had engaged in so much abstract discussion about the evils of discrimination that they began to feel it was incumbent upon them to act according to their beliefs. Otherwise it was all empty talk, philosophizing in the worst sense of that word. Each had presented himself to the others as a concerned and responsible citizen, a person with deep moral convictions, and one who would challenge existing practice where it was clearly wrong. By not acting on these self-professed values, each person's reputation would be diminished in the eyes of the others. In a curious way, then, the four students policed each other and in so doing ensured that each would act like the person he said he was. They provoked each other into action, according to Franklin McCain: "There were many words and few deeds. We did a good job of making each other feel bad" (Carson 1981, 15).

COMMITMENTS IN SELMA

In the Selma voting rights drive, we have a slightly different example of people becoming increasingly committed to a course of action that they did not necessarily wish to follow. As the stakes of this campaign increased, and participation correspondingly grew more dangerous, it became more difficult for an individual to bow out without losing face. Although many in the campaign were probably reluctant to place themselves in the life-threatening situations that arose, the dynamics of the campaign and in particular the escalation of the conflict increased their commitment to their fellow activists to the point where they had to—as the saying goes—finish what they had started.

Commitments can sneak up on an individual. Becker (1960) calls this process "commitment by default." An individual, through a series of small acts, works himself into a situation in which he must follow a course of action or risk suffering a serious consequence. Each minor act in the chain enters the individual into a side bet that can be collected only if he maintains "a consistent line of behavior"; if he does not, he loses it all. It is, according to Becker, as if a person made a steady stream of contributions out of his wages to a nontransferrable pension fund; each separate contribution could be lost without great pain, but after a sufficiently lengthy period, the potential loss would be so great that the option to change jobs would be effectively foreclosed.

When civil rights activists led by Martin Luther King, Jr., invaded Selma, Alabama, in January 1965, they fully expected Sheriff Jim Clark to do something rash that would draw the public's wrath against him and increase its sympathy for the civil rights movement. For weeks, however, Clark, well-known for his lack of self-control, refused to take the bait. Local officials had conspired to keep a lid on him, and Clark himself seemed determined to deny the protesters an issue to rally around. King gave speeches and led daily marches to the voter registration building, where blacks attempted to get themselves added to the voting roll. A few minor skirmishes and the odd act of violence drew limited media attention to the campaign but on balance the situation at the end of the month remained well contained and uncontroversial. This strange turn of events left the activists dismayed and disappointed. Campaign leaders, surmising that nothing succeeds as planned, contemplated packing their bags and resuming the registration drive elsewhere. But precisely at this point, "just as," observed John Herbers, a *New York Times* reporter, "the campaign seemed to be on the verge of dying" (Garrow 1978, 48), Sheriff Clark refused to leave well enough alone and launched four mass arrests over two days that, in a striking instance of deus ex machina, breathed new life into the movement. On the first day, according to plan, King was himself arrested, along with two hundred and fifty other marchers who deliberately violated a local parade law. That same day, in a separate incident, an additional five hundred schoolchildren were also arrested. On the following day, while King remained in jail after refusing to post bail,

Clark made two more mass arrests involving hundreds of schoolchildren and adult marchers (47–48).

Although Clark's impulsive crackdown at the beginning of February reinvigorated the activists enough for them to carry on, the campaign still languished through the remainder of the month and failed to grab the national spotlight. King upped the ante in the first week of March when he called for a protest march from Selma to the state capital, Montgomery, where a petition of grievances would be presented to Governor George Wallace. The decision was sparked by the shooting of Jimmie Lee Jackson (referred to in chapter 2) in the nearby town of Marion. Jackson had been mortally wounded by a state trooper while retreating with other demonstrators from a scheduled march to the town courthouse. A number of other blacks, along with several newsmen, were also bloodied in the vicious confrontation, which drew front-page headlines in the national press.

In the estimate of Albert Turner, a participant, about 50 percent of the six hundred protesters who arrived at Brown's Chapel to participate in the march to Montgomery had come from Marion (Raines 1977, 195). Many of the marchers brought with them backpacks and other camping equipment in anticipation of a long trek. On the other hand, others, like SNCC leader John Lewis, never figured to march on that day the entire fifty-mile route along the highway from Selma to Montgomery. It couldn't be done: "We hadn't set up tents along the way; we didn't have any place to stay. Apparently the idea was that we would march outside of Selma that night and them come back, and then the next morning we would continue. But our plan was not to go from Selma to Montgomery straight. That was just impossible" (Raines 1977, 206).

Neither group, it happened, had the right idea about how events would unfold on that fateful sunny Sunday afternoon. On their way out of Selma, the marchers had to cross over the Edmund Pettus Bridge which spanned the Alabama River. There at the bridge they were met by Sheriff Clark and his notorious posse, mounted on horseback, and a bevy of state troopers led by Major John Cloud, who ordered the marchers to retreat. When the protesters held their ground, the posse and troopers assailed them with billy clubs, bullwhips, cattle prods, and tear gas, quickly forcing them to flee for their lives after they had tried momentarily to resist nonviolently by huddling in prayer. Not content with merely turning the marchers around, Clark's posse chased them down and savagely beat them as they struggled desperately to reach the sanctuary of their church. All the while, television cameramen and still photographers recorded the events on film and in pictures that would be shown to a shocked and outraged national audience that evening and in the following days.

In the aftermath of Bloody Sunday, King, who had returned earlier to Atlanta to deliver a sermon and had missed the march, rushed back to Selma to organize a second march on the following Tuesday. At the same time, hundreds of sympathetic onlookers from out of state who had seen pictures of Sunday's attack were moved to travel to Selma to show their support for the civil rights activists.

President Johnson, however, wanted the proposed march to be canceled, and word was passed to King that Federal District Court Judge Frank Johnson would issue a restraining order if necessary. King resisted these attempts to dissuade him but gave signals that he was prepared to compromise with the administration. A deal was tentatively struck when administration representative LeRoy Collins got King to agree to retreat upon reaching the officers' line if he (Collins) obtained agreements (which he subsequently did) from Sheriff Clark and Colonel Al Lingo to restrain their troops (Garrow 1986, 402).

The deal, however, was unbeknownst to other civil rights leaders, and the assemblage of two thousand marchers who congregated at Brown's Chapel early Tuesday prepared to finish what had been so brutally interrupted the previous Sunday. After a morning of rallying, King arrived in the early afternoon and delivered what, considering his intentions, was a highly unusual speech exhorting the throng of marchers to persevere in the task at hand despite the great danger facing them: "I have made my choice, I have got to march. I do not know what lies ahead of us. There may be beatings, jailings, tear gas. But I would rather die on the highways of Alabama than make a butchery of my conscience. . . . I ask you to join me today as we move on" (Sitkoff 1981, 192).

By now the marchers were energized and braced for anything that might stand between themselves and the capital. Having taken King's message to heart, they filed out after him singing "Ain't Gonna Let Nobody Turn Me 'Round," one of the anthems of the movement. When they reached the Edmund Pettus Bridge, there to greet them once again on the other side were Major Cloud and the state troopers. King led his ranks across the bridge but halted at the line of officials, whereupon he was commanded by Cloud to cease and discontinue the march for reasons of public safety. King then requested and was given an opportunity to lead his group in prayer. Moments later, to the shock and amazement of his followers, he turned and directed the marchers back to the chapel. "Although each rank of the column," Garrow (1978) writes, "wheeled in turn and followed King back into Selma, the surprise—and anger—at the meek retreat was widespread and strong among the SNCC workers and Selma teenagers, who had not received word of the late-morning negotiations" (87). Nevertheless, Matusow (1984) adds, "Most of the two thousand marchers . . . were no doubt pleased by their unanticipated reprieve from Martyrdom" (183–84).

Fager's interpretation of the reaction of the marchers to the turnaround is corroborative:

> There were those who were disappointed at this outcome, and they
> were to make their dissatisfaction noisily evident when the march
> was over; but they were a small minority. Most of those who
> walked over the bridge were simply relieved that, after nerving
> themselves to face death itself, they were in one piece, walking back
> through downtown Selma singing and smiling. (105)

PRIVATE VS. PUBLIC PREFERENCES

It is difficult to understand the reasons behind this peculiar mix of emotions in the marchers—first anger over having been repelled initially at the bridge, then relief over being stopped a second time—but let me offer the following explanation.

The perpetrators of violence want to deter the activists by magnifying the costs of participation. But although violence frightens, terrorizes, and deters, it also challenges the pride, honor, and courage of the activists, and oftentimes these intangible and emotional factors will cancel out the dampening effects of violence. The fear of being known as a coward, a quitter, or a person who cannot be depended on in a crisis can counteract the fear of being physically harmed. Therefore if free ridership is accompanied by shame, disgrace, dishonor, and other reputational damage, individuals may continue to prefer participation to nonparticipation irrespective of the rising cost of participation.

Sometimes, however, group members, having been pushed around by the opposition, will calculate that it is not worthwhile to escalate a conflict because of the prohibitive costs they will likely have to bear. If group members arrive at this conclusion collectively, through open, candid discussion, then we would expect them to refrain from acting rashly. A preference for participation is conditional upon other people also participating; should there be a general exodus, then each individual will have no compunction about also bailing out, since courage and cowardice after all are largely relative notions. If I choose to be a free rider while everyone else perseveres in the face of great danger, I am a coward, but if we *all* decide to throw in the towel in this situation, then perhaps we are simply prudent.

It is, however, precisely in these situations that pride and anger can undermine any forthright assessment of one's predicament, since such emotions typically cloud prudential considerations. Although each individual may secretly prefer that the group retreat from further confrontations with the opposition, each is also likely to want to maintain a brave face. Therefore, in Selma, the fear of being labeled a coward may have pressured a number of individuals to agree to march despite their reluctance to do so. Private preferences may have been suppressed in order to protect one's reputation and to avoid public humiliation.

The contradiction between each group member's private and public preferences can be seen as follows. (See fig. 3.2.) Privately each person wants the entire group to withdraw (DD). Barring that outcome, he would like to withdraw surreptitiously while everyone else persevered (DC). Lastly, if he is going to participate, he would rather do so in concert with others than all alone (CC > CD). Defection is therefore the dominant private strategy of every individual. If everyone could make a free choice, unencumbered by social pressures and preoccupations with his reputation, a withdrawal would be the natural outcome.

In contrast, a group member's public preferences are strikingly different. Public preferences are those cues and messages that he is providing to others. Because he prefers to be perceived as courageous rather than fainthearted, each individual professes to want to take tough measures against the opposition. Each individual, in fact, prefers to "out-tough" the other, gaining a bit of satisfaction from the pusillanimity of his compatriot (CD > CC). Nothing is worse than appearing cowardly before another's fearlessness.

Order of Private Preferences	Order of Publicly Stated Preferences
1. DD (Everyone defects)	1. CD
2. DC (Everyone participates but him)	2. CC
3. CC (Everyone participates)	3. DD
4. CD (Everyone defects but him)	4. DC

FIGURE 3.2. Private vs. Publicly Stated Preferences

Of course everyone's pluckiness in the face of adversity creates in each individual's mind a misleading impression of other people's intentions. This in turn leads to a collective response that is suboptimal for the participants. Instead of staying out of the fray, the group returns for another round.

The Selma episode shows that a person's choice may reflect his underlying preference or it may not. Participation that is motivated by expressive and participatory benefits, consideration for the welfare of others, inaccurate calculation of one's own expected (self-interested) benefits, or heartfelt moral beliefs accurately reflects a preference for action over inaction. On the other hand, participation that is induced by social pressure or fear of punishment or retribution reflects a choice of action over inaction but conceals (sometimes transparently) an underlying preference for inaction over action (cf. Sen 1973). Thus, the anger of the Selma marchers quickly turned to relief when they realized they were retreating from the bridge and returning to the chapel. They had expressed their readiness for combat, only to be spared the ordeal, an outcome that satisfied both their private and public preferences.[12]

SYMPATHY AND MORAL CONCERNS

As I suggested earlier, people do not always have to be pressured to do the honorable thing. Indeed, many people will choose to act morally and refuse to take advantage of others even when an opportunity to do so presents itself. In such cases, uncooperative but narrowly rational behavior will be passed up even when it can be undertaken with impunity.

In many of the instances cited above, those who were pressured by others to participate undoubtedly were already inclined to do so for moral and altruistic reasons, and their reluctance was due to the extremely high cost of involvement. The social pressure that was applied to them was therefore the marginal incentive that was required to push them over the threshold separating nonparticipation from participation; it was, however, hardly the sole motivation for their eventual cooperation.

---

12. As Schelling (1966) observed in discussing the mixed motives of the game of chicken, "One of the values of laws, conventions, or traditions that restrain participation in games of nerve is that they provide a graceful way out. If one's motive for declining is not lack of nerve, there are no enduring costs in refusing to compete" (120).

In chapter 5 I will argue that individuals who have internalized the norms so wholeheartedly that the temptation to free ride is extinguished may constitute the essential force behind collective action in its earliest and most uncertain stages. However, it is unclear to me how we can disentangle the motivations that impel such people to behave in the manner that they do. Are their actions essentially expressive in character, in that they reflect a need and a desire to voice displeasure and moral outrage over current practices? Or do the actions simply represent the logical extension of a well-socialized citizen who has learned the lesson not only that it is prudent to possess other-regarding concerns, but that it is best to develop genuine feelings for others so that one plays fair instinctively rather than strategically?

As I suggested earlier, moral behavior is more honored when it is not seen to be driven by ulterior motives; hence, it may be in one's self-interest to develop genuine concern for others. In this vein, Michael Scriven (1966) contends that it can be rational for someone to submit to being socialized into a society that fosters altruistic concerns. While each person within such a system must occasionally make sacrifices in helping others, each is more than compensated by the assistance he receives in return. "In the usual circumstances of society, each citizen's chances of a satisfying life for himself are increased by a process of conditioning all citizens *not* to treat their own satisfaction as the most important goal" (239–40).

Acting morally, according to Scriven, is akin to obeying orders instinctively in the army. If everyone in the armed forces acts selfishly and refuses to take directions, each person's chance of survival in a military conflict is greatly reduced. It is therefore in the soldier's interest that he and his colleagues undergo rigorous training and learn to follow commands automatically. It is also in his interest that soldiers be taught to make great personal sacrifices for their country, since heroism and personal valor are among the most prized resources an army can possess; naturally, the gains that extreme patriotism and self-sacrifice bring to the collectivity and in particular to his chances of survival would have to exceed the greater risk to his own life that a commitment to heroism entails. In other words, it is advantageous to be a member of a squadron of heroes only if, as a result, the probability of being saved through the sacrifice of others is greater than the likelihood that one will have to give up his own life in the interests of another.

Moreover, "instinctive unselfishness" effectively reduces the community cost of supporting a prestige system, since the reward for conforming is divided thereupon between an external social payment (overt incentive and punishment) and an internal self-payment—the good feeling one gets "automatically" from upholding an ideal (Goode 1978, 21). Therefore the *internalization* of norms through an elaborate socialization process, which has typically appeared superfluous in a rational choice calculus, may be viewed as a community cost-saving device in the institution of a moral system of rewards and punishment. If people are unselfish only under the watchful eye of an authority, then unselfish behavior will in practice be uncommon. People cannot be monitored and policed continuously in all facets of their lives; the penalties instituted may be insufficient to command the desired behavior; out of ignorance or incompetence, people may miscalculate that it is in their interest, given the penalties, to comply; people will behave selfishly whenever they calculate that there is little likelihood that penalties will be enforced. In sum, the well-trained conscience is the best policeman. It is "inescapable, incorruptible, immediate, and inexpensive" (Scriven 1966, 245).

Of course the moral system outlined by Scriven works only if people honor their commitment to unselfishness when the opportunity presents itself and do not simply pay lip service to the credo as long as they benefit and do not have to live up to it themselves. The system collapses when people revert to selfishness once they are called upon to make a sacrifice. For this reason it is preferable that people internalize their moral views to the point where the temptation to act selfishly when one should act morally is removed, so that the moral alternative becomes the *preferred* alternative. For one so committed to a moral life, actions are taken not because they are rewarded or because alternative action is punished but because such actions are morally right. The decision to choose a moral life was made for prudent, long-run selfish reasons, and this decision cannot be reversed for short-run selfish reasons.

> A man now moral is not contaminated by his past; he is not now *secretly* amenable to selfish arguments because *once* he was. He is motivationally no different from a man who is moral because he has been brought up that way, and such a man would not be persuaded. However a man gets to be moral, he *is* moral if he does what is moral *because* it is moral. So the moral life is a rationally stable solution to the problem of how to live. (Scriven 1966, 260)

Proportionately few people, it would seem to me, have developed the commitment to moral behavior that Scriven recommends. Nonetheless, even limited, self-serving personal commitments that a person will accumulate in the normal course of affairs to friends, family, and associates will tend to constrain his freedom to act selfishly in all circumstances. Commitments tend to bind an individual "to act in a more altruistic manner" than he would have had he not made such commitments originally (Harsanyi 1969, 523). The response of the civil rights activists in Selma, recounted above, shows how severely one's rational choice can be constrained by personal commitments.

Moreover it seems equally clear that the same ongoing social exchanges and interactions that provide people with an incentive to uphold their obligations to others are also conducive to the development of genuine concerns about others. Community gives rise to both fair play and affection, and the closeness of social bonds will determine the degree to which people will cooperate with others not only out of self-interest but out of sympathy as well.

Therefore not all cooperation that is motivated by social concerns will be coerced or involuntary. The same factor that makes it important for us to maintain an agreeable reputation—membership in groups whose members depend on each other for at least part of their well-being—also promotes mutual trust, sympathy, and solidarity. For example, Carson (1981) tells the stories of two SNCC staff members who, through different but equally fortuitous means, grew increasingly attached to the civil rights cause and the people they worked with.

John Perdew was a junior attending Harvard University when he decided to go with some friends to Albany, Georgia, during their summer vacation in response to a SNCC recruitment drive. Perdew knew little about the civil rights movement and he volunteered mainly because he was looking for something "adventurous" to do. But once in Georgia he had a rude awakening to the brutal treatment of blacks in the South. He also discovered that the civil liberties he took for granted back home were routinely trampled upon by Georgia officials. Twice he was arrested for participating in demonstrations; the second time he was imprisoned for three months on a bogus insurrection charge. When he was finally released, his education to become an activist was complete and he chose to remain with SNCC's field staff.

The second SNCC staff member, Bill Hall, participated in his first civil rights protest in order to be close to his girlfriend: "If I wanted to be with her, we were going to be on the line together picketing" (Carson 1981, 72). After this innocent introduction, Hall began attending meetings and participating in the activities of a nearby SNCC affiliate. As Hall was drawn increasingly into the movement, his grades at Howard University were compromised and he failed in his first attempt to win entrance to medical school. This freed even more time for political activism, so that when he eventually gained acceptance to medical school, his priorities had so changed that he declined and decided to remain with SNCC. "I just became so involved," he explained, "so much in love with the people" (ibid.).

These examples illustrate how initial recruitment into a relatively costless political activity can prepare or ready an individual for subsequent recruitment into riskier forms of participation. The first foray may occur almost accidentally or be the result of mild social pressure; one might attend a rally out of curiosity, or a demonstration at the urging of a close friend one does not wish to offend or disappoint. Attendance at the political event, however, introduces the novice into a different social network, informs him of the nature of the cause, exposes him to new ideas, attitudes, and values, and leads him to develop sympathies toward others (McAdam 1986). In this manner, participation in time-consuming, perilous forms of political activity that cannot be explained by conventional notions of self-interest may be an outgrowth of more routine activities that can be attributed to narrowly rational instrumental motives.

Summary

Several issues have been addressed in this chapter. I argued that social interaction is better modeled as an iterated prisoner's dilemma than as a single-play game. Consequently individuals have an incentive to develop decision-making strategies that are contingent on the cooperative or uncooperative behavior of others. Contingent strategies, such as tit for tat, are extremely effective in generating and maintaining cooperation in two-person prisoner's dilemma interactions; but such strategies are less effective in large-number situations because monitoring is difficult and mass defection to punish a lone defector is impractical.

I examined Hardin's proposal that large-scale cooperation can be manufactured out of small-scale relationships. According to this argument, people cooperate in large-scale ventures because otherwise their small-scale partners will punish them in the course of their local (e.g., dyadic) agreements. But this solution is unworkable: the defector's partner in the dyadic relationship will also want to defect from the large-scale agreement; but even if he cooperates in the larger venture, he will have no incentive to punish as long as their small-scale arrangement continues to be profitable.

Alternatively, I suggested that people will cooperate out of reputational concerns. An esteemed reputation has considerable instrumental value in a society. Individuals who fulfill their obligations are more attractive to others as friends, associates, and partners than those who are known to shirk their duty.

A series of examples from the civil rights movement illustrated the prevalence of reputational concerns in people's decisions to participate in various campaigns. I also argued, however, that these personal commitments were augmented by genuine concerns and sympathy for others. Social interaction is conducive not only to the development of obligations and commitments but also to the formation of other-regarding interests.

4 | *Narrowly Rational Expressive Benefits*

> *Revenge is a kind of wild justice.*
> Francis Bacon, *Essays*

One stumbling block of a rationalist approach is that it leaves little if any room for behavior that is not so much means-end as expressive in character. Whenever I teach the logic of collective action to classes of undergraduates, I have difficulty convincing them that it has anything to do with reality. Invariably they object that the "logic" is both empirically false and misleading as a prescription for action. At the heart of their unease is a stubborn belief that people do not want to be free riders. Instead, "they want to be a part of collective action because they *enjoy* participating." I have no doubt that these students are in some sense correct. In essence, they are echoing a point made by economist Albert Hirschman (1982), who likened taking a free ride when one has the opportunity to participate in public action to declining a delicious meal in favor of a satiation-producing pill.

Eagerness on the part of participants is obviously inconsistent with claims that people have to be dissuaded from free riding either through selective incentives or the threat of penalties. Eighteen-year-old Cordell Reagon, for example, crashed civil rights demonstrations in Nashville after having been told to stay away because he was considered too young (Branch 1988, 525). The obvious reason why people like Reagon clamor to participate is that they derive considerable expressive pleasure from the act of participation itself. That is how Walter Lippmann explained the motivations behind the famous American revolutionary John Reed:

> He is a person who enjoys himself. Revolution, literature, poetry, they are only things which hold him at times, incidents merely of his living. Now and then he finds adventure by imagining it, oftener he transforms his own experience. . . . He is the only fellow I know who gets himself pursued by men with revolvers, who is always once more just about to ruin himself. I can't think of a form of

disaster which John Reed hasn't tried and enjoyed. (Rosenstone 1975, 4)

Political activists, it appears, not only wish to achieve particular political objectives, such as a change in government policy, and to fulfill their obligations, but also to voice their convictions, affirm their efficacy, share in the excitement of a group effort, and take part in the larger currents of history. "Life is action and passion," observed Oliver Wendell Holmes. "I think it is required of a man that he should share the action and passion of his time at the peril of being judged not to have lived."

Expressive behavior is so-called "because its importance to the actor is in expressing support for the cause, regardless of whether it produces the desired visible consequences. The question is not one of acting rationally or irrationally: the advocate wants to 'do something,' to 'go on record,' to 'strike a blow' for the cause" (Turner 1981, 11). Turner takes the inherent uncertainty of the effectiveness of political activism to be evidence of its nonrational basis: "The complex, opaque, and slowly evolving situations within which most social movements operate make assessments of any but the most immediate effects extremely difficult. . . . Consequently most action must be governed by the accepted symbolic significance attached to a course of action, which is the criterion for expressive rather than effect-rational behavior" (ibid.).

I will use the term "expressive" in the broadest sense to encompass the variety of noninstrumental benefits that one might receive from political participation. Some may quarrel with my choice of terminology for such a general category of benefits. Expressive benefits, for example, that stem from voicing one's opinions are separable from the good feelings that one gets from doing the right thing, as well as from the important lessons that one learns from taking part in the political process. Unfortunately there is no widely accepted classification for these ill-defined incentives. Scitovsky (1976) discusses our continual "pursuit of novelty" and our need for "stimulating activity." Hardin (1982) evaluates a broad class of "extrarational" motivations, which includes both moral and participatory goals. Margolis (1982) examines three types of "noncontingent" benefits: (1) demonstration benefits, (2) consumption benefits, and (3) psychic or moral benefits. Elster (1985) considers "process-oriented motivations for cooperation" (147). And Hirschman (1985) simply studies "noninstrumental" activities "such as the pursuit of truth, beauty, justice, liberty, community, friendship, love, salvation, and so on" (12).

It is not difficult to find evidence for the expressive value of political participation. If we accept at face value the testimony of abolitionists, populists, civil rights activists, feminists, environmentalists, antiwar protesters, and other participants in causes large and small, political activism is often driven by a desire for self-respect and personal empowerment. Even participation in more conventional political activity seems to be significantly motivated by these considerations. For example, in her study of members of four prominent public interest organizations—the League of Women Voters, the Conservative Caucus, the ACLU, and Common Cause—Cook (1984) discovered that the development of a feeling of efficacy was the reason respondents most frequently gave for joining. The desires to pursue a policy and to fulfill one's civic duty were the second and third incentives cited most commonly. "Political information" was the most frequently cited "material" incentive for membership, but it was seldom regarded as the primary reason for joining. Based on her examination of open-ended interviews with group members, Cook comments that for many of the respondents, the act of joining is akin to enlisting in an "ideological crusade." The comment of one respondent provides some insight into the logic of his membership, which may not be atypical of public interest activists: "The organization has the freedom and recognition to raise issues that I, as an individual, do not have the courage or time for" (419). For this individual, then, the organization provides the vehicle for the expression of his own beliefs. The effectiveness of the organization in the political arena gives him a vicarious source of pleasure.

Student protest, for good reason, has been more frequently characterized as an expressive form of activity than other types of collective action taking place outside of the campus environment. Students are a uniquely marginal and yet privileged group in society. Although most are of legal age, they are not yet perceived as adults and typically do not carry the responsibilities and obligations of adults. They possess more disposable time to engage in political activism than the average person; they have more opportunity in the socially and politically conscious university environment to attach themselves to established organizations and campus political groups; they study, dine, and traverse in a highly concentrated geographical area, so that communication is rapid and organization and mobilization relatively easy; and they enjoy a special immunity because they are students and for that reason are expected, in the normal course of their college career, to indulge in a certain amount of rabble-rousing activity.

Because it is a relatively low-cost form of participation, many question the seriousness and even the sincerity of student protest. To Gordon Tullock (1971), student protest has little to do with the purported social or political goal of the protest, and much to do with the pure entertainment value that the activists derive from what amounts to a social gathering. If student radicals were so dedicated to their political goals, Tullock asks pointedly, why don't they leave the sanctuary of the campus and take to the streets, where they would be far more likely to have an impact on both the public and the government?

Tullock is not alone in his skepticism. In line with this view, Filler (1978) has observed that "as the youth movement reached its height, little separated the spirit behind festivals from that of demonstrations, except the rhetoric and placards necessary to the latter" (171).

THE BENEFITS OF PARTICIPATION

Recently Hirschman (1982) has made an extreme case for the importance of expressive benefits in motivating participation in all forms of public action (not just those with low costs attached to them) by arguing that the costs normally attributed to participation should instead be regarded as part of the benefits. The motivation behind political activism, he contends, lies in this special nature of the cost-benefit calculus. In the conventional view, people do not wish to spend the time, energy, and money that it costs to acquire a public good they desire. They would forego this cost if possible. Against this view, Hirschman argues that participation in collective action is one of those activities that, like play, are believed to be worthwhile in their own right. Like old-time athletes who played for the love of the game, political activists relish the competition and conflict of the political arena.[1]

There is, in other words, no clean partition between the *end* being sought (truth, liberty, justice) and the *process* by which this goal will be reached. Fighting the good fight is ennobling and uplifting and it carries its own rewards. For this reason, Hirschman contends that the normal cost-benefit calculus associated with collective action must be revised to reflect the utility that people derive from the act of striving for their goals, independent of the utility of the goal itself. Instead of treating the costs and benefits of participation as separate entities on opposite sides of the cost-benefit ledger, he proposes that the various

1. Or like some descendants of old-time players: when Brett Hull, a former bench warmer, was asked how it felt to be traded from a team that eventually won the Stanley Cup, the son of hockey legend Bobby Hull replied matter of factly, "I didn't want to stay; I wanted to play. How much fun is a Stanley Cup ring if you earned it by sitting in the stands?" (Sexton 1990, 35).

costs of participation should actually be counted as benefits because that is how they are regarded by the activists themselves. Time, energy, and expense, the argument goes, are not costs but in fact benefits, because the activist relishes not only the attainment of the public good but the struggle that he undergoes to achieve it.

> Indeed the very act of going after the public happiness is often the *next best thing* to actually *having* that happiness. . . . Once this essential characteristic of participation in collective action for the public good is understood, the severe limitations of the "economic" view about such participation, and about the obstacles to it, come immediately into view. The implication of the confusion between striving and attaining is that the neat distinction between costs and benefits of action in the public interest vanishes, since striving, which should be entered on the cost side, turns out to be part of the benefits. (1982, 85–86)

Since costs are indeed benefits, Hirschman continues, the free rider problem falls by the wayside. It behooves one to contribute one's share to collective action because to do otherwise would lead to a reduction in one's total utility.

Why is this fusion between cost and benefit more characteristic of public-regarding than private-regarding activity? Hirschman (1982, 89–90) speculates on three possible reasons. First, the relationship between effort and outcome tends to be more predictable and deterministic in private endeavors than in public ventures. An employee knows the relationship between the time he spends on the job and his remuneration; consequently there is a natural tendency to conceptualize the process in terms of inputs and outputs, or costs and benefits. In contrast, public action is typically fraught with uncertainty; no one can say for certain whether it will ultimately bear fruit. This indeterminacy lends a quiet dignity to those who are willing nonetheless to brave these uncharted waters. It is *as if*, Hirschman says, the pleasure received from striving compensates for the possibility that the goal will not be attained.

Private pursuits on the job, I might add, have the quality of being coerced. Routinized hours constrain when an employee is supposed to work, so that no matter how hard he tries to persuade himself that he enjoys his job, the manifest features of his employment—a daily schedule, weekends off, limited vacations—give his activity the appearance of work rather than play.

Public action, on the other hand, is typically voluntary, so that each participant controls the level and timing of his contributions. The usual perception of costs and benefits is less likely to be applied. Even the pursuit of truth and beauty can be turned into a chore for the scholar and artist if they are regimented to a fixed daily schedule. What makes these pursuits pleasurable is not only the uncertainty of achieving results but also the unforced conditions in which they are undertaken. Anyone with firsthand experience with these sublime activities knows how suddenly they can be transformed into mundane tasks with the imposition of deadlines.

A second reason people find pleasure in striving for social goals is that there are few activities that give them a comparable sense of mastery over their society. Many participants are intoxicated by the idea that they are party to a collective force which has the potential to bring about great social changes. This prospect drives and sustains them, even though realistically their chances of success may be slight.

Third, people believe that public-regarding activity fosters personal growth and development. Political participation educates one about the competing interests of society, the workings of the political process, and the disparate views that can be heard on public issues. One is therefore bettered in the course of participation even if the designated purpose of public action is unfulfilled.

SELF-SERVING EXPRESSIVE BENEFITS

Limits on the extent that one can participate will cause some people to choose not to participate at all. Hirschman ventures that in democracies in which voting is the primary vehicle available to citizens for expressing their political preferences, many people will abstain from going to the polls because it is "so watered down a form of participation" (Hirschman 1982, 108). Voting does not permit those with the most intense feelings about an issue or candidate to register the strength of their beliefs; therefore as an instrument of political participation, the vote will be a source of frustration to those citizens who wish to increase their influence on political affairs.

Most southern blacks, of course, were denied even the option of voting, but they had the opportunity to participate in the political process through various organizations. Of the major organizations, CORE, SCLC, and SNCC had the advantage of being known for using direct action tactics that in effect lifted the ceiling on political involvement. Unlike the NAACP, which followed a legalistic strategy and required limited involvement from its following beyond a membership fee, the more radical groups offered blacks a greater opportunity to invest their time and energy in a cause. Direct action gave the ordinary person an opportunity to participate actively rather than passively in the civil rights movement. Instead of making a minimal financial contribution to the NAACP and thereby delegating responsibility to that organization to represent him in the struggle, an individual could instead get a hand in the action himself. In addition, those who could not afford to contribute money were nonetheless able to contribute their time and energy to those organizations that encouraged mass participation.

For many blacks the key word was involvement, but in particular involvement in an enterprise that gave them a feeling of efficacy and accomplishment. If involvement is predicated on a desire to get a reaction or a response from the opposition, to upset or disturb the authorities, then an individual will choose to participate only when he is reasonably assured that enough others will also participate to produce the desired effect. SCLC leader James Lawson understood this motivation well:

> Many people, when they are suffering and they see their people suffering, they want direct participation. They want to be able to say, what I'm doing here gives me power and is going to help us change this business. . . . That's one of the great successes when you do something like a school boycott . . . or an economic boycott. Because here I am, mad already, with the racism I see, and now you tell me, okay . . . here's a chance for us to do something. (Aldon Morris 1984, 124)

The motivation to participate in this instance is like a desire to gain revenge. To appreciate this parallel, imagine that you have been tormented repeatedly by a gang of neighborhood bullies. With each confrontation your anger toward them builds, but as only one individual against many, you are helpless to retaliate. If only you had some allies, however, you would be able to work in concert with them to face and rout the hoodlums.

Suppose these allies emerge, but instead of working with you, they offer to do your fighting for you so that you will not have to place yourself at risk. Chances are that given the pain and humiliation you have endured, you will decline the offer and relish the opportunity to become directly involved in getting revenge on your antagonists. As Barrington Moore (1978) noted, "Vengeance means retaliation. It also means a reassertion of human dignity or worth, after injury or damage. Both are basic sentiments behind moral anger and the sense of injustice" (17).

Whether one is seeking revenge or striking out against an oppressor, the end that is being served is personal, and the means toward that end arguably is narrowly rational. A person who wishes to influence another person or group but who can do so only in combination with the coordinated efforts of others will contribute to that collective effort. The same grievances are likely to be expressed through private acts of resistance and destruction when coordination is difficult to achieve because community ties are weak, people are geographically dispersed, or leadership is absent. James Scott (1985), for example, has studied the strategies characteristic of unorganized peasant resistance such as "foot dragging, dissimulation, false compliance, pilfering, feigned ignorance, slander, arson, sabotage, and so forth " (29). Similar tactics were also used by rebellious slaves in the antebellum South. Their repertoire included several "subtle forms of noncooperation—feigned illness and stupidity, arson, neglect of crops and livestock—with their owners" (White 1985, 11).

Of course if the rank and file of a movement seek confrontation with the opposition in order to satisfy their own personal aspirations (to develop self-esteem, personal identity, etc.), it is essential that the leadership channel this energy into projects that serve the collective interest. Otherwise there is the danger that collective action will degenerate into reckless acts of violence and destruction which may serve personal desires, but harm the purposes of the movement.

The revenge or retaliation motive makes provision of the collective good a consequence of private acts, even though these private acts are typically manifest only in a group context. When collective goods are produced as a by-product of private actions, however, they may be accompanied by unwanted external effects. Private consumption that is not explicitly aimed at generating the collective good indeed may go awry and create a public bad even while the producers continue to satisfy their private concerns.[2] A boycott or a riot therefore may serve equally well for releasing the frustrations of group members and boost-

2. Here I disagree with Elster (1985), who maintains that "the benefits from participation belong in the class of states that are essentially by-products. . . . One cannot get them if one engages in collective action solely to get them." But I agree with his subsequent observation: "This, of course, is not to deny that some individuals might believe this shortcut to be possible and join collective action on such grounds. To the extent that the efficacy of collective action depends on the sheer number of partici-

ing their self-esteem, but they are not likely to be equally effective political strategies for the group as a whole.

In his discussion of the internal disputes within the CORE organization, Kenneth Clark (1966) illustrates how fine the line is between activism that is personally satisfying but politically ineffective and activism that fulfills both personal and collective goals. Local CORE groups, he notes, had taken to initiating unruly but unfocused demonstrations. Although these activities were politically unproductive, the motivation behind the participants in them was readily ascertained:

> Whatever the anarchism of these locals and the inadvisability of demonstrations not directly related to concrete grievances, there is something to be said for the observation that, when multitudes are inconvenienced or threatened with discomfort, the very random quality of the action reflects the desperation of the demonstrators and has some impact, even if only irritation, upon the white majority. To the Negro, white irritation and anger is at least a *response*. (253)

More intense and more costly forms of participation may also be more attractive to altruists than less taxing, easier activities. Those dedicated to increasing the welfare of a group may not be content to perform rudimentary tasks that appear to have little bearing on whether the major goals of collective action will be accomplished; rather they will seek more important roles in the movement in order to provide themselves with greater responsibility. This helps explain why some activist groups are eager to provide their members with input into the decision-making process and to provide them with duties that enhance their feeling of involvement. Stoney Cooks, a participant in the Selma march who had just arrived from Indiana, was amazed by how quickly he was given some responsibility: "People like myself who show up from no place, express a desire to participate and to work *with*, and readily there was something for you to do or someone to bring you in and give you a feeling of meaningful participation" (Raines 1977, 216).

It is paradoxical, then, that positions of responsibility are parceled out to the altruist as a selective incentive for him to contribute. Unlike

---

pants, such free riders on the movement—to use that term in a nonstandard sense—could actually help it. If, however, dedication and long-term planning are needed, those who are into collective action just to realize themselves will not contribute much to the success and may well detract from it" (147–48).

egoists, who may require side payments to offset their cost of participation, moralists are attracted by incentives that increase their cost but upgrade the amount they contribute to the group's utility.

PERCEPTIONS OF COSTS AND BENEFITS

It is appropriate to ask how prevalent expressive behavior would be in the absence of an audience or a public. People do, as Turner suggested, want to go on record with their preferences, their indignation, and their outrage; they are interested in the demonstration effect of their actions, not merely in the cathartic pleasure of carrying out the action itself.

Tullock was right in suggesting that student protest was "fun," but he could have added that it was socially profitable as well. "Students at Rutgers, Berkeley, Minnesota, Yale, and Antioch," writes Newfield, "rushed to the center of sit-in activity to get arrested. . . . [They were] beginning to realize a jail record could be a badge of honor" (Newfield 1966, 40–41).

Similarly, Hodgson (1976) writes that "commitment to the civil rights movement or to draft resistance . . . was among other things a way of competing, a way of showing off, a way of being in the fashion or of setting it" (309). The social instrumentality of participation therefore helps explain why the students of the sixties were not gathering at religious revivals or conservative caucuses but at civil rights protests, peace demonstrations, free-speech rallies, and other liberal and left-wing concerns. Obviously they did not simply want to show others that they were politically active but that they were *socially-concerned* activists. Even those who attended mainly for the social mixing, we can presume, still required that the party and entertainment be sponsored by the correct political faction.

Although it seems undeniable that political participation is sometimes a noninstrumental activity that carries its own reward, Hirschman and those sharing his viewpoint have underestimated the extent to which participation is a socially instrumental activity in the manner discussed in chapter 3. One's presence at historical events can often be parlayed into future benefits, in both the short run and the long run. By participating, an individual enhances his reputation among his colleagues. He has fought the good fight when it counted, demonstrated his dependability in group efforts, shown a willingness to contribute his fair share, and shown that he is a person of action.

His participation in collective action also makes him a more interesting person to others. He acquires a collection of stories and memories to trade on. In effect, the experiences he has had are a rare commodity; contrary to the popular phrase, one cannot "relive history." These social benefits greatly increase the attractiveness of cooperation.

I also doubt whether the argument that political activists turn costs into benefits can be sustained in its entirety. While the standard costs of participation are in many respects perceived as benefits by the political activists themselves, the line separating costs and benefits is seldom so blurred that people are unable to distinguish between the two. Costs contain the seeds of benefits in that part of the reward for achievement is tied up in the struggle itself; but although costs may be so discounted, they continue to be an important factor in determining whether or not people will participate in collective action.

Even the most dedicated civil rights activists made rather mundane cost-benefit calculations in deciding the extent to which they wished to become involved. When, in 1931, Walter White of the NAACP wrote to Roy Wilkins about the possibility of filling the vacant secretary's position at the organization, Wilkins, then a newsman in Kansas City, could hardly contain his excitement.

> I read the letter several times, my heart thumping. This was no invitation to bury myself in the business department of *The Crisis* but an offer to work side by side with the most exciting civil rights leader of the day. I pulled out my typewriter and tapped out a two-paragraph reply. Anything overeager, I cautioned myself, might spoil my chances. (Wilkins 1982, 104–5)

The *Crisis* remark refers to an earlier offer that the NAACP had made to Wilkins to take over business managership of the association's news and literary magazine. Wilkins had declined this invitation, partly because he did not fancy himself in a position that had the outward appearance of being fairly sterile (as he alludes in the passage cited), but also because the salary accompanying the job offer was slightly less than what he was then making at his newspaper the *Call*. To be sure, the prospect of living in New York, where the NAACP was headquartered, as opposed to Kansas City—a city he was growing to despise—held forth obvious compensatory cultural benefits, but all the same, these benefits came with a significantly higher cost of living. In the end, Wilkins decided the offer wasn't sweet enough.

On the other hand, the position of secretary was obviously much more to his liking. Wilkins relished the idea of working in New York on the front lines of the best known and most effective civil rights organization in the country. As he put it: "These [the NAACP] were people who were getting things done" (105).

Still, for the second time around, the organization almost failed to recruit him. After Wilkins successfully interviewed for the job in New York, the delicate issue of salary was finally raised, and to Wilkins's consternation, the NAACP was offering quite a bit less than he wanted.

> I knew that the Depression had hurt the N.A.A.C.P., but I was not prepared to go broke working for it. At the time I was earning $2,600 a year at the *Call*, and I told Walter and Dr. Du Bois that I would have to have $3,600 a year to absorb the cost of moving and maintaining Minnie and me in New York. As diplomatically as he could, White said that the board had been thinking about a salary along the lines of $3,000. I felt a stab of disappointment. I told him that the issue of money wasn't paramount, but I would have to talk the matter over with my wife. We shook hands all round. It was clear that I had the job—if I could afford to take it. (Wilkins 1982, 106)

Ultimately Wilkins did a little haggling and got the NAACP to agree to split the difference between its offer and his asking price; that and the assurance of a future raise got Wilkins on board, although it appears he would have settled for somewhat less.

Wilkins's money wrangles at the NAACP did not end there. Later, following the resignation of W. E. B. Du Bois, Wilkins was appointed to edit *The Crisis* by the NAACP Board of Directors. This new assignment was on top of his other responsibilities, which had already left Wilkins feeling overburdened and exploited. "For two years I had done the office work and publicity chores of two employees who had been lost to Depression austerity. Between them, they had earned $3,300 a year. Delighted with this savings, the board voted to pay me $20 a month to do their work. There were days when I felt like Bob Cratchit in thrall to Scrooge" (ibid., 155).

Organizers of collective action are certainly aware that the costs and benefits of participation will weigh heavily on the potential contributor's mind. When E. D. Nixon was contemplating whether to organize a boycott of the Montgomery bus system following the arrest of Rosa Parks (for failure to relinquish her seat on a crowded bus to a white passenger), he knew that practical and economic considerations would impinge on the likelihood that blacks would support the boycott. Consequently it wasn't until he calculated that virtually all blacks were within walking distance of their places of work that he decided to go ahead with his plan (Raines 1977, 44–45). Subsequently the costs of supporting the boycott were reduced further when local black cabdrivers volunteered to transport boycotting passengers for the price of a bus ride. Student activists also did their share by running a car pool service that picked up boycotters at the stops where they normally waited for the bus.[3]

Another problem with equating costs and benefits is that by so doing, we trivialize the sacrifice that some political activists have been known to make in the service of a cause. Not every jailed activist can claim the experience of birth control activist Margaret Sanger, whose only regret seemed to be the brevity of her stay.

> From her own account . . . her stretch [in prison] was something of a lark. She wrote in her diary that it was "tragic, to see human beings forced to so low a level" as the drug addicts and prostitutes she encountered in jail. But she enjoyed the exotic experience and her status as a heroine among the other female prisoners. The romantic glow of her long-awaited martyrdom must have heightened even more when she emerged through the prison gates on March 7 to find her comrades greeting her with the "Marseillaise." (Kennedy 1970, 87)

In contrast, the freedom riders, by all accounts, had a miserable time in the jails. They were crowded into small, filthy cells, forced to sleep on concrete floors, fed unpalatable food, prevented from maintaining personal hygiene, intimidated, harassed, and sometimes beaten by unfriendly guards. On top of the physical privation was the sheer boredom of the jail experience. Denied recreation, reading material, or any other diversion to wile away the time, they tried among themselves to institute their own daily schedules with song, prayer, and discussion sessions interspersed between bouts of sleep.[4]

3. A half century earlier, hackmen and draymen provided substitute forms of transportation at discounted fares for blacks boycotting Jim Crow streetcars (Meier and Rudwick 1969, 764).

4. On the other hand, Fager (1974) describes King's experience in a Selma jail: "For Dr. King, of course, going to jail was like a vacation, a blessed respite from the punishing nineteen and twenty-hour days he put in outside, and he and [Ralph] Abernathy set about making the most of it once they were in the quieter quarters of the city jail. The two had been to jail together almost every time they had been arrested, and had long since developed a routine for passing the time constructively. . . . They were perfectly safe, and except for the fact that the bedding was lumpy and uncomfortable, in no hurry to end their interlude" (55).

Even the noble Gandhi could not entirely transmogrify the costs of incarceration into benefits. While awaiting imprisonment for the first time in South Africa for demonstrating against that country's "Black Laws," Gandhi was horrified to find himself worrying not about the cause he was championing but about how he was going to survive in jail and about "what would become of his home, his legal practice, [and] his public life" (Mehta 1976, 122). The irony did not escape him, as he indicates in his diary:

> How vain I was! I, who had asked the people to consider the prisons as His Majesty's hotels, the suffering consequent upon disobeying the "Black Act" as perfect bliss, and the sacrifice of one's all and of life itself in resisting it as supreme enjoyment! Where had all this knowledge vanished today? . . . This . . . train of thought acted upon me as a bracing tonic, and I began to laugh at my own folly. (ibid.)

Having thus regained control of himself, Gandhi enjoyed a relatively comfortable and productive stint in prison. He wiled away the sentence by exercising, meditating, reading, and writing, and emerged with an even stronger conviction in the power of the single individual to prevail over tyranny.

MORE ON THE PERCEPTION OF COSTS AND BENEFITS: "AS IF" PREFERENCES

Civil rights activists, we should note, often behaved (for strategic reasons) as if the punishments threatened by the authorities for engaging in protests and demonstrations were a benefit rather than a cost. When the jail-no-bail tactic was initiated, for example, southern authorities were shocked to discover that protesters chose prison over an opportunity to pay a small fine and be free. The confusion shown by the authorities was understandable, since the threat of imprisonment had historically been the strongest deterrent against political activism. When the protesters turned around and revealed a preference for being jailed, this erased the most effective penalty possessed by local officials. The potency of this tactic illustrates Schelling's (1966, 42) point that it is sometimes in the interest of someone not to appear coolheaded and completely rational. "Reckless" strategies that are pursued by individuals in the course of a conflict (like the freedom rides or the policy of jail-no-bail), which risk their lives and well-being, may also exact a significant cost from their adversaries—enough of a cost that they are more willing to negotiate.

In the eyes of civil rights demonstrators, of course, there was nothing pleasant or attractive about the prospect of prison. Organizers behind the jail-no-bail strategy usually found it difficult to sign up recruits, and those who did agree to the undertaking typically did so with serious reservations and trepidation. In the 1961 Rock Hill, South Carolina, demonstrations against dime store operators, students set to embark on a jail-in had second thoughts up to the moment of action. "As we walked uptown," one participant recalls, "some of us wondered whether any of our group would change his decision on the way and withdraw. None did" (Meier and Rudwick 1975, 188).

Some leaders, notably Martin Luther King, Jr., were more effective than others at making the rank and file come to prefer in their hearts (to adopt as their *real* preferences, in other words) the option of staying in jail by refusing bail. King possessed an extraordinary capacity to make his followers focus on the pleasures rather than the travails of their struggle to achieve racial equality. His message was that the struggle itself was sufficiently worthwhile and ennobling to compensate for the great price that each participant would have to pay. The hostilities, threats, and injuries that each would have to endure were a testimony to their dignity, self-esteem, and courage. As Bayard Rustin recalls, "In the black community (before King's inspirational lectures) going to jail had been a badge of dishonor. Martin made going to jail like receiving a Ph.D." (Raines 1977, 56).

"As if" preferences, however, are hard to keep in practice. During the freedom rides, a number of volunteers vowed to remain in jail if arrested, but discovered that the actual experience was more grueling than they had bargained for. While in prison, not all of the freedom riders accepted their sentences with equanimity, nor did they all share the same enthusiasm for further sacrifices to protest the conditions of their imprisonment. Some freedom riders were reluctant to give up their mattresses as a price for continued singing. Only some prisoners fasted, precipitating "fistfights through the bars when non-fasting prisoners aggressively slurped their food in front of those trying not to eat" (Branch 1988, 484). This only shows that pretending to relish some form of privation is obviously easier when your own associates do not reveal your bluff. James Farmer recalls the sudden turnabout: "We had trouble with some of the Freedom Riders because the training had to be hasty, and many of the people who rushed in, including some of the SNCC people, were not prepared for this sort of thing. 'We're gonna stay in 'til hell freezes over.' But after two days, 'You got money to bail me out?'" (Raines 1977, 126).

CORRELATED COSTS AND BENEFITS

Hence, when we examine the experience of participation from the perspective of activists, it is apparent that they separate costs from benefits, and that the costs are the conventional ones that are generally recognized: money, time, pain of punishment, etc. Benefits, on the other hand, are often tied to the ability of activists to effectively express their anger or disapproval over a policy or existing state of affairs. Participation in collective action for this reason is an expressive but narrowly rational activity.

An amendment to the "costs are benefits" notion is that benefits are some function of costs. The two elements are positively correlated. We are able to transform society and to "make history" by way of collective action only when there is a worthy opponent that must be subdued. Otherwise the socially instrumental and expressive value of participation in a cause is likely to be greatly diminished. Whether change is regarded as revolutionary depends greatly on the nature of the opposition: How strong is it? How alien are its values and institutions to the revolutionaries? How much has to be overcome?

Mansbridge (1986) observes that both the proponents and opponents of the Equal Rights Amendment (ERA) exaggerated the effects of the amendment in order to mobilize activists more effectively. This tactic was understandable insofar as the participatory benefits that people are likely to receive from their involvement in collective action will be affected by their perception of the historical magnitude and significance of the cause. If the ERA were portrayed as a symbolic but trifling amendment to the Constitution, the movement for its passage could hardly be described as a watershed event in the evolution of the rights and status of women in this country.

Likewise, civil rights activists needed to feel challenged. Alabama was an oft-chosen site of demonstrations and marches because that state constituted perhaps the greatest obstacle to the movement. Similarly, members of the more radical civil rights groups—especially SNCC—went out of their way to tackle difficult projects that required tremendous courage and dedication (Wilson 1973, 184). Hard victories provided the largest payoffs. This strategy is a double-edged sword, however, since an intransigent and difficult opponent will also foster disillusion and frustration in the movement; moreover, when the opposition is strong, all but the most eager activist will be deterred from participating until there is some safety and security in numbers.

Later I will argue that participatory benefits are really "potential" benefits, since they are not fully reaped unless collective action is successfully executed. Futile attacks on a powerful opposition may prove extremely costly but because of the impotence of the effort will not provide much in the way of expressive, moral, or other socially instrumental benefits.

Jerry Rubin recognized the correlation between the costs and benefits of activism when he declared the worthlessness of any "movement that isn't willing to risk injuries, even death" (Matusow 1984, 320). This outburst occurred after the leaders of a huge Berkeley-to-Oakland antiwar march chose to retreat rather than have a showdown with a large contingent of Oakland police officers who were determined to block the marchers at the Oakland boundary.

Rubin's harsh assessment suggests that political activists can "artificially" upgrade the level of their benefits by escalating the conflict with their opponents. Many civil rights demonstrators took to direct action for this reason. "Nothing showed this more clearly," according to Meier and Rudwick (1975), "than the loud singing and chanting on many picket lines, and the sagging of morale when a victory came through negotiations rather than through direct action" (228). This preference for action over talk, everything else being equal, makes sense in terms of both expressive and socially instrumental benefits. Whereas direct action involves many, negotiations are necessarily conducted by a few, so the ability to claim credit for a successful outcome is significantly reduced if it is achieved peacefully rather than through a protracted conflict. Moreover, courage, fortitude, bravery, and dependability are more easily demonstrated on the streets than in the bargaining room; therefore even the leaders of the negotiating team for the activists may prefer to achieve a victory through their leadership on the battlefield.[5]

5. For these reasons, militant factions or organizations in a movement are sometimes able to "outbid" their more moderate counterparts for the services of the most highly motivated activists seeking participation in the cause. Competition among organizations for followers, however, can be kept in check if cooperation among the organizations around a coordinated strategy is crucial for the movement as a whole to succeed. During the March on Washington, for example, the leading civil rights organizations submerged their differences (albeit only temporarily) in order to place concerted pressure on the Kennedy administration to pass the civil rights bill then before Congress.

5 | Creating the Motivation to Participate in Collective Action

Contemporary man lives constantly outside himself and only knows how to live in the opinion of others.

Jean Jacques Rousseau

The social and psychological benefits of participation are not unconditional, as is often implied, but instead are usually contingent upon the successfulness of collective action. Brian Barry (1978) speculated about the general relationship between benefits and success in *Sociologists, Economists, and Democracy,* though he did not elaborate:

> Whatever the reason why a person may attach himself to a cause, more enthusiasm for its pursuit is likely to be elicited if it looks as if it has a chance of succeeding than if it appears to be a forlorn hope. Nobody likes to feel that he is wasting his time, and that feeling may be induced by contributing to a campaign which never looks as if it has a chance. (30)

I would add that this sense of futility predominates whether one participates for socially instrumental or noninstrumental expressive reasons. Take the case of the noninstrumentalist. Hirschman suggests that for the noninstrumentalist, there is a transformation of costs into benefits. If we structure the payoff matrix in the fashion he suggests, we would find that an individual is always better off when he participates than when he does not, regardless of the actions of his colleagues; participation is therefore a dominant strategy in this revised game, whereas nonparticipation was the dominant strategy in the original prisoner's dilemma game. Even in the extreme case when *no one else* has taken action, it is still better for an individual to participate because he will still enjoy the fruits of his labor (though not the spoils), which is better than nothing (the outcome when no one, including him, participates). (See figure 5.1.)

But this is surely bizarre and not an implication that Hirschman intended. No one can march on Washington by himself because that is neither a march nor an event, let alone a historic event, but a symptom

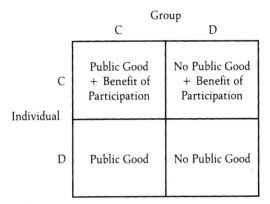

FIGURE 5.1. The Costs-Are-Benefits Model. Entries are payoffs to the individual.

of megalomania. Without the involvement of other activists, there will be no history made and consequently no participatory benefits for the brave iconoclast. Moreover, the isolated protester typically will not enjoy the same expressive benefits he would if he were acting in concert with others. Much of the expressive pleasure of public action comes from having been able to make others stand up and pay attention to your protests; consequently unless he is already famous, the lone activist needs the company of others if he is to have any chance of attracting public attention to his message. There may be some visceral relief but little expressive value to shouting in the wilderness.[1]

SOCIALLY INSTRUMENTAL VALUE

Likewise, the instrumental value of participation depends on the viability of collective action. The instrumentalist supports the cause in the abstract but will contribute to it only if it will pay dividends to him personally. This is not as ignoble as it sounds; everyone, I'm convinced, to some extent supports values and carries out good deeds because it is wise from a cost-benefit calculus. The instrumentalist in effect is making an investment in a political experience. What type of experience would we expect him to "purchase"? A safe bet is that he would try to limit his contribution to those instances of collective action that have

1. The unusual story of white postman William Moore's solo "Freedom Walk" illustrates how we view such mavericks who are determined to go it alone. Moore embarked on a solo march from Chattanooga to Mississippi carrying signboards promoting racial equality and desegregation, but his trip was abruptly terminated when he was brutally murdered on the highway. He was subsequently memorialized by the movement, even though he had earlier been refused sponsorship for his actions by CORE, which had regarded him as a kook (Branch 1988, 747–50).

good prospects of being successful. No one remembers losers in politics, just as no one remembers them in sports. For this reason, participation in an anemic social movement is a far cry from participation in a triumphant campaign. A movement that succeeds at achieving its objectives receives widespread recognition and publicity, and participants in the movement receive credit for having done their fair share for a worthy cause.

Unsuccessful movements are denied such publicity; people are consequently less likely to have heard of these movements or to be aware of the exploits of the participants. For example, veterans of the civil rights movement look back fondly on their experiences and continue to receive the plaudits and esteem of others for having been leaders in their time. In contrast, participants in, say, the nuclear freeze movement may well be accused of wasting their time. Indeed, whereas winners are praised, losers may be scorned. Olson (1971) made a passing comment on this point in *The Logic of Collective Action:* "Selfless behavior that has no perceptible effect is sometimes not even considered praiseworthy. A man who tried to hold back a flood with a pail would probably be considered more of a crank than a saint, even by those he was trying to help" (64).

Fruitless activity, therefore, even when it is selflessly devoted to the interests of the group, will probably go unrewarded. This claim runs against the grain (correctly, I believe) of various equity theories (Homans 1974; Adams 1965) which stipulate that people are inclined to make a connection between an individual's effort to achieve a goal and the rewards that he deserves as a consequence. By this account, if I work diligently to achieve some objective, I should be repaid for my efforts, even if the product of my labor in itself merits little esteem. On the contrary, I suspect that bad acting, bad piano playing, bad cooking, and bad political activism are not judged any better simply because we discover that the practitioner has trained long hours or dedicated himself to the task. There is perhaps a tendency in us to *want* to praise the industrious worker. As a result, we may seek something admirable in his work and for this reason selectively grade his performance more highly than that of a less dedicated individual.

On the other hand, while there may be a weak tendency for our evaluation of a person's performance to be favorably affected by the amount of effort he has expended, there is probably a stronger contrary tendency for our evaluation of his character to be diminished by the failure of his actions. A movement's failure, for example, may cast doubt on the wisdom, tactics, and efforts of the participants and make them the targets of derision as opposed to social esteem. Witness the cold shoulder accorded veterans of the Vietnam War in comparison to our treatment of those who served successfully in World War II.

FULFILLING OBLIGATIONS

Lastly, members of a group will feel *obligated* to participate in a large-scale movement only when it is clear that collective action is likely to survive and have real meaning. There is little if any obligation to participate in a hopeless cause. If the pressure to participate in any cause originates from the obligation not to take advantage of the efforts of others (but to contribute one's share if the collective effort benefits everyone including oneself), then that obligation is lifted in lost causes. Since collective benefits are not forthcoming, there is no advantage to be taken. In his study of protest in Tokugawa Japan, for example, White (1988, 50) found that noncooperative villagers were more likely to be pressured by other villagers, not at the inception of protest, but after protest had begun to enjoy some momentum.

If it appears that the venture will fail, each individual can decide for prudential reasons—with a clear conscience—to withhold any contribution on the grounds that it would be good money thrown after a bad cause. This decision would not likely harm his reputation for being an honorable person who lives up to other (mutually profitable) agreements. Under better conditions, he would do his duty, but mitigating circumstances make it conscionable for him to refrain from in essence sacrificing himself: "acts, including speech acts, are to be evaluated by their probable consequences; no one is morally required to take risks unless the probable consequences are beneficial; what is commendable is regard for the best results, not futile gestures" (Hill 1979, 83).

Not everyone will subscribe to this consequentialist view of morality; some will hold that a person must make an effort irrespective of the balance of forces in the situation. One must do all that one can do to correct an unjust situation, however ineffective that might be. In other words, the principle is held up as an absolute dictum, like "never tell a lie," or "always help those in need," or "always go to the aid of a victim." You may, for example, sell your stock in a company that is guilty of unfair labor practices; since someone else buys the stock, you have not harmed the company, but you have given expression to your values and behaved in a manner that is consistent with your principles.

Nonetheless, the absolutist position is difficult to defend when the cost of upholding a principle is prohibitive. I am not obligated to go to the rescue of another if to do so would only guarantee my death as well as his. The point is that the moral pressures that emanate from belief in such norms and values as justice, fairness, equality, and liberty will be negated (or neutralized) under particular circumstances, namely, when the act of adhering to the norm will probably inflict grievous harm on oneself or others without improving the well-being of anyone. Consequently, there will be no moral incentive to motivate an individual into the political arena that compensates for the absence of either self- or group interest.

It so happens, however, that most instances of political activism take on this long shot quality. There is usually uncertainty regarding the prospects of proposed collective action; therefore it is difficult to expect much in the way of deterrents or retribution for noncooperation. Moreover, because of the inherent ambiguity surrounding political activism, less scrupulous individuals can conjure up numerous reasons or arguments for why they are justified in not getting involved: e.g., protest will backfire by causing the opposition to dig in its heels and become even more repressive; poorly executed tactics will cause the public to withdraw its sympathy and support for the aggrieved group; working within conventional channels will be more productive than less organized but more disruptive tactics. Thus, in order for large-scale cooperation to occur, there must be at a minimum a general agreement that the proposed project is clearly to the benefit of the group. Consensus on the advantages of the endeavor generates a conditional willingness to participate as well as a disposition to punish defection from it, both of which are crucial for the emergence of large-scale cooperation.

But even this may not be enough. My desire to contribute my share to a collective good and to avoid taking advantage of others will lead to an actual contribution only if I assume that others are going to do their part in supporting the collective good. As Parfit (1986) observes, "If we are reluctant to be free-riders . . . [a]ll that is needed is an assurance that there will be many who do A [cooperate]. Each would then prefer to do his share. But a reluctance to free-ride cannot by itself create this assurance. So there are many cases where it provides no solution" (40).

The conditional status of personal obligations to make sacrifices for the collective good is the central element of George Klosko's (1987) "fairness thesis": "The strength of A's feeling that he is obligated to make sacrifices or bear burdens (in order to provide presumptive public goods to his society) will be heavily influenced by his views concerning the extent to which other individuals are making similar sacrifices or bearing similar burdens" (358).

As evidence that people actually operate according to this rule, Klosko cites a study by Song and Yarbrough (1978) on the relationship between taxpayers' ethics and their beliefs about the behavior of other taxpayers. The strongest obligation to comply with tax laws was felt by those who believed that most other people filed their taxes honestly. Similarly, other studies cited indicate that people are more disposed to cheat on their taxes when they believe that not everyone is contributing his fair share to the nation's coffers. Both tax avoidance and tax evasion therefore undermine the public's allegiance and conformance to the tax system and seem to encourage dishonesty more than high tax rates per se (ibid., 360–61).

Elster (1985) supposes that even altruists will make sacrifices only so long as they do not suspect that others are playing them for fools. "Altruism may be pure and disinterested, in the sense that you derive positive utility from the well-being of another, regardless of his character or conduct, but more frequently you act altruistically towards someone as a function of his character, a minimum condition being that he is not trying to cash in on your altruism" (144).

In sum, the social and psychological benefits that are associated with collective action usually will be operative only when collective action has reached fairly sizable proportions and shows signs of being successful. Consequently for a given individual the receipt of such benefits is contingent upon the actions of other potential activists. Each individual is thus forced to make certain prospective calculations before he can ascertain the benefits he will derive from his own participation. Will enough others participate so that collective action stands a good chance of being successful? This calculation must be made carefully. No one—neither the instrumental nor the noninstrumental activist—wants to invest in a lost cause.

The most difficult part of organizing a movement, therefore, is the task of building up the movement to the point where an obligation or incentive to contribute to it arises. Usually the initial stages of coordination will follow a different dynamic from that of the latter stages. A group of highly motivated individuals—purists, zealots, moralists, Kantians, what have you—will have to provide the leadership required to convince others that large-scale coordination will be a profitable activity. This is likely to occur through a combination of propaganda, communication, and—perhaps most importantly—successful models of collective action. Genovese (1974) points out, for example, that while southern slaves often resisted white authority and sought their freedom, the chance of any sustained movement was inhibited by the strength of their masters and a shortage of successful precedents. "Thus, the slave might know of small groups of desperate holdouts here and there, but he had no example of an autonomous black movement to guide him" (591).

Successful models of protest do not have to originate from within the movement itself. Groups can be inspired by the exploits and experiences of other causes and movements, past and present. Women, minorities, and other disadvantaged groups, as well as student protesters in South Korea and China, for example, have tried to replicate the civil rights movement's exemplary model of collective action. Similarly, present-day campus protest activity frequently takes a page from the tactics employed by student demonstrators in the 1960s, the most recent heyday of college activism.

It is noteworthy in this regard that the collapse of communist governments across Eastern Europe in 1989–90 appears to have been patterned on the same model. By the time the wave of popular protests swept Czechoslovakia, events there were almost a replay of earlier protests in Poland, Hungary, and East Germany, "only a month later and a bit faster" (Schmemann 1989, 6). Czechoslovakia may have benefited most from these precedents. Not only did it take Czech citizens only a week of demonstrations to remove the Communist Party leader, but it seemed as though the entire population became convinced all at once of the need for major reforms. The Communist Party's last hope was that the workers would not come out in support of the students and intellectuals. Instead, millions of workers, inspired by reforms elsewhere, participated in a two-hour general strike that crippled the operation of the country.

The availability of successful models of protest raises expectations about the chances of success. Only when coordination is shown to be advantageous to the group will group members have the obligation and incentive to form a convention and institute the system of rewards and punishments required to sustain it. In most cases, this is a difficult hurdle to climb. When William Lloyd Garrison founded the New England Anti-Slavery Society in 1831, he was able to enlist only a dozen members who would commit themselves to advocating immediate emancipation. Nor did the Society thereafter gain new adherents easily; rather, the cause appealed mainly to small numbers of Quakers, young upstart revivalists, and free blacks from northeastern and midwestern states. Dillon (1974) explains: "Important and influential though the converts to abolitionism came to be, their numbers remained relatively few, simply because the number of persons capable of sustained moral commitment at the level of intensity demanded by that stage of the antislavery movement is always limited. . . . [N]ot many [wished] to subject themselves to the hostility and ridicule (51–52).

Moreover, before collective action begins to pay dividends, there are likely to be numerous detractors who disagree with the tactics of the activists. (Garrison's ranks were too extreme for many other abolitionists who called for an end to slavery on moral grounds but never envisioned a society in which blacks would participate as equals with whites.) Elster (1985) comments that Kantians ("unconditional cooperators") who are inspired to act according to duty often cause more trouble than good. Would-be heroes in social movements produce a collective bad when they induce the authorities to punish the entire group, including those innocent of participation. For this reason, Elster suspects, we hold an "ambiguous attitude toward Kantian behavior in collective action. On the one hand, society needs people who act morally without considering the consequences when misperception of the consequences is easy or likely. On the other hand, blindness for consequences may be disastrous" (151).

For example, when the four college students protested the use of segregated lunch counters in Greensboro, they encountered, paradoxically, muted support from a few female white customers but vehement criticism from a black female store employee. The woman scolded the activists, ironically blaming "their kind" for perpetuating the inferior status of blacks. "That's why we can't get anyplace today, because of people like you, rabble-rousers, troublemakers. . . . This counter is reserved for white people, it always has been, and you are well aware of that. So why don't you go on out and stop making trouble (Raines, 77–78).

As the woman explained later, she was afraid she would lose her job because of the sit-in. Nonetheless, she was sufficiently proud of the outcome of the Greensboro sit-in that she attended a latter-day celebration of the event, proving Elster's point.

Similarly, gay activist Randy Wicker encountered strong resistance from other homosexuals in the early 1960s, before the gay rights movement took root. Wicker's goal was to make people realize that most homosexuals looked and acted like everyone else, and that they were not all flamboyant "queens." But many closet homosexuals felt that it was in their interest to preserve the flamboyant stereotype in order to ensure that they would never be suspected. Wicker threatened to lift the veil (D'Emilio 1983, 158).

The resentment of the group toward those who disturb the status quo is evident in a variety of contexts.[2] In general we distrust those who appear too reckless or rash because we rely on others to guide our own reactions to life situations. "When people mobilize to protect cherished values," McNall (1988) writes, "they often look to friends and neighbors to determine whether they are doing the right thing" (227). For this reason, we prefer to be around people who have the same sensibilities as we do, so that we can take our cues from them about the proper course of action. The behavior of other people provides us with a baseline for how to act in a given situation and establishes standards for bravery, cowardice, selfishness, and generosity. Because leaders typically establish unusually high standards of behavior for others to emulate, few people are able to uphold these qualities, nor do they wish to under ordinary circumstances.

Birmingham civil rights leader Fred Shuttlesworth, for instance, made some people nervous because he did not provide the same cues and signals as other members of the movement. Known to be a fearless man, Shuttlesworth did not recoil from the harsh tactics of the opposition as others did. One colleague commented only somewhat facetiously that he did not want to be around Shuttlesworth on campaigns because the man was oblivious to danger (Aldon Morris 1984, 72). Nevertheless, such exemplary behavior by some can place considerable pressure on others to follow suit. Leaders can therefore set the tone and prompt those who would normally remain apathetic to commit themselves to the movement. In general, passive members of a group who submit to an inequitable status quo can be shamed by those who do not accept their station in the community, or who simply behave in a manner that is inconsistent with it.

Many of these problems concerning the initiation of collective action were on prominent display during the civil rights movement.

2. Research on prison populations, for example, has found that the renegade inmate who stands up to a guard more often than not draws the wrath of fellow prisoners. "Only to a very limited degree did the other prisoners regard him as a welcome symbol of courageous opposition. More often they treated him as a fool, as one who upset the delicate system of compromise and corruption that was the basis of prison society. To other prisoners he appeared as one who sacrificed the well-being of the inmate population as a whole, for the sake of childish emotional outbursts" (Moore 1978, 73).

Among blacks, there were very real fears that political activism would annoy the white authorities and worsen rather than improve their living conditions. In the aftermath of the 1943 race riots, many black leaders believed that large-scale direct action campaigns were ill-advised and detrimental to the interests of blacks. In place of these controversial tactics, they suggested that blacks pursue a more moderate and quieter course of progress through litigation in the courts and lobbying in the legislatures. The prevailing wisdom was that blacks should avoid radical measures that would jeopardize their relations with white liberal allies (Barnes 1983, 60).

When CORE entered the picture in the postwar years and promoted selected direct action campaigns to combat segregation, it had to overcome this bias against more aggressive forms of political participation. CORE began as a small, tightly knit, exclusive organization. Its members were expected to be well steeped in the philosophy of non-violence and dedicated to following a set of Gandhian tactics which CORE employed in its political campaigns. A person who wanted to join CORE had to demonstrate his suitability to the organization. "Commitment and dedication were deemed more important than size, and prospective members were carefully investigated and interviewed before being admitted" (Meier and Rudwick 1975, 8). CORE had difficulty attracting followers because of its incipient status as a new, generally unknown and untested organization. People were especially reluctant to subject themselves to the considerable risks required of CORE members because CORE's techniques were unproven. Although CORE initiated local projects in cities around the country aimed at ending discriminatory practices in housing, accommodations, employment, and schools, it counted only a limited number of victories, and almost all of these involved the integration of public facilities such as restaurants. Therefore not only was white opinion aligned against more substantial changes in race relations but the black population in the 1940s was unprepared to rally behind the new tactics of the relatively unknown CORE organization.

In the absence of either a strong national leadership or a coherent national policy to combat racial discrimination, CORE struggled and survived as a small organization whose limited resources and manpower restricted the types of projects it could undertake. The "up or out" rule that normally applies to the career paths of individuals in organizations described the early development of CORE. Despite the high level of commitment and dedication among its members, local CORE chapters regularly disbanded when they were unable to mount enough pressure against a discriminatory business or organization to force a policy change. They also frequently disbanded, however, following a victorious campaign when after having completed their task, they were unwilling or unable to take the next step in attacking discrimination in other, more sensitive areas of American life.

In other words, members of a local CORE unit often chose not to marshal their resources when it was apparent that such efforts would be unsuccessful. The Saint Louis CORE group, for example, according to Meier and Rudwick, found itself at an impasse after successfully desegregating downtown dining facilities in that city. Members of Saint Louis CORE had not been drained by the campaign they had recently completed, nor were they uncertain over which issue they should address next. Agreement existed that discrimination in employment was the most pressing problem. However, CORE felt ill-equipped to tackle the problem. In order to be successful in this area, CORE's method of boycotting and picketing business establishments required widespread mass support, which CORE did not enjoy even in the black community. Consequently, CORE activists "regarded their techniques as inadequate and inappropriate for this type of campaign. Actually what they lacked was power" (Meier and Rudwick 1975, 63).

CORE's lack of a mass following had hurt it in the past, even in its campaigns to desegregate public accommodations. In 1943, a Chicago CORE group targeted Stoner's, a downtown restaurant. After unsuccessful attempts at negotiating with management and mobilizing public opinion against the restaurant, CORE proceeded with its ultimate tactic—direct action—which in this case called for a sit-down protest in the restaurant. The problem was that CORE only numbered in the tens while the restaurant seated over two hundred customers (ibid., 13).

CORE's experiences were typical of the less established civil rights organizations that were trying to build up their credibility in the black community. SCLC encountered similar trepidation among the black townsfolk in Saint Augustine, who sought improvements in their living conditions but feared that demonstrations would bring retaliation and increased repression. Consequently, local blacks shied away from protests until they were confident that collective action could generate favorable results (Colburn 1985, 27).

SUCCESSFUL COLLECTIVE ACTION

Successful collective action, however, alters the complexion of political participation. Inducements and rewards that were absent when the movement was unable to make headway come to the fore and alter the cost-benefit calculations of prospective activists. What was once a losing proposition becomes profitable; what was once a chore becomes a crusade.

Another example drawn from the Montgomery bus boycott illustrates how preferences can change as a movement gathers momentum. At the start of the boycott, the leadership role was foisted on black ministers for two reasons. They were immune from economic pressure and the church was the best institution available to serve as the basis for organizing collective action. News of the boycott could be spread more efficiently through the church than through the available black media, and church congregations already possessed the solidarity and leadership that would make them easy to mobilize.

The black ministers, however, only reluctantly assumed leadership and, if the boycott had received scant support from the black community in the first few days, they "doubtless would have quietly but quickly disengaged themselves." But because the black community instead threw itself enthusiastically behind the boycott, the ministers felt obligated to retain their leadership position or risk being "branded as cowards and traitors" (Fairclough 1987, 18).

The ministers became more enthusiastic, however, as the boycott endured against strong opposition from the white authorities. The more the conflict intensified, the greater the admiration and respect they received from the black community. The media spotlight cast on the boycott prompted the ministers to shed their anonymity so that they could bask in the publicity they received. So great was the transformation of the preachers' attitudes toward participation that when they were arrested for violating the state's antiboycott law, they were not in the least troubled but reacted instead with good humor and pride (ibid.). On the other hand, ministers who had been excluded from the leadership were chastened and regretted their nonparticipation, as we would expect in a successful campaign. "The boycott had so captured the imagination and the loyalties of the city's blacks that the failure of a black minister to be included occasionally as a speaker at the frequent mass meetings which were the movement's backbone demeaned him in the eyes of his congregation" (Thornton 1980, 211).

From a broader perspective, the success of the Montgomery boycott had a tremendous psychological impact on the black population across the country. King announced that the Montgomery boycott had demonstrated, among other things, that "we can stick together for a common cause" and that "our leaders do not have to sell out" (Branch

1988, 195). Blacks in general came to realize that they could improve their standing in society through organized collective action, and much of the uncertainty then prevailing about the benefits of coordinating their efforts was thereby eliminated (Morris 1981, 751).

In general, as direct action tactics proved their mettle in disputes around the country, civil rights activists took to the streets with a new-found vigor and determination. By the early 1960s, direct action was widely recognized by both its proponents and its opponents as an extremely potent tactic. In northern cities particularly, local officials and entrepreneurs, after witnessing the destructive pattern of interracial conflict in the South, often made concessions at the mere threat of direct action. Those in positions of authority anticipated that change was inevitable and therefore sought to prevent the damage that a protracted conflict would inflict on their communities.

When even weakly organized protests began to win concessions, civil rights activists developed a confidence in their ability to transform society that bordered on hubris. Genevieve Hughes, a CORE official, after noting that the civil rights issue had reached the top of the political agenda in the country and placed whites on the defensive, rejoiced in her belief that: "We can do everything we want. . . . [I]t may be that the day has finally come when no matter what CORE does or how it does it, it still wins" (Meier and Rudwick 1975, 229).

CORE's newfound confidence, a 180-degree turnaround from its demeanor in the 1940s and 1950s, propelled the organization to tackle projects that would have been unthinkable a few years earlier. Retail outlets, banks, city governments, utility companies, industrial firms, and other employers were targeted for protests because they used discriminatory hiring practices. No project seemed too ambitious. A few CORE chapters in California and the midwest tried to reform the hiring practices of entire downtown districts in one fell swoop by negotiating simultaneously with dozens of shops and businesses (Meier and Rudwick 1975, 233).

6 | Coordination Problems in Assurance Games

> *You can't always get what you want.*
> Rolling Stones lyric

If social and psychological benefits operate in the way I suggest, then their inclusion in the cost-benefit calculus does not resolve the collective action problem in a trivial manner but rather reconstitutes it into an alternative but equally interesting form. In other words, even if we grant that some people are driven to validate publicly their political convictions and relish an opportunity to be present at the making of history, while others feel pressured or obligated to do their fair share, it does not follow straightforwardly that these individuals will be able to collaborate successfully.

To see why this is so, let me illustrate, through figure 6.1, how the choice facing the potential activist changes when we incorporate social and expressive benefits in the manner I suggest. The addition of these selective incentives removes the temptation to free ride. As before, the individual can either participate or not participate in collective action. But now if all others participate, he also wishes to participate, receiving in the process not only his share of the public good but also the satisfaction and benefit (both immediate and long-term) of having played a role in the collective endeavor. On the other hand, if the rest of the group does not participate, the public good will not be obtained, and the individual will only be wasting his time and energy if he chooses to go it alone; there will be few or no compensatory social and expressive benefits. Therefore each individual wants to do what everyone else does, but he prefers everyone to participate rather than to abstain.

COORDINATION VS. PRISONER'S DILEMMA PROBLEMS

This is no longer a prisoner's dilemma but a type of coordination game known as an assurance game (Sen 1967, 1974; Schelling 1960; Elster 1979). The coordination problem in the assurance game differs in many significant ways from the prisoner's dilemma. Because it is in

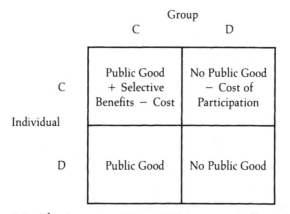

FIGURE 6.1. The Assurance Game. Entries are payoffs to the individual.

the interest of the players to work together in the assurance game, they will do so if they can reassure each other that they share a common understanding of their predicament. Both mutual cooperation and mutual defection are equilibria, but CC is preferred by all to DD. If everyone else cooperates in the assurance game, then one has an incentive to cooperate as well. In contrast, those engaged in the prisoner's dilemma are better off when they all cooperate than when they all defect, but each is better off defecting while the others cooperate. Therefore in a prisoner's dilemma, mutual cooperation is difficult to achieve since each player has an incentive to double-cross his partners. Even when communication is possible in the PD, each player will be tempted to violate any agreement to cooperate unless he has cause to fear retaliation from the other players in subsequent interactions.[1]

In coordination games more generally, it is in the mutual interest of the parties to coincide on a given outcome. The parties win or lose together. In pure coordination situations, the parties have a complete interest in collaborating, while in nonpure coordination situations, the interests of the parties in collaborating outweigh the idiosyncratic preferences they have for particular outcomes (Ullmann-Margalit 1977). For example, consider two friends who have planned to have lunch together but forget to decide beforehand at which of the two nearby downtown cafés they are supposed to meet. In a pure coordination game, the friends share a common preference order for the two cafés

1. Elster (1979, 146) argues that the conditions necessary for cooperation in the n-person PD supergame (viz., small stable communities with shared premises and information) are also likely to foster mutual affection and common expectations and therefore to transform the PD into an assurance game.

(see figure 6.2a); but if it is a nonpure situation, the friends prefer different cafés, although their desire to meet has a higher priority (see figure 6.2b).

Coordination is often achieved simply in an assurance game in which one outcome is preferred to all others by every player. If, in the

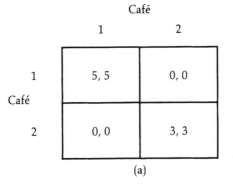

(a)

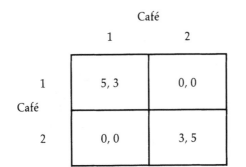

(b)

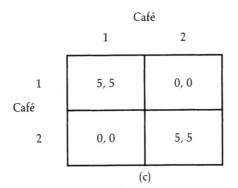

(c)

FIGURE 6.2. (a)–(c). Coordination Games

case of the lunch date, each person prefers the same café, is aware of the other's preference, and is aware of the other's awareness, then it is a simple matter for them to coordinate their choices. Even without communication, the two people should be able to reach through tacit coordination the superior outcome in the game. Each knows that the other prefers the same alternative and will choose that alternative as long as there is reason to believe that he will do likewise. Knowledge that the other person is similarly inclined reduces one's hesitation to choose the preferred alternative. At the same time, each person knows that as his hesitation declines, the hesitation of the other person to choose the preferred alternative also declines because the two share a common analysis of their predicament. This process of removing doubt about the likely action of the other feeds upon itself until each person is extremely confident that the other will choose the preferred alternative (cf. Taylor 1987, 39).

More serious coordination problems arise when the parties are faced with more than one optimal outcome. This occurs when there are multiple coordination equilibria, any one of which is satisfactory. If the two friends are indifferent toward the two cafés, then each must try to anticipate the other's move. (See figure 6.2c.) In practice, each person is likely to consider any auxiliary information he possesses that might suggest which of the two cafés he ought to gamble on. Perhaps this problem arose in the past and, on that occasion, the two guessed right and managed to arrive at the same café. That being the case, each might assume that the other will repeat the choice that proved successful the last time around.[2]

When a precedent is unavailable, other salient cues might make one of the two restaurants the more obvious choice. For instance, one of the two cafés might be much better known than the other, one café may be more centrally located, or one of the cafés—as luck would have it—may have been reviewed in that morning's paper, which each person reads and knows the other reads too.

Schelling (1960, 53–80) examined a number of pencil-and-paper coordination problems in which players tried to match strategies based on some salient features of the situation that each believed would be

2. But keep in mind David Lewis's (1969) caveat: "Of course, we could never be given exactly the same problem twice. There must be this difference at least: the second time, we can draw on our experience with the first. More generally, the two problems will differ in several independent respects. We cannot do exactly what we did before. Nothing we could do this time is exactly like what we did before—like it in every respect—because the situations are not exactly alike" (37).

noted by the others. One such problem consisted of sixteen small squares arranged in a four-by-four square formation. The object of the game was to choose one of the sixteen squares; if all players chose the identical square, they won a sum of money. Another problem involved arranging the letters ABC in some order; if all players arranged them in the same order, they were rewarded with a cash prize. In a third problem, two players were rewarded if, choosing independently of each other, they could agree on calling either heads or tails. In each instance, the players tried to follow what they surmised to be the most common and predictable strategy.

LYNCH MOBS

The psychologist Roger Brown (1965) analyzed the dynamics of a lynch mob based on an assurance game model. In Brown's model, the members of a lynch mob congregating outside of a jail must choose between two courses of action: either (1) storm the jail to confiscate the prisoner or (2) hold back and do nothing. Everyone of course relishes the idea of "expediting" the criminal justice process by hanging the prisoner that day; but at the same time each recognizes that challenging the local police carries obvious risks and dangers. To charge the jail impulsively might get one shot or thrown in jail.

On the other hand, the risk of punishment for an individual is greatly reduced if he acts not alone but in concert with the other members of the mob. There is safety as well as strength in numbers. Large numbers make people feel anonymous and give them the impression that their actions are endorsed and supported by the entire community. As Brown points out, the reasoning in the mob is that "if everyone would participate in the lynching then no one could be punished for it and no one would be criticized for it. If everyone would help lynch the prisoner then everyone could enjoy the prisoner's agony without fear of punishment and perhaps even with some sense of having helped to uphold an ideal" (754).

Consequently, according to Brown, each individual in the mob hopes that everyone will storm the jail.[3] The flip side is that each individual fears that he will storm the jail and find himself unsupported by the rest of the mob, thereby placing himself at the mercy of the

3. Compare Brown's assumptions about the lynch mob to Twain's in the *Adventures of Huckleberry Finn*. In the lynch mob scene, Sherburn derides the mob that has gathered in front of his house and impugns their motives. None wants to be there, he sneers, but they're afraid to chicken out: "You didn't want to come. The average man don't like trouble and danger. *You* don't like trouble and danger. But if only *half* a

Others

Lynch   Not Lynch

	Lynch	Not Lynch
Lynch	+ +, + +	− −, +
Not Lynch	+, − −	0, 0

Individual

FIGURE 6.3. The Lynch Mob

prison guards. Brown summarizes this problem using a game matrix showing the individual's predicament in relation to the rest of the group. (See figure 6.3.)

Starting with the bottom right entries and moving counterclockwise: if no one tries to lynch the prisoner, then nothing is gained and nothing is lost. If an individual acts alone, he will be swiftly and harshly punished (− −), an outcome (Brown ventures) that will give the rest of the group a small amount of cathartic, albeit sadistic, pleasure. An all-out effort by the individual and the rest of the group, however, produces satisfaction for all concerned. Lastly, if the group storms the jail while the individual refrains, Brown surmises that the members of the group will run the risk of punishment (− −) while the individual enjoys some vicarious pleasure (+). This outcome therefore is the reverse of the outcome when the individual goes it alone. I might add here that the payoffs associated with the final outcome are appropriate only if we assume (probably unrealistically) that the group (minus the sole abstainer) will not successfully lynch the prisoner.

Now if each individual in the crowd regards his situation in the way depicted by the matrix and in addition knows that everyone else shares his preferences, it is a foregone conclusion that the crowd will turn into a lynch mob. Because all individuals prefer lynching to not

man—like Buck Harkness, there—shouts 'Lynch him, lynch him!' you're afraid to back down—afraid you'll be found out to be what you are—cowards—and so you raise a yell, and hang yourselves onto that half-a-man's coat tail, and come raging up here, swearing what big things you're going to do. The pitifulest thing out is a mob; that's what an army is—a mob; they don't fight with courage that's born in them, but with courage that's borrowed from their mass, and from their officers. But a mob without any *man* at the head of it, is *beneath* pitifulness" (1985, 190–91).

lynching and are aware of each other's preferences, they will quickly coordinate their actions and storm the jail.

In practice, however, coordination will probably be more difficult to achieve than the game suggests. Brown points out that the crowd members will have doubts about each other's willingness to participate in a lynching. "Do the others," each person will ask, "really want, above all, to have a lynching or to let themselves go in a religious frenzy?" (Brown 1965, 756). Therefore to make sure they are "on the same page," the members of a lynch mob go through a "milling" phase during which they convey their preferences to each other. Milling "seems to be a process of informed communication, a process by which members learn that they are of one mind, that they are individually eager to lynch, riot, or otherwise, 'let go'" (Brown 1965, 756). This process might continue indefinitely as crowd members try to reach some consensus about the nature of their predicament.

GRAPHS

Following Schelling (1973, 1978), we can represent graphically how the payoff accruing to an individual varies continuously in prisoner's dilemma and coordination games according to the distribution of cooperative and uncooperative choices in the group. On the ordinate we plot the respective payoffs to a given individual for contributing or not contributing. On the abscissa we indicate the number of individuals, ranging from 0 to n, who have elected to contribute (by implication, n minus the number of contributors equals the number of noncontributors). Two payoff curves result, one for each alternative.

In the case of an n-person prisoner's dilemma,[4] the payoff curves will have the following characteristics (see figures 6.4 and 6.5 for examples). The two curves will not cross; each curve will be monotonic; and the curve representing the dominant choice will always be above the curve representing the dominated choice. Lastly, there will be some coalition k that will be able to do better by choosing the dominated alternative than by defecting with everyone else.

4. Schelling defines a multiperson prisoner's dilemma as having the following characteristics: (1) there are $n + 1$ individuals, each faced with the same binary choice having identical payoffs; (2) each individual has the identical dominant choice; (3) no matter which choice an individual makes, the dominant or dominated, his payoff varies directly with the number of others who choose the dominated alternative; (4) there is some number k such that k or more individuals can do better by making the dominated choice when all others have made the dominant choice.

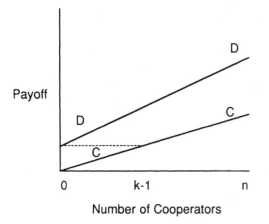

FIGURE 6.4. *N*-Person Prisoner's Dilemma

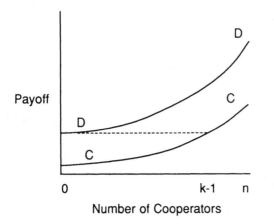

FIGURE 6.5. *N*-Person Prisoner's Dilemma

Consider what happens when the payoff curve for abstention criss-crosses the payoff curve for participation, as in figures 6.6 and 6.7. Now we have a coordination problem. There are two equilibria, one corresponding to total abstention and the other to total participation. Although total participation is the preferred equilibrium for the group, thus making it an assurance game, it may be difficult to achieve this outcome because each individual will prefer to abstain unless a certain number (determined by the point $v - 1$ where the two payoff curves intersect) in the group choose to participate.

In any of these cases with two or more equilibria, the problem (if there is a problem) is to get a concerted choice, or switch, of enough people to reach the superior equilibrium. There may be no need for coercion, discipline, or centralized choice; it may be enough merely to get people to make the right choice in the first place, and this expectation may be achieved merely by communication, since nobody has any reason not to make the right choice once there is concerted recognition. (Schelling 1973, 407)

But as Schelling points out, "People can get trapped at an inefficient equilibrium, everyone waiting for the others to switch, nobody willing to be the first unless he has confidence that enough others will switch to make it worthwhile" (ibid.).

One interesting feature of the assurance games is that there is—as in the case of the PD—a viable coalition of size k (located where the C payoff exceeds the D payoff when everyone defects) that can profitably cooperate. Should this coalition emerge, its members will do better than if they had defected like all the rest. The problem is that by contributing to the public good, they also improve the lot of the defectors. Hence, there may be some tendency for members of this coalition to defect themselves and reap the higher payoffs enjoyed by those who have abstained. Unfortunately, members who give in to such temptation may destroy the viability of the coalition and force an exodus toward the suboptimal equilibrium.

Alternatively, if the coalition can recruit enough additional mem-

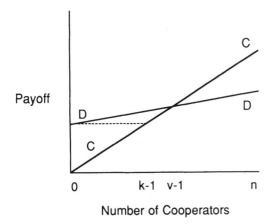

FIGURE 6.6. N-Person Assurance Game

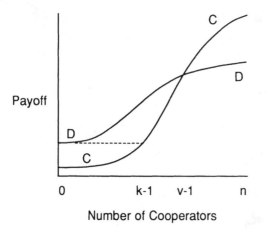

FIGURE 6.7. *N*-Person Assurance Game

bers (to equal the point $v - 1$), then participation will become the dominant choice and all those formerly abstaining will be induced to jump on the bandwagon. Before this critical mass is reached, however, the situation continues to be a prisoner's dilemma: each abstainer is better off free riding on the efforts of the participants in the coalition. The coalition is sufficiently successful to sustain itself but not attractive (or coercive) enough to compel those outside it to contribute their fair share. Only when the coalition expands its membership to achieve some threshold level does it provide the requisite incentive for all others to join.

COORDINATION AMONG POLITICAL ACTIVISTS

Whereas coordination problems are relatively simple to overcome in everyday interactions, they can severely impede efforts to initiate mass political activism. The members of an aggrieved group may harbor a strong desire to participate in collective action, but they must nevertheless reassure each other of their willingness to contribute. This prerequisite is more difficult to satisfy than it may appear at first glance, largely because of the size and concomitant vagaries of a social movement.

In textbook assurance games, the players make their choices on the basis of the same payoff matrix, and they know that other players' choices are also based on this matrix. Moreover, in textbook games, the payoffs for mutual cooperation are directly related to the level of contributions. If, for example, the players are political activists who are unhappy with the status quo and eager to confront the system, they know that they will be successful if a sufficient number of them combine their efforts to press their demands on the government. In addition, if these budding activists can communicate with each other, they will quickly agree to challenge the system together, since each activist stands to benefit by becoming involved if enough other activists agree to participate. As I explained above, even without communication, they should still be able to find tacit means to coordinate a challenge to the status quo because they possess perfect information about each other's preferences.

What makes this example unrealistic is that (1) the payoff for collaboration is certain and foreseeable; and (2) the activists share, and know they share, a common understanding of their predicament. In reality, however, there is likely to be considerable doubt in the minds of prospective activists about the merits of any particular level of cooperation, as well as about the perceptions and preferences of fellow group members.

In contrast to textbook assurance games, then, coordination is difficult to achieve because people are not completely informed, and because coordination at designated levels does not guarantee success. The ability of the leaders of the movement and their followers to mobilize their resources in pursuit of a goal is a necessary but insufficient condition for the attainment of that goal. Much depends also on the responsiveness of the petitioned party—whether local authorities, Congress, or the administration—to these coordinated demands.

Consider how these sources of uncertainty alter the payoff matrix facing the activists (see figure 6.8):

The matrix in figure 6.8 contains the following assumptions: No collective good will be produced if fewer than k individuals cooperate; only a cost c is incurred. The minimal efficacious subgroup requires k contributors. If between k and $v - 1$ individuals cooperate, some collective good b (which exceeds c) is produced, but it remains advantageous to be a defector if the level of cooperation remains within these bounds. However, if v or more individuals cooperate, the movement takes off and generates both more of the collective good $(2b)$ and selective social and psychological incentives b' for contributors which exceed the cost of participation. If at least v individuals cooperate, every

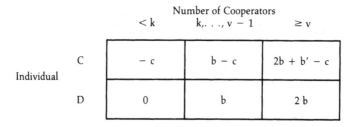

FIGURE 6.8. An Assurance Game with Uncertainty. Entries are payoffs to the individual.

individual will prefer cooperation to defection. Therefore although there are high start-up costs to collective action, the attraction of individual cooperation increases with the total level of contributions.[5]

Because k and v are unknown, and because estimates of these parameters waver across group members, collective action is inherently uncertain. For any given level of cooperation, the possibility of success has to be balanced by the prospect of failure. Perhaps a combined effort will pay dividends, perhaps not. Whether it ends in success or failure depends on the number of cooperators as well as on the responsiveness of the authorities. Acting together, in other words, when there are too few participants (less than k) may be no better than acting alone—both may be futile, if not outright dangerous. In such cases where collective action is destined to fail, each individual is better off abstaining than participating. On the other hand, cooperation is a more palatable strategy when there are between k and $v - 1$ cooperators, but each cooperator is still being exploited by the defectors in the group, who do better by free riding.

In this predicament, each activist's decision will depend on his subjective estimate of the likelihood that collective action will be successful, as well as his beliefs about the perceptions and calculations of other activists. Someone who thinks that collective action has little chance of succeeding will set very high levels for k and v; in the most pessimistic case, k and v will exceed the size of the group seeking benefits—this means that even total cooperation will be assumed to be futile.

Even if some activists hold out hope for success at feasible levels of

5. Figure 6.8 assumes a step collective good. The amount of the collective good that is produced varies in discontinuous steps rather than continuously with the level of contributions. Therefore the thresholds in figure 6.8 are not identical to those in figures 6.6 and 6.7. In particular, there is no break-even point where individuals are indifferent between cooperation (C) and defection (D).

cooperation, they must still estimate the likelihood that such levels will be reached. The benefits of cooperation and defection are contingent upon the likelihood of different levels of participation. If we define $P(\cdot)$ as the estimated probability that the indicated level of cooperation will be reached, then the expected values of cooperation and defection are obtained by taking a weighted sum of the payoffs for each strategy at various levels of cooperation:

$$EV(C) = -c \times P(<k) + (b - c) \times P(k, \ldots, v - 1)$$
$$+ (2b + b' - c) \times P(\geq v) \qquad (6.1)$$

$$EV(D) = 0 \times P(<k) + b \times P(k, \ldots, v - 1) + (2b) \times P(\geq v). \qquad (6.2)$$

Cooperation is the best strategy only if the difference between these two values, $d = EV(C) - EV(D)$, is greater than zero. This condition is satisfied when:

$$d = [-c \times P(<k) + (b - c - b) \times P(k, \ldots, v - 1)$$
$$+ (2b + b' - c - 2b) \times P(\geq v)] > 0. \qquad (6.3)$$

Because the sum of probabilities equals 1, this reduces to:

$$d = [b' \times P(\geq v) - c] > 0. \qquad (6.4)$$

Therefore $d > 0$ if

$$P(\geq v) > \frac{c}{b'}. \qquad (6.5)$$

This means that an individual will cooperate only if he estimates that the probability that at least v individuals will cooperate is greater than c/b', the ratio of costs to selective benefits. Therefore everything else being equal, developments that lower the cost of participation, increase the selective benefits accompanying contributions, or raise the probability that total participation will reach the critical threshold—which might be accomplished by reducing v itself—will abet the cause. As I have noted, however, estimates of the value that v must take will vary among group members depending on their assessment of the prospects of collective action; and estimates of the probability that there will be at least v cooperators will also be unsettled. To further complicate matters, not only will an individual be uncertain in his own mind about these parameters, but he will also know that others are uncertain about them too, and that others are aware of his uncertainty. These combined sources of uncertainty are prone to undermine anyone's confidence in collective action.

Prospective activists in communication with each other will obviously be in a better position to agree on an optimal course of action. But even if they decide to rally against the authorities, each activist might remain nervous about the dependability of others to uphold their end of the agreement. Because of the vagaries of the situation, each activist may develop doubts about the probability of success, the preferences of his fellow activists, and ultimately the wisdom of his choice.

We can think of this collective action problem more generally as an iterated assurance game or supergame in which prospective activists must continually make decisions about whether to participate based on the information they receive about the outcome of the game in preceding trials (i.e., previous campaigns of the movement). The early trials of this supergame allow participants and spectators to evaluate the nature of the game they are playing and, in particular, to estimate the values of b, b', c, k, $P(\geq k)$, v, and $P(\geq v)$. The parameters of the game therefore are established by the changing fortunes of the movement. Early forays by the movement in its nascent stages provide information about the relative difficulty or ease of attaining the group's objectives, the number of people who support the cause, the force of social pressures and other selective incentives, and so on. The initial plays of the game reveal both the strategies of the players in the community and the payoffs for those strategies. This trial-and-error process clarifies the shapes of the payoff functions for cooperation and defection at different levels of cooperation. These functions are ambiguous to the participants and become defined gradually by the participants' experiences in the political process. Moreover, these functions are constantly being reevaluated as old campaigns wind down, and new ones are begun.

TIPPING PHENOMENA

Because of the uncertain prospect of collective action, most potential activists are likely to be risk-averse. Even though they have a conditional willingness to participate, they will adopt a wait-and-see attitude to determine if collective action is likely to be viable before tossing their own hats into the ring.

Here I'd like to elaborate on the concept of "thresholds" based on the work of Thomas Schelling (see also Granovetter 1978 and Granovetter and Soong 1983). Schelling's (1978, 102–10) description of the "dying seminar" illustrates a "tipping" phenomenon that most of us have experienced at one time or another. The dying seminar refers to the way that seminars, after enthusiastic beginnings, fade out of existence as fewer and fewer people turn up for each session. The reason the seminar collapses is not that no one is interested—after all, people seemed *very* interested at the start—but that people drop out when the size of the seminar falls short of the ideal size needed to guarantee their continued participation.

In essence, there is a "run" on the seminar just as there is a run on a bank. Each participant will attend the seminar only if a certain number of other people also attend, and he will refrain as soon as the attendance drops below that level. In any sizable gathering of people, attendance thresholds will vary across individuals so that individuals will be triggered to depart under different circumstances: some will give up if there are only a few no-shows, while others will stick it out until attendance is so sparse that the function can no longer properly be called a seminar. Unless there is the right mix of participants to produce a viable equilibrium, the seminar will dissipate as early dropouts reduce the attendance level to the point where additional dropouts follow; this in turn stimulates further departures, and so on, until the sole survivors decide to give up on the whole effort.

Schelling (1978, 155–66) gives other examples of the tipping phenomenon, including a discussion of how neighborhoods may become racially segregated even if few or none of its inhabitants are strict segregationists. As in the dying seminar model, an individual prefers to do something if the right combination of people share his preference; in this case, he will reside in a neighborhood if it contains a certain minimum proportion of his race but move out if that ideal balance is disturbed. If everyone has a different level of tolerance for proportions of the other race, it is possible that the first residents of a racially mixed neighborhood who move away because of dissatisfaction with its composition will disturb the equilibrium sufficiently to set off a chain reaction out of the neighborhood. In this manner, the degree of racial segregation in a residential zone eventually might greatly exceed the average level of tolerance among its inhabitants.

Translate the model to the case of political participation. I have argued that each potential activist has in mind some threshold size v that collective action must reach (with a sufficiently high probability) before he is willing to make a contribution. In other words, as long as the number of activists is likely to remain below v, he withholds his contribution. Given this assumption, unless there is a fortuitous distribution of thresholds among the potential activists, collective action will never get off the ground.

Even without specifying exact numerical thresholds that people have in mind before they find collective action profitable, it is apparent that there will be coordination problems in the real-life version of the assurance game. One major obstacle is that these thresholds (when we are dealing with protest movements) will be much larger than the size of any particular individual's primary and reference groups. Unlike the two-person or small-n-person games, complete multilateral synchronization is not possible; instead each person has to operate as best he can on the basis of limited information—good information, perhaps, about how his immediate circle of acquaintances will behave, but considerable uncertainty about the likely choices of those who are beyond his social circle. As Schofield (1985) points out, "the fundamental theoretical problem underlying the question of cooperation is the manner by which individuals attain knowledge of each other's preferences and likely behavior. Moreover, the problem is one of common knowledge, since each individual, i, is required not only to have information about others' preferences, but also to know that the others have knowledge about i's own preferences and strategies" (218).

Hence, although the nature of the game facing potential activists has changed from a prisoner's dilemma to an assurance game, we still have a serious collective action problem, albeit of a different kind. In the prisoner's dilemma, the problem is that each individual prefers free riding to participating. In the assurance game, this problem potentially vanishes; each individual prefers participating to free riding but only under a certain problematic condition—only if there are enough other participants to make collective action likely to succeed. The danger is that everyone will stand around waiting for others to pay the heavy start-up costs needed to initiate the process. In terms of our graphic representation of the PD and coordination problems, the payoff for defection exceeds the payoff for cooperation until some threshold level of participation $v - 1$ is reached, at which point the payoff curve for cooperation intersects with the payoff curve for defection. Until a certain number of people commit themselves, all prospective activists find themselves in a PD situation.

REAL ASSURANCE GAMES

Fantasia's (1988) description of a wildcat strike in a New Jersey foundry shows how the emotions, preferences, and behavior of workers change dramatically after the critical threshold is reached. The strike was first contemplated following the sudden dismissal of a popular maintenance worker who had fallen asleep on the job. Several angry co-workers, impatient with the normal union-management grievance procedure, began to organize a work stoppage:

Men started moving from their work stations toward the center of the finishing department. But contrary to romanticized images of workers acting in forceful unison, there was definite hesitation on the part of many at this initial stage of the action. A walkout was clearly "illegal" according to the union contract, and the workers faced certain dismissal if they were unsuccessful. Action that would jeopardize one's livelihood was not to be taken lightly and would not occur without a certain amount of careful deliberation and negotiation. (82–83)

As in the case of the lynch mob, the negotiation occurs tacitly as workers provide each other with cues and signals about their respective degrees of commitment to the proposed action. Fantasia breaks the evolution of this particular wildcat strike into three phases, the first of which was crucial. In the initial phase, the shop foreman confronted the workers and ordered them back to work, threatening them with the loss of their jobs. The workers at this point were still feeling their way through the strike and could be divided according to their level of commitment. The boldest workers—in effect, the leaders of the strike—stood up front, backed by a second, more scattered group, which was in turn backed by a third group whose members strayed only a slight distance from their work stations. In this critical phase, the leaders of the strike faced down the foreman and gave him the impression that they were a united group. This action, in turn, showed their less committed co-workers that collective action could prevail over the opposition of the company.

In the second phase, the workers, now similarly committed—at least as indicated by their actions—moved out of their department toward an outdoor courtyard. Fantasia observes that the workers at this stage were still extremely tense and apprehensive. They moved in "amoeba-like fashion" (ibid., 85) since no worker wanted to stand out as an individual.

The third phase of the movement was entered when members of the different departments emerged in the courtyard area.

At this point, workers converging on the courtyard found themselves among a larger group of workers from other departments, giving rise to a clear change in the mood of the strikers. The tension of the previous twenty minutes or so, caused by a real fear of losing one's job, dissolved into near jubilation as workers enthusiastically greeted co-workers from other departments. . . . Their expressions almost resembled those of school children as they rush out the doors of a grade school on a warm spring day, laughing and jostling good-naturedly. The workers sensed that there was little doubt now who would have the upper hand. (ibid., 87–88)

In our terms, the workers suddenly realized, upon meeting up with their colleagues, that they were engaged in an assurance game in which success was guaranteed and mutual cooperation was clearly the best strategy. Up until that point, each worker continued to wonder if his actions would cost him his job. Not surprisingly, in the aftermath of the strike, workers tried to claim credit for their role in the successful action. "Tales of bravado abounded, with each worker trying to outdo the other about how he had 'stood up' to the company and won" (ibid., 91).

What the successful wildcat strike also did was create a precedent or convention for subsequent collective action. Several months later, when another grievance arose—regarding inadequate heating in the department—workers more readily committed themselves to another work stoppage. Not only were workers more assertive and confident this time around, but company officials were more responsive to the new demand, knowing full well that the potential for a total walkout existed. Fantasia speculates that if the first strike had been forcefully halted—with accompanying firings—the second strike would never have taken place. "Had the first action not succeeded, the 'culture of solidarity' at Taylor [the foundry] would presumably have been destroyed, and possibly even replaced by an atmosphere permeated by fearfulness and selfishness" (ibid., 112).

As this case illustrates, it is difficult to ascertain in loosely structured collective action where the C and D curves crisscross. People therefore tend to edge their way toward this point if they are willing to venture at all. Social solidarity among potential participants will tend to reduce the threshold, because people will feel obligated to participate at an earlier stage of collective action than they would in the absence of social pressure and personal commitments to the group. Selective benefits (b') therefore will be operative at lower levels of cooperation. In addition, a movement that is able to squeeze concessions from the opposition will effectively lower the threshold because successful collaboration will demonstrate to nonparticipants that they can obtain sufficient returns for their efforts. Cooperation can also be assisted, for similar reasons, by favorable historical precedents and traditions which serve to increase the prospects of success in the estimate of group members. Leipzig's long and fabled tradition for opposing authority, for example, dating from the Protestant Revolution may help to explain why the mass protests that toppled the Communist Party in East Germany started in that city before spreading elsewhere (Binder 1989).

Factors that lower the threshold also tend to raise estimates of the probability that there are enough cooperators prepared to meet that threshold. Successful past collective action proves that a considerable number of people are willing to participate in collective action. Social pressure presumes that people are linked by membership in the same community and therefore share common bases of information. People who share a tradition of successful collective action will have higher expectations that fellow citizens will cooperate and will consequently be more likely to cooperate themselves. In this regard, media coverage of the movement can also help to resolve coordination problems by shaping and informing public perceptions about community alignments, public opinion, and the level of participation in collective action (Taylor 1986, 161).

In general, uncertainty about the preferences of others is removed and coordination is facilitated when people work through social and political networks and organizations. Groups are more readily mobilized than individuals. Individuals in groups bonded by a distinct ethnicity, race, or social status, ties of friendship and kinship, and common membership in religious, fraternal, social, and political clubs, associations, and organizations have greater solidarity and are in closer communication than groups that are not constrained by similar functional and social linkages. Solidarity and affection in turn go hand in hand with the development of personal obligations and selective social incentives. For these reasons, civil rights leaders mobilized the masses by working in concert with existing organizations such as churches, college and school groups, unions, and professional and fraternal organizations. Members of these preexisting networks had reputations to protect, respect and affection for each other, and reliable information about the preferences and probable behavior of others.

It is when a movement evinces little hope of achieving its goals, because either community relationships are weak or authorities are indifferent or hostile, that the crossover point for the C and D curves will be unduly high. Nonparticipants will be reluctant to cooperate until the movement has grown to a considerable size—which, by the way, it never will so long as everyone makes this assessment of its prospects. Should the movement get off the ground but encounter recalcitrant authorities, the activists will soon feel that their efforts are in vain; each activist will come to believe that not enough people are contributing to be able to produce the desired outcome, and that everyone who is cooperating is a sucker. Each member of this group will come to see himself as part of a coalition that is not sufficiently powerful to attain the results it seeks. These conditions presage the start of a bandwagon in reverse, fueled by a self-fulfilling prophesy. Once everyone fears that the collective action is doomed and his efforts are in vain, everyone will behave in a manner that will ensure the demise of the movement. Each participant will prefer to opt out of the movement altogether rather than expend additional resources on an ill-fated campaign. Cutting and running will be the order of the day.

To rescue the situation, what is typically required is a core of highly dedicated, extremely moral—some might say extremely "irrational"— individuals who are willing to assume leadership roles and to constitute in effect the critical mass that instigates the growth of collective action (cf. Oliver, Marwell, and Teixeira 1985; Oberschall 1980). Such individuals are either the most morally committed individuals within the entire social movement or they are risk-taking entrepreneurs who initiate activity on the assumption that they are investing in a collective endeavor that will ultimately be profitable.

The leaders will have to intercede and dispel the fatalistic mood by persuading their followers that they will eventually prevail if they are patient and persistent; in addition, the leaders will have to double their efforts to squeeze some concessions out of their opponents in order to buoy the sagging spirits of their followers. A successful coalition can turn around the prospects of collective action. By extracting concessions from the opposition and holding out the promise of further benefits, this coalition may be able to exert enough social pressure on nonparticipants to bring additional cooperators into the fold.

In any mass endeavor, it is essential that the leaders retain the confidence of the followers and that the followers sustain their conviction that they are doing the right thing by participating.[6] The significance of credible leaders in the movement is emphasized in Popkin's (1979) treatment of peasant rebellion:

> Whether the entrepreneur is directly exchanging immediate individual benefits for peasant inputs or trying to convince the peasant that

6. Charismatic leadership (e.g., King, Gandhi) is commonly believed to be attractive to followers for irrational reasons. A more rational interpretation of this bond can be made if we consider these leaders to be the die-hard element that is crucial in any collective action. People—viz., joiners—need to believe that they have a chance to prevail before they are willing to sacrifice their time, energy, and perhaps even their lives to achieve some collective goal, and a charismatic leader instills this belief or faith in them.

his actions can have a perceptible and profitable impact on the collective good, he must be concerned with increasing the peasant's estimates of the efficacy of his contribution to secure the promised returns. This means that the peasant's subjective estimates of the would-be entrepreneur's capability and credibility will directly influence the entrepreneur's ability to organize peasants, and that, *ceteris paribus,* a situation with more credible organizers is likely to be a situation with more effective organizations. (259)

Popkin also indicates that the credibility and trustworthiness of both Communist and religious political entrepreneurs were furthered by displays of self-abnegation. Peasants assumed that leaders practising self-denial were more likely to use their contributions to further collective rather than selfish ends (ibid., 261).

For similar reasons, SNCC organizers enjoyed success in Mississippi because of their reckless, fearless, devil-may-care attitude. Amzie Moore, a local resident, recalled that he "found that SNCC was for business, live or die, sink or swim, survive or perish. They were moving, and nobody seemed to worry about whether he was gonna live or die" (Raines 1977, 236). Local blacks therefore knew that SNCC did not plan to stay in town just long enough to stir up trouble, leaving them to suffer the consequences. Rather, SNCC activists became a part of the community and worked to build a grass-roots movement. They learned the identities of the local leaders and used these people as conduits to attract new recruits. By their deeds, therefore, SNCC activists demonstrated a willingness to stand up to whites even at the risk of their lives. This left an indelible impression on the black townsfolk.

During the Montgomery bus boycott, the organizers worked hard to bring prominent people from around the country to the city to demonstrate their support for the boycott. This made the local people involved feel that the movement was in good shape and that their sacrifices would soon pay off. Bayard Rustin observed that "the fact that important people from all over America were coming to see this was a great psychological boon to the people who had to put up with walking to work, losing jobs, wondering whether they'd ever win" (Raines 1977, 54).

In general, people of renown are particularly suited to play a vital role in the early stages of collective action. By attracting media coverage, public figures reduce the risk of participation in more dangerous forms of collective action for rank-and-file activists. The presence of the media serves as a protective umbrella for the movement as a whole, even though its focus is on certain key participants. By lending his name and energy to a cause, the celebrity draws public attention to it, and at the same time his endorsement gives the cause more credibility. Publicity and credibility, in turn, are qualities that in the public mind are associated with the likelihood that the cause will be successful.

While celebrities can provide extraordinary collective benefits to a cause, they are also in a position to reap greater benefits than the average political activist. The social esteem or honor paid out to a celebrity will be greater because he will be perceived to be risking a greater loss than an ordinary person. Goode (1978) suggests the rule that "the greater the potential loss . . . and the more successful the exploit, the greater the honor" (344). For this reason, he explains, a member of the upper class who risks his life for the benefit of the group will be more highly praised and rewarded than a member of the lower class who acts in the same way: a person's social status is a measure of his worth and therefore of the risk he takes when he places his life on the line to aid others.

It follows that a person's prestige within the community also rises with the perception that he is subject to greater danger than the average individual. This corollary sometimes encourages perverse behavior in the heat of collective action. Following the Montgomery boycott, for example, a number of black leaders were the targets of bombings. Because these attacks were commonly assumed to reflect one's stature and importance within the black community, it became a mark of distinction to be bombed, as well as a source of envy:

> Some resented the fact that Abernathy's prestige rose dramatically because he was the only leader bombed both at church and at home. Graetz's stature grew because on the most recent night of terror his home had been the target of two bombs, one of which did not go off. . . . When the rumor mill passed the word that one of the Graetz bombs had been meant for a methodist preacher within the MIA, that preacher actually became consumed with regret that he had not been bombed—to the point that he later had a mental breakdown. Rev. Uriah J. Fields, the "traitor" of the previous summer, was temporarily restored to leadership because the church he had regained, Bell Street Baptist, suffered the most destruction on the night of the bombs. (Branch 1988, 200)

Ironically, public figures involved in collective action probably benefit unduly from the misapplication of Goode's rule. As I suggested, a celebrity's renown can protect him from personal harm and actually make it less costly for him to participate. For instance, while campaigning with SNCC in Mississippi, the comedian Dick Gregory became a hero among activists and local black residents because of the audacious way he stood up to white policemen: "I'd have a guy tell me, say 'Here come that nigger.' I'd say, 'Your momma's a nigger'" (Raines 1977, 292). Despite his habit of posturing and taunting the police, the high-profile Gregory survived untouched. In retrospect, he marveled: "I never went to jail in Mississippi. That's unreal. . . . They have arrested everybody but me. They arrested three or four hundred people. I have *never, ever* been arrested in Mississippi" (ibid.).

Asked why he was so fortunate, the comedian speculated that it was because of his fearless attitude but then conceded part of the reason may have been that "I always had federal agents around me, and I was still Dick Gregory, and they'd have to be careful about what they were gonna do" (ibid.).

The public figure therefore benefits twice from his notoriety. He pays a lower price for his participation in the cause compared to the typical activist, and yet he gains more prominence and social esteem for his efforts. Nonetheless, the comparative advantage enjoyed by the public figure also works to the benefit of the collectivity, which uses his name and contribution as an advertisement for the cause.

Political Entrepreneurs

The rationality or irrationality of leaders of causes is open to debate. Political entrepreneurs are conventionally described as people who will pay the costs of soliciting and coordinating contributions in exchange for individual benefits such as power, prestige, or a share of the profits derived from collective action (Hampton 1987, 256). One might get the impression from this that any number of individuals can step into the breach if the cost-benefit calculus is favorable. In practice, however, there are likely to be only a few members of a community who have the credentials and social standing necessary for effective and successful leadership. Consequently there may be substantial community pressure on such individuals to lend their prestige and the leadership skills associated with their current roles to the new political enterprise, especially if it is perceived that collective action is impossible without the active involvement of these pivotal individuals. Such pressures will likely lower the rate at which these individuals can discount the future repercussions of their actions (cf. Frohlich, Oppenheimer, and Young 1971).

In this fashion, community leaders occupying nonpolitical positions may be drafted into the political arena because of the unique resources they possess. The combination of entrepreneurial opportunity and conformity to social pressure therefore helps explain why the leaders of public-spirited collective action tend to be community leaders with considerable resources already at their disposal. Existing leaders command respect, manpower, and monitoring capabilities which increase their chances of favorably (i.e., profitably) resolving coordination problems. At the same time, these capabilities carry responsibilities and obligations which the community may demand that the leaders fulfill as a price for its allegiance to them.

This is consistent with the argument I made earlier (in chapter 3) that reputational concerns will often motivate people to follow a consistent line of action. People regarded as leaders in one context, such as ministers, schoolteachers, and prominent business men and women, will hurt their status and credibility if they do not uphold their reputations in other situations which call for them to marshal their resources. For this reason, black ministers felt obliged to take a central role in community boycotts and other political campaigns or else they would be diminished in the eyes of their congregations.

Leadership therefore extends beyond the purview of a particular position; rather it is a capacity that is often transferable from one realm to another. In their effort to recruit high school students into the Birmingham campaign, James Bevel and Diane Nash started by targeting the campus leaders—in this case, the basketball stars at the school, who readily agreed to assume leadership roles in this phase of the movement (Branch 1988, 752). Undoubtedly these athletes, like the ministers, realized that the burden rested on them to use their resources in the interests of the movement, since they were among the small number of focal individuals who had the potential to coordinate a collective venture.

In connection with reputational concerns, I also discussed earlier how unselfish commitments can originate from commitments that were originally undertaken for narrowly rational reasons. Altruistic concerns and sympathy therefore can be a natural product of long-term cooperative relations with others. In the course of these social exchanges, we develop not only mutual obligations but mutual trust and affection as well. The combination of altruism and "strong" moral commitment—according to which people do what is right because it is right and not because it will serve their self-interest ("weak" morality)—can account for the unconditionally cooperative behavior that is demonstrated by the organizers of collective action.[7]

It is my impression, however, that efforts to reduce the behavior of leaders to selfish motives are typically unsatisfactory. Religious belief propelled many devoted civil rights activists and in the darkest moments of the movement may have provided the essential motivation. For example, King acknowledged in a sermon that he was frightened to death in the early stages of the Montgomery boycott. But "'on a sleepless morning in January, 1956, rationality left me. . . . Almost out of nowhere I heard a voice that morning saying to me, 'Preach the gospel, stand up for truth, stand up for righteousness.' Since that morning I can stand up without fear'" (Garrow 1986, 89). Indeed, E. D. Nixon was chagrined to find too little faith among the Montgomery leaders. In the midst of the boycott, some ministers retreated from their commitment to participate in a mass meeting after learning that press photographers would be present. Nixon tore into them:

> Somebody in this thing has got to get faith. I am just ashamed of
> you. You said that God has called you to lead the people and now
> you are afraid and gone to pieces because the man tells you that the
> newspaper men will be here and your pictures might come out in
> the newspaper. Somebody has got to get hurt in this thing and if

---

7. Altruistic and moral behavior, of course, need not go hand in hand. I can do something for another because I get pleasure from the other person's pleasure (altruism); but I am not necessarily motivated by moral concerns, which are impersonal in nature (Elster 1985, 148). Similarly, my moral behavior toward another may not involve any desire to increase his welfare. Sen's distinction between "sympathy" toward others and abstract "commitment" to a moral ideal is instructive here. Both pertain to behavior that is other-regarding; but whereas sympathy is egoistic (I am pleased by another's increase in fortune), commitment entails a personal sacrifice. To illustrate: two boys have two apples between them, a small apple and a large one. The first allows the second to choose the apple he wants, whereupon the second immediately takes the larger apple. Seeing this, the first boy cries out indignantly over the unfairness of the outcome, prompting the second boy to ask the first how he would have chosen. The first boy declares adamantly that he would have taken the smaller apple of course. "Well then," the second boy responds smugly, "you got the one you wanted all along." Obviously the first boy was acting out of commitment rather than sympathy (Sen 1977, 95).

In the context of public-spirited collective action, however, moral and altruistic motivations—commitment versus sympathy—will often be difficult to partition. Most civil rights activists were driven by both moral ideals and principles and sympathetic concerns for the welfare of blacks.

you preachers are not the leaders, then we have to pray that God
will send us some more leaders. (Garrow 1986, 23)

Nevertheless, many people, like Assistant Attorney General Roger
Wilkins, speculated that Martin Luther King, Jr., was just another
publicity seeker who would turn on and off with the microphones and
television cameras. But in Wilkins's case, this idea was completely dispelled when he saw King spend hours of his time speaking to ghetto
children in Chicago—"holding a seminar in nonviolence"—during the
time when King and his family were living in slum neighborhoods to
study and publicize the dilapidated condition of housing for impoverished blacks in the city. As Wilkins observed, in awe: "Here is this Nobel
Prize laureate, sitting on the floor, having a dialogue with semi-articulate
gang kids. . . . For hours this went on; and there were no photographers
there, no newspaper men. There was no glory in it. . . . He was a great
man, a great man" (Matusow, 1984, 204).

It was clearly difficult for King to quell accusations of status seeking. Charges of selfishness trail even the most idealistic political activists. As King friend and associate Stanley Levinson shrewdly observed
in an unpublished letter to *Time* magazine: "Ironically, there are those
who have argued that Dr. King is so extraordinarily self-sacrificing that
he must be seeking martyrdom, while now a new voice charges that he
avoids sacrifice [upon being released from jail in Albany]. He is indeed
damned if he does and damned if he does not" (Branch 1988, 558).

One could similarly entertain the notion that the four students
from North Carolina Agricultural and Technical State University who
initiated the sit-in movement in 1960 in Greensboro were driven by
instrumental concerns. Prior to their bold act, none of the four was
prominent on the A and T campus; none played on a sports team or
was a member of a fraternity. But after they had taken their courageous
stand at Woolworth's, they became celebrities. "It was everyone on
campus speaking to them, people in lunch lines giving up their places
to them. It was every fraternity on campus issuing bids, and news-
papermen asking for stories and interviews" (Wolff 1970, 95). "Across
the nation they became known as the Four Freshmen, and the honors
began to come in. For them that spring was a time for classes to be
forgotten, ROTC drills missed, a time to bask in the glory of something
they still weren't sure of. In the campus newspaper, an English profes-
sor . . . wrote a poem for the demonstrators" (ibid., 103).

Yet only a hardened cynic would suggest that the four young men
traded the prospects of fame against the costs of participation in their

decision to protest Woolworth's policy. Although undoubtedly aware they were taking a dramatic and newsworthy stance, they could not have foreseen the outpouring of support they received, or that their actions would spark hundreds of sympathetic sit-ins throughout the country. I suspect that while they may have had vague dreams of making history, of "making a difference" in their lifetimes, and of receiving the plaudits that accompany such accomplishments, their main purpose was simply to protest an immoral and irrational policy in their community. Such an interpretation is consistent with their backgrounds. Although unexceptional for the most part, they had been exposed to idealistic values more than the average youth during their formative years. Their parents supported and participated actively in the civil rights cause; their high school teachers taught them to value their civil rights and made them aware of the rights they were being denied.

Almost forgotten in this whole episode is the man who was pivotal in implanting the idea of protest in the minds of one of the four young activists. Robert Johns, a white man in his forties, was a clothier whose business was located at the edge of the black section of Greensboro. Active in the local chapter of the NAACP, he was well-known, and in many white quarters widely disliked, for his liberal views on racial issues.

What is interesting about Johns for our purposes is the peculiar life he led before he assumed the role of provocateur in Greensboro. Ever since he was a youngster, Johns had been a media hound. For a number of years, Johns's claim to fame was his ability to sneak into major sporting events and be photographed alongside the star attractions. Gate crashing championship boxing matches seemed to be his forte. In the confusion at the end of a fight, Johns would rush into the ring and embrace the victor, raise his arm, or simply crowd in alongside him. Johns usually succeeded in being photographed together with the champion by the press, and these pictures would be published in the days and weeks ahead.

From all appearances, then, Robert Johns was a maverick, as well as a publicity hound who moved from one venture to another seeking attention. Reportedly he believed that he deserved more credit than he received for his role in the movement. "He sees all the publicity and honors many of the civil rights leaders are getting, and he feels that some of this should be coming to him" (Wolff 1970, 184). Nonetheless, a purely instrumental explanation of Johns's actions seems to fall short, as it did in the case of the four A and T students. Johns certainly relished publicity, but he was also a man who had become well integrated within the black community; he had their respect and friendship and their trust that he could be depended upon in a pinch. Joseph McNeil relied on Johns to coordinate the sit-in because, he explained, "In my heart I felt this guy was not going to leave me to the vultures" (Chafe 1980, 82).

This affinity between Johns and the black community appears to have instilled in him an enduring sympathy for the problems experienced by blacks. Without this sympathy it is unlikely that Johns would have endured the harassment and intimidation he received from the white community for contesting segregation practices in Greensboro. A telling indication of Johns's sincerity occurred when he agreed to assist the A and T students upon their request on condition that his involvement would remain secret. Therefore given what turned out to be his greatest opportunity to achieve a measure of lasting fame, Johns chose to remain anonymous.

One problem with being too closely wedded to rational choice explanations of social behavior is that we risk foreclosing by our assumptions the possibility of alternative explanations that do not rest on the egoistic motivations of the actor. If the mental set is sufficiently ingrained, even the most seemingly other-regarding and selfless behavior can be reduced—by the ingenious rational choice theorist—to narrow economic calculations. Alternatively, we may simply accept that people do take the welfare of others into consideration and that there are instances of truly altruistic and moral behavior that do not spring from selfishness. "Altruism, trust and solidarity," Elster (1979) contends, "are genuine phenomena that cannot be dissolved into ultra-subtle forms of self-interest. This argument . . . points to the need for a broad notion of rationality. *Economic man* may be defined through continuous preferences and narrow self-interest, but *rational man* may have non-Archimedean preferences and be moved by concern for others" (146).

For our purposes, whether we wish to characterize such moral and altruistic behavior as rational or not is less important than the observation that such actions are likely to be rare. According to R. M. Kanter, few people are able to feel an identity between their personal goals and the goals of the group. It is the uncommon individual who is so committed that "what he wants to do (through internal feelings) is the same as what he has to do (according to external demands)," so that "he gives to the group what he needs to nourish his own sense of self" (Zurcher and Snow 1981, 459).

Reporters covering the recent democracy movement in China, for example, observed that there was a shortage of "assertive leaders who dare to command the ranks. The newly formed student organizations still have no presidents, only committees that are so large that they are ungainly, and many of the most talented students are afraid to take an official position in an organization that is branded illegal" (Kristof 1989, 7). Potential leaders were deterred by the prospect of imprisonment or a dreary job assignment in a distant outpost. The government still controlled the careers of college students and could punish activists when they graduated. Because of these concerns, younger (first- and second-year) college students tended to be at the forefront of demonstrations—apparently because the shadow of the future was not quite as oppressive to them as it was to those nearer to graduation. A third-year student explained: "Those who walk in the front row of the demonstration and get caught are not the most important leaders. They are young people in their first or second year. They are 17 or 18. For them, it's not so bad. But those in their third or fourth year are more careful" (ibid.).

The availability of people who have extremely low or *no* thresholds to participation may be pivotal in determining the success or failure of the movement. Kantians, or "unconditional cooperators," are special in that they cannot be suckered by other players, since they value cooperation irrespective of the actions of the other parties. Conversely, conditional cooperators also want to participate, but only under the condition that other people join in the enterprise with them. In my discussion of political activism, this additional proviso may be enough to sink efforts to produce a public good, since every potential collaborator may rest on his heels until he thinks that the venture has shown sufficient promise for him to lend his assistance. Conditional cooperators do not wish to free ride, but they are nonetheless wary of being played for suckers. In their concern to protect themselves, they may allow the opportunity to organize mutually profitable collective action to fall by the wayside—unless there are enough unconditional cooperators to take up the slack and start the process in motion.

Altruists can therefore provide the impetus behind the movement and pave the way for conditional cooperators. They may tip the recruitment process into motion so that people with increasingly high thresholds are drawn steadily into the movement. Moreover, in conventional entrepreneurial terms, altruists can assist the movement by providing selective incentives, monitoring individuals, and casting shame on those who shirk their responsibility (Taylor 1987, 110).

The idea that people have varying thresholds marked by different levels of commitment helps to account for the way that political activism typically unfolds. We do not find instances of collective action emerging with full force as we might anticipate if people felt unconditionally obligated to contribute to a group objective because of their personal ties. People who saw that it was in their long-run interest to participate would presumably decide at the same time to do their part in the social movement. In other words, people would join the campaign en masse.

Instead what we tend to observe is a gradual accretion in membership or participation in a cause. Publicity about the initial engagements of the early participants or encouraging results obtained by them gives the movement a shot in the arm and attracts new recruits, and subsequent developments determine the future course of collective action. As the status of the movement changes, some people develop an interest in participation that they did not have formerly. If people decide at different points when it is worth their while to contribute, the order of participation in collective action will be staggered rather than simultaneous. For example, during SNCC's campaign in Mississippi to persuade local blacks to register to vote, individuals who chose not to register because they feared retaliation nonetheless pointed out those in their midst who had the fortitude to resist the pressure and come forward. In this way, SNCC activists discovered who had the lowest thresholds to participation and therefore the greatest propensity to join the campaign in its earliest stages (Raines 1977, 247). In Cleveland, Mississippi, Bob Moses realized that SNCC workers would have to establish the critical mass themselves, because "the adults here will back the young folks but will never initiate a program strong enough to do what needs to be done" (Branch 1988, 330–31).

The concept of thresholds also helps us to account for the difficulty of resurrecting large-scale collective action after it has collapsed. If people have different thresholds, it is necessary that collective action be built up in stages, with those having the lowest thresholds playing the role of initiators (cf. Marwell, Oliver, and Prahl 1988). Therefore when collective action comes unglued, it cannot be reconstituted wholesale. The foundation for collective action has to be laid down again in order to attract those latecomers to the movement with the highest thresholds. Civil rights leaders in Louisville learned this lesson the hard way in the midst of a campaign to desegregate public accommodations, after they had agreed to halt demonstrations as a goodwill gesture:

It was extremely difficult to resume marching and picketing on a large scale. The large marches and the publicity received from the mass arrests had drawn new groups, such as white professionals and other blacks, to the downtown struggle and had the students—the backbone of the marches—more involved than ever, only to see all of their energies halted on May 6. Discontinuing the demonstrations in early May sapped the momentum that had been built up since February. Demonstrations started again in midsummer, but for the remainder of 1961 only a handful of people participated. (Wright 1982, 205)

GREENSBORO

The dynamics of the 1960 Greensboro sit-in campaign epitomize how an assurance game is successfully played. The original four participants wanted desperately to go through with their plans; nevertheless, they were nervous about how people would respond to their actions. They also harbored some lingering fears that not everyone would show up, but their close friendship allayed most of these concerns. It was after all their friendship that in the first instance provided them with the security and confidence to devise their bold scheme. "I think the thing," recalled Franklin McCain, one of the students, "that precipitated the sit-in, the idea of the sit-in, more than anything else, was that little bit of incentive and that little bit of courage that each of us instilled within each other" (Raines 1977, 75).

Although the Greensboro students sought to pressure Woolworth's to change its policy of refusing lunch counter service to blacks, they also wanted simply to register their disapproval of the policy. Therefore successful coordination by the four in defiance of the lunch counter prohibition amounted to a major victory for them irrespective of the subsequent repercussions of their actions. McCain describes how he felt when he refused to leave the lunch counter when asked to do so by the store waitress:

> If it's possible to know what it means to have your soul cleansed—I felt pretty clean at that time. I probably felt better on that day than I've ever felt in my life. Seems like a lot of feelings of guilt or what-have-you suddenly left, and I felt as though I had gained my manhood, so to speak, and not only gained it, but developed quite a lot of respect for it. Not Franklin McCain only as an individual, but I felt as though the manhood of a number of other black persons had

been restored and had got some respect from just that one day.
(ibid.)

As we would predict in a situation requiring mutual assurance, after
McCain and his collaborators set the example at the Greensboro Woolworth's lunch counter, others sympathetic with the action came to the
store to lend their support. Twenty of their schoolmates joined the sit-
in at Woolworth's when it resumed the following day; then white students from the area became involved. Soon people were pouring in
from universities throughout the area to protest Jim Crow service
wherever it was practiced in downtown Greensboro. Support by students in the area was virtually unanimous. "'Everyone wanted to go.
We were so happy'" (Carson 1981, 12). From there, sit-ins spread rapidly through dozens of cities in the South. "It was," Sitkoff observes,
"as if an entire generation was ready to act, waiting for a catalyst.
Greensboro provided the spark, but young blacks through the South
provided the tinder for the response that followed" (Sitkoff 1981, 95).

As Sitkoff suggests, many of the young men and women who
joined the sit-in protests in the South had *wanted to participate* in the
civil rights movement for quite some time. Nevertheless, it took the
Greensboro sit-in to create the opportunity and provide the example
and impetus for these people to finally get involved. As one young
black student explained, "all rejoiced [over the Greensboro sit-in], and
we all felt the opportunity was here; and the fact that college students
were doing it is one of the powerful reasons for participating ourselves
. . . but more than anything . . . we all realized we had been *wanting
to do something* and now was the time" (Fishman and Solomon 1968,
365–66). Likewise, a student participant likened the movement to
"waiting for a bus. . . . You know where you're going all the time,
but you can't get there 'til the right vehicle comes along" (Carson
1981, 16).

Many of these youngsters explained that they had harbored a
strong desire to assert their opposition to segregation ever since learning of the *Brown* decision a number of years earlier. Participation in nonviolent protest gave these people a dignified, legitimate manner in
which to express their anger and discontent, personal efficacy, and in-
dependence of mind and action.

Preexisting organizations and social networks were crucial in coordinating the response of the students. Morris's (1981) research on
the origins of black student sit-ins in the late 1950s revealed that "most
of the organizers of the early sit-ins knew each other and were well

aware of each other's strategies of confrontation" (750). Not only were the participants in a particular local sit-in well acquainted with each other, but the leaders of roughly concurrent sit-ins conducted across various locales tended to be friends who had coordinated their tactics. Churches, civil rights organizations, and student groups connected the participants in the sit-ins. These groups were already well schooled in confrontational methods; "little time was lost on debates as to whether sit-ins should be adopted" (ibid., 765). The existence of wide-ranging social and communications networks ensured that the sit-in tactic would diffuse rapidly. Strong community ties eased coordination problems and sustained the protests, despite concerted efforts by local authorities to derail the movement by using repression, mass jailings, and news blackouts.

One chronicler of the Greensboro sit-in suggests that the black population was so primed for political action that it made little difference who took the initiative in challenging the practice of segregation, just as long as there was someone or some people who had the courage and boldness to start the ball rolling (Wolff 1970, 101). It was significant, however, that the four A and T students were able to hold their ground long enough to attract attention to their actions and draw supporters to their cause from the surrounding college community. Fortunately for the protesters, "repression tended to occur in the later phases of diffusion in the deep South, at a time when the sit-in tactic had widely diffused and a broad social movement was already taking shape" (Oberschall 1989, 48). This suggests that the bandwagon probably would have been stopped in its tracks had the authorities aggressively removed the original participants and the first few waves of reinforcements. One student participant from neighboring Raleigh noted that it was about "a week or more before most of us realized that the persistence of the Greensboro students was sparking the nucleus of a gigantic movement with mass appeal" (Wolff 1970, 102).[8]

8. A parallel can be drawn to the hunger strikers who barricaded themselves in Tiananmen Square during the democracy movement in China. Although Beijing residents had earlier tolerated the student protests and been mildly critical of the inconvenience they were causing in the city, they became increasingly supportive as the students persevered: "The city's citizens, from the young entrepreneurs in business suits to the old ladies sitting in front of their homes, compete in praising the students" (WuDunn 1989, 6). As the momentum of the movement shifted in favor of the students, people who were normally reluctant to take part in the protests sought to become involved. "Sensing that this is a historic time that they want to play a part in, many workers have come to help. Often that means buying food and drink for students, even if they don't ask for it" (ibid.).

DATA ON THE STUDENT SIT-IN PARTICIPANTS

Data collected by Matthews and Prothro (1966) comparing student participants and nonparticipants in the southern sit-in movement substantiate many of the expectations we have regarding the dynamics of the assurance game. Some preliminary observations first: an overwhelming majority of black students (85 percent) approved of the sit-in movement, while the proportion disapproving was minuscule (5 percent). More remarkably, almost one-quarter of all black students participated at some time during the first year of the sit-in movement. Many of the participants reported receiving some sort of punishment for their political activity—either formal sanctions such as being arrested and jailed, or informal deterrents such as being taunted, threatened, or beaten. Plainly students were presented with enough negative inducements to make them want to keep their distance from the movement (ibid., 413–15).

Variations in the degree of threat facing students did affect who participated and who abstained. Two factors correlating with the rate of student participation were the size of the community in which the student was raised and the proportion of it that was black. Participants were more likely to come from large cities in which the black population constituted a significant but not terribly threatening (to whites) percentage of the whole. "They tended to come from areas with enough Negroes to create a genuine 'Negro problem' but not so many as to result in extreme repression by whites; they tended to come from cities where race relations were, relatively speaking, more benign than in the countryside" (ibid., 418–19). Therefore students who had grown up under less fearsome circumstances were less deterred from participating in collective action.

Another significant characteristic of the participants is that they were much more likely than nonparticipants to believe that white southerners were able as well as willing to change their ways. Participants were not as inclined to agree that all white people were prejudiced against blacks, to believe that blacks were denied due process in the South, or to believe that the attitudes of white people in the South would never be changed. Even more revealing is that the participation rate was much higher among students who believed that less than half of white southerners favored strict segregation than among those who believed that all or most white southerners favored it (ibid., 421–22). Thus being Pollyannaish (and incorrect) about white dispositions and unduly sanguine about the prospects of reforming southern society were helpful in encouraging black students to assume the risk of political participation. Students without such optimism and hopefulness were far less inclined to make an investment in collective action.

If nonactivists encountered more repression than activists, and saw less reason and purpose in collective action, they also had fewer opportunities to participate—if we are to take them at their word. Roughly a quarter of the nonparticipants were unable to articulate a particular reason for their inactivity, but of those who could, about half cited a lack of opportunity or, what amounts to the same thing, excessive distance from the protest sites. Another 6 percent indicated that they either had not been asked to participate or did not know how to get involved. The remainder cited various costs of participation, including possibly being fired, being expelled from school, being rejected by parents or teachers, or running into white opposition (ibid., 416).

REFUSING TO LEAVE WELL ENOUGH ALONE

If the leaders of collective action have trouble initiating or resuscitating a campaign, the opposition forces may do so inadvertently through their overzealous behavior. Time and again throughout history, we witness instances of unraveling and dying campaigns being revived by the ill-advised roughhouse tactics of the opposition. Commonsensically we attribute the second wind of the activists to their moral outrage over the callous and inhumane actions of their opponents. A good indignation, Emerson noted, brings out all of one's power. Personal pride and ego also come into play as the activists see their courage being severely tested. In chapter 3 I showed how the importance of saving face can motivate participation even when most people would rather abstain from the action. The private preferences of the activists are submerged beneath their publicly stated wishes to retaliate. Doubts about the wisdom of such action are kept to oneself, thus allowing a form of groupthink to take over (Janis 1972).

Repression can also reinvigorate activists by redefining the elements of the game they are playing. When activists are severely rebuffed in their attempt to stage a demonstration, organize a rally, engage in a peaceful protest march, or participate in some other legitimate or morally justified form of political participation, what takes on immediate and utmost importance for them is to be able to show their opponents that they cannot be repelled in this manner. Therefore the activists usually vow to resume the campaign (e.g., in the case of a terminated march) at the precise point where it was so brutally suppressed, or to disregard a ban on some form of proscribed activity.

In this fashion, for example, the South inadvertently fueled the abolition movement when its politicians tried to stem the flow of antislavery petitions to Congress as part of a comprehensive campaign to silence the slavery debate. The ensuing debate in Congress on the question eventually led to passage of the infamous "gag rule," which did not ban antislavery petitions but nevertheless allowed them to be tabled upon receipt. To evince their disdain of the gag rule, abolitionist leaders launched a campaign to inundate Congress with a flood of new petitions. The successful campaign not only registered the abolitionists' disapproval of the congressional action but also initiated countless petition signers to the abolitionist cause. "The mere act of signing one's name to an antislavery petition meant personal commitment and identification with the movement. Thus the petition campaign created a network of loyal workers who had actually taken part in the movement against slavery" (Dillon 1974, 102).

In such cases the objective of collective action shifts from the long-term goal of bringing about the desired social change to the short-term goal of defying the authorities. Success is no longer defined by the concrete achievements of the campaign but by whether or not the activists can sustain their protests in the face of severe opposition. In other words, successful coordination per se becomes the aim of the campaign and not the means to the end.

The consequences of such a restructured assurance game can be easily discerned. Because defiance is now the aim of the game, each player prefers to be an activist rather than a spectator so long as there are enough other people to constitute a defiant front. But since defiance is an end in itself in this restructured game, there will no longer be a tendency as before for individual members to bail out when it appears that the opposition is not willing to make concessions. Instead, coordination in this instance constitutes its own reward, so that no participant has an incentive to break the collective pact once it has been successfully formed.

To give a second illustration of this process: in 1934, in the midst of the NAACP's campaign for a federal antilynching law, U.S. Attorney General Homer Cummings organized a national conference on crime to be held in Washington but neglected to include the problem of lynchings in the South on the conference's agenda. When Roy Wilkins suggested to Walter White that the NAACP picket the conference,

White floated the idea as a trial balloon to his associates in Washington, who in turn communicated back that such a protest would scarcely get noticed.

Wilkins disagreed and decided to mount a picket with but *three* sympathetic friends. Together the four traveled to the hall where the conference was convened and brandished crude and awkward sandwich-board signs protesting the absence of a federal antilynching law. Within minutes they were arrested for violating the municipal sign law. As Wilkins (1982) recounts, it was the best thing that could have happened:

> Word of our arrest spread quickly through the NAACP Washington
> branch. The timidity that had dogged the demonstration vanished
> in a rush of indignation. Not only was the Justice Department going
> to wink at Judge Lynch, it seemed, it was also going to violate the
> spirit, if not the letter, of the First Amendment, arresting four men
> who had the temerity to challenge its crime conference. In short or-
> der, the branch resolved to set up the protest. (135)

With great vigor and determination, and armed with a well-thought-out legal strategy, the new troops took to the streets, traveling to the conference hall in separate cars and via different routes to circumvent parade laws. When threatened with arrest, they challenged the police's interpretation of the laws and threatened them with lawsuits on grounds of false arrest. This time the police conceded and left the picketers to their business.

Brimming with satisfaction, one of the original four protesters, George Murphy, a journalist, reflected on his experience: "My going to jail for protesting against lynching in this country was a cost, though small, of which I shall always be proud" (Wilkins 1982, 136).

I should add that thinking of such instances of collective action in terms of the prisoner's dilemma leads to a very different prediction about the effect of repression. Increasing the cost of participation would deter political action and make free riding even more attractive. In other words, where the PD model pertains, repression should always dampen political activism. Instead, repression often invigorates a movement by giving the activists a more immediate purpose to rally around. Even extreme repression, such as that which took place in Selma, may stimulate a movement by placing the reputations of the activists on the line, thereby giving them no choice but to stand up for their rights.

SUMMARY

To summarize, I have presented an alternative way to think about the collective action problem—one that explicitly incorporates the social and participatory benefits that result from political activism. These social and participatory benefits, I claimed, do not solve the collective action problem but rather alter it from a prisoner's dilemma game to an assurance game. The reason we still have a collective action problem, I argued, is that these benefits are contingent upon the successfulness of collective action. This is true whether people participate for instrumental or noninstrumental reasons. Consequently a potential activist will assess the prospects of collective action and decide to join only when he feels that enough others will participate to make it viable. The problem is that every potential activist may be thinking along these lines, so that everyone stands around waiting for others to build up collective action to the point where he is willing to contribute.

What is needed under the circumstances are some highly dedicated, morally committed activists who will contribute to collective action when few others are willing to do so. These might be the people Hirschman referred to—who equate the costs of participation with its benefits. They provide the leadership in the movement and constitute its critical mass. However, such self-starters—gamblers, really—who are willing to support collective action in its earliest, least promising stages are relatively rare, I suspect. And, I would argue, it is because they are a rare breed that public-spirited collective action is uncommon.

Thinking about collective action in terms of an assurance game therefore reveals why collective action is difficult to initiate and at the same time explains why individuals spurn free rides and relish or savor political participation when the right opportunity arises.

7 | A Formal Model of Collective Action

There's no better way to make men part of a movement than to have them give something to it.

John Steinbeck, *In Dubious Battle*

In the preceding chapters I argued that public-spirited collective action resembles an assurance game in which potential activists will participate if they can be confident that enough other activists will also participate to make the campaign worthwhile. Since spontaneous mass coordination does not occur, someone or rather some group of leaders and dedicated activists has to get the ball rolling by taking the initiative and setting an example for others to follow. Furthermore, the masses of potential activists have to be organized and marshaled for protest, which requires the development and mobilization of organizations, associations, and other social groups. Lastly it is necessary that the nascent movement be reinforced by both symbolic and tangible successes so that veteran activists will stay the course and new ones join the cause.

The game-theoretic analysis set up the problem facing supporters of a cause. It structured the choices facing each individual and made the outcomes of those choices contingent upon the decisions of other similarly minded individuals. By stripping down the elements of the movement to a simple game, we were able to infer how such factors as organization, leadership, government responsiveness, repression, violence, sympathy, morality, and obligation were likely to affect the probability that the movement would succeed or fail.

In this chapter I will explicitly incorporate into a simple dynamic model those elements that determine how a social movement unfolds or changes over time. This model builds on the individual level assumptions developed in the preceding chapters about the factors that motivate political participation. The purpose of the model therefore will be to show how the individual decisions to join or quit a movement translate into collective outcomes.

The model represents the underlying dynamics of a movement as a process of supply and demand. In order for the proponents of change to achieve their goals, they have to build and sustain a popular movement that, through a combination of disruption, pressure, and moral persuasion, will motivate or force local authorities and the federal government to accede to its demands. The model will be used to spell out and verify (within the logic of its assumptions) a number of points discussed earlier: the importance of leadership, organization, incremental success, government responsiveness, steadfastness in the face of setbacks, and resistance to intimidation and harassment from opponents. Exactly how these factors interact over time to determine the path of a social movement is specified by the model. After deducing a number of general results from the model, I will show, in this chapter and the next, how it applies to various campaigns that took place over the course of the civil rights movement.

An advantage of this type of model is that it allows us to trace the separate and combined effects of a number of key factors or parameters on the development of a social movement. By making different assumptions about the relative values of the parameters—i.e., by varying theoretically the rate of government responsiveness, the strength of social networks and organizations, and other factors—we can offer numerous deductions about how these changes will affect the course of the movement over time. Another strength of dynamic models is that the mathematical theory underlying them allows us to specify precisely the equilibrium and stability conditions of the system under consideration. Given any set of assumptions about the parameters of the model, we can establish the equilibrium of the dynamic system as well as whether the equilibrium will be realized. Perhaps the major benefit of the supply-and-demand model in particular is that it is able to explain a large variety of seemingly unrelated observations about collective action and social movements, although it is based on a relatively simple and parsimonious set of assumptions. While many of these observations have been made elsewhere in different contexts, they have not heretofore been incorporated within a single model.

The model presented here was inspired by an elegant analysis of consumerism by William McPhee (1966) in the mid-1960s. McPhee wanted to know what accounted for the fate of consumer products in our societies. Some products gain a foothold in the society while others are wiped off the market just as soon as they appear. Periodically a new product will be introduced that captures the imagination of the buying public and starts a fad or fashion. For McPhee, the fate of consumer products follows two simple rules of supply and demand: (1) people get what they want, and (2) people want what they get. Therefore depending on the responsiveness of the producers to demand and the reciprocal stimulation of demand created by supply, the levels of supply and demand will follow one of several paths over time: supply and demand will flatten out and reach an equilibrium or steady state; supply and demand will be overresponsive to each other and spiral upward out of control; supply and demand will be aborted; or supply and demand will oscillate.

The same set of scenarios can be said to constitute the possible outcomes of political demand through collective action. Depending on the results it achieves, collective action can sputter and disband, stabilize at a particular size, escalate and grow into a mass movement, or ebb and flow episodically.

Nevertheless there are important differences between the dynamics of commercial and political demand. In the McPhee model, supply and demand refer straightforwardly to the number of units of a particular commercial product, such as record albums or hula hoops, that are desired and produced. Demand comprises two components: a certain amount of basic demand, which is constant across time periods, and an additional amount of demand that is stimulated by the level of supply in the current time period. Supply in turn is a function of a basic constant level of supply plus some additional amount of supply that is prompted by the level of demand in the immediately preceding time period. Supply and demand therefore fuel each other within a single dynamic system.

In the model of political supply and demand proposed here, I assume that demands are registered through political mobilization. In other words, the more people want, the more they have to mobilize in order to get it. And the more they mobilize, the more they want. People therefore mobilize in order to express their demands in the political marketplace and whether these demands are fulfilled or not depends upon the extensiveness of political mobilization. As in McPhee's model, supply and demand enjoy a reciprocal relationship. Popular demand is answered with government policies, which in turn affect the level of subsequent demand.[1]

The dynamics of the Montgomery bus boycott, for instance, illustrate how the demands of protesters escalate as a movement gathers

---

1. In chapter 9, demand and the level of mobilization are treated separately, although the level of mobilization is still driven by the number of outstanding demands.

momentum and strength. In the beginning, boycott leaders requested only a few relatively minor changes in the practices of the bus company. They wanted black drivers to operate the buses serving black neighborhoods, better treatment of black customers on the buses, and a more "reasonable" application of the color line on the bus that would allow blacks already seated in the rear of a filled bus to retain their seats even as additional white passengers boarded. When the Montgomery leadership balked at making even these modest reforms, the protesters intensified their efforts and adjusted their demands correspondingly. For their all-out campaign, which required extraordinary devotion, sacrifice, and coordination, the boycott leaders and their followers upped the ante from their initial token demands to a call for complete racial integration of the buses (Chafe 1982).

The notions that political mobilization induces supply—that there is, in effect, power in numbers—and that supply encourages mobilization form the central premises of the model. A complication, however, is that supply and demand are not homogeneous, since there are many kinds of political demand as well as various types of policies that can be supplied by the government. In the simplest of cases, there is political mobilization in favor of change and reform as well as countermobilization to maintain the status quo. Likewise, supply can refer either to policies and concessions that are agreeable to those who advocate change or to measures that are favorable to those who oppose change.

Given these two forms of demand, I assume that the amount supplied in any time period depends on government initiatives that either promote or inhibit reform—which by definition are independent of popular demand—and on government responsiveness to the proponents and opponents of social change:

$$S(t) = i + r_1 M(t - 1) - r_2 O(t - 1), \qquad (7.1)$$

where:

$S(t)$ is the level of supply in period t;

$M(t - 1)$ is the level of mobilization in favor of change in period $t - 1$;

$O(t - 1)$ is the level of opposition to change in period $t - 1$;

i is the amount of government initiative in each period;

r_1 is the rate of government responsiveness to proponents of change; and

r_2 is the rate of government responsiveness to opponents of change.

"Supply" is intended to be an extremely abstract concept. It refers to any output produced by the target of collective action that can be construed as a concession to activists on either side of the conflict. The target of collective action is usually the government, whether at the local or national level, but it can also be private corporations, businesses, universities, or other key institutions in society. Therefore in different contexts, "supply" can refer to the concessions made by a business to alter its practices, a court decision, an executive order, a decision to form a commission to study the problem at hand, an agreement to enter negotiations, or passage of a new law. Supply that runs against the interests of the protesters takes on a negative value of $S(t)$. All of these forms of supply are admittedly difficult to quantify in terms of amounts, and I make no attempt to resolve the measurement problem beyond suggesting that the various concessions or outputs are in principle reducible to a common underlying scale.

What causes fluctuations in demand? Of the two types of demand, opposition to change plays a secondary role in the model insofar as such opposition is assumed to be entirely reactive to efforts to promote social reform. In other words, I assume that opponents of social change mobilize only in response to the mobilization of those who wish to alter the status quo:

$$O(t) = pM(t), \tag{7.2}$$

where:

$O(t)$ is the level of opposition to change in period t;

$M(t)$ is the level of mobilization in favor of change in period t;
and

p is the opposition's rate of countermobilization.

This does not rule out the possibility that such opposition will have an important effect on the fate of the reform movement. As indicated in equation (7.1), opposition forces can limit the concessions made to the reformers through effective political pressure on the government and other agents of supply; in addition, through harassment, violence, and other forms of intimidation, opponents of change can directly deter individual participation in such movements (this possibility is incorporated in equation (7.3)).

It may have been, for instance, the *failure* of the prolife movement to react to abortion rights activists that eased the way for the Supreme Court's 1973 *Roe* v. *Wade* decision. The prolife faction, according to Luker (1984), was caught completely off guard by the success of prochoice activists. Prolife proponents made the inaccurate assumption that people with prochoice views constituted a small minority of the population. They took it for granted that there was a consensus among

Americans that the embryo was a person. Abortion laws and practices were consequently liberalized before prolife advocates could register significant organized opposition.

The heart of the model deals with how advocates of reform initiate and sustain collective action. This process is represented by an equation that relates the level of mobilization in any period to such factors as the number of leaders in the movement, the past successfulness of collective action, the strength of social networks connecting activists, the contagion of the movement, and so forth. This equation specifies how those factors which affect the likelihood that someone will participate in collective action combine to produce the aggregate level of mobilization in any given period.

I assume first that there are two types of activists in the movement—"leaders" and "followers"—who are marked by significantly different degrees of attachment to political protest. Leaders may be professional activists who maintain organizational or institutional positions that overlap with, or are closely related to, their activities as instigators of mass collective action. However, even when activism is not an extension of the professional roles of leaders, it is for many at least an avocation. Large blocks of leisure time are devoted to gathering information about current affairs, organizing and attending meetings with other activists, propagating new ideas to the public, and protesting government policies.

Followers are latecomers to collective action and are a more amorphous group than leaders. They possess far less intensity about political issues, are less ideological, radical, and single-minded, even while being sympathetic to the general goals of the cause. As a larger, more anonymous collectivity, the followers enjoy much less interaction among themselves than is the case among the leaders. For the typical follower, the immediate issue or cause is the magnet drawing him to make a contribution.

Leaders, by contrast, have more programmatic concerns and regard each conflict as an integral part of a broader, long-range plan. In essence, hard-core political activists identify with ideological goals that encompass a variety of social changes, and consequently their activism is sustained, whereas followers exhibit a more tenuous and transitory identification with activist causes. Because leaders are also more likely to have central roles in their communities, they have their reputations to protect. They are subject to closer scrutiny and cannot easily discount the future consequences of their present choices and actions.

For these reasons, leaders and followers are treated separately in the model of supply and demand. The number of leaders plus the number of followers equals $M(t)$, the total number of people who have been mobilized in period t. The size of the leadership is represented by a constant term, a, that is independent of both the level of mobilization and the level of supply. This means that leaders are persistent across time periods and remain in the movement even though it has neither attracted followers nor reaped benefits. In contrast, followers are fickle; their representation in the movement is a function of the levels of mobilization and supply. This is based on the assumption that people will join a campaign for two reasons: (1) because it has already proven successful and therefore shown prospective activists that it is a worthwhile investment; and (2) because, successful or not, a sufficiently large number of other activists have already committed themselves to the campaign.

I will call the first effect, in which people join a movement when the going is good, i.e., when it has achieved a modicum of success, a "bandwagon" effect; and I will label the second effect, in which activists rush to join a movement because other activists have already enlisted, a "contagion" effect. The size of the bandwagon effect in any given period is equal to the product of the bandwagon rate, b, and the level of supply in that period, $S(t)$. Similarly, the size of the contagion effect in any given period is equal to the product of the contagion rate, c, and the level of mobilization in the preceding period, $M(t - 1)$.[2]

These are two types of effect that we expect to occur in assurance games. The assurance problem resides in the doubts that people have about the chances of collective action. Doubts over what is required for successful collective action—which hinder coordination—will be alleviated by either of two developments. First, as the number of activists increases, so will assessments of the power of collective action. In particular, the greater the number of "other" activists who have decided to add their efforts to the cause, the more likely an individual on the sidelines will choose to become an active participant. Individual activists, for reasons given earlier, base their decision to participate or abstain on the perceived viability of collective action, which is directly related to the size of the movement.

Similarly, if the nascent campaign manages to extract concessions from the opposition, this will immediately demonstrate its viability

---

2. This does not rule out the possibility—indeed likelihood—of mixed motives. Someone might join partly because the movement has proved successful and partly because others are already participating. Consequently this person contributes (in appropriate proportions) to both the bandwagon and contagion processes.

and in so going attract new recruits. A history of success is the best way political activists can demonstrate to potential activists that collective action is efficacious and a worthwhile investment. To quote sociologist Neil Smelser (1962), "limited successes of a movement, especially unanticipated successes, often 'prove' the efficacy of a given method of agitation and stimulate more agitation of this type" (295).

Both successful achievement of goals and successful mobilization make collective action more attractive to prospective participants by offering more in the way of participatory benefits and by placing greater moral and social pressure on them to conform and do their part in the interest of the group.

Oberschall (1980) has offered a similar specification of the factors underlying participation in mass collective action. In his model, there is a small group of individuals who value the collective good more and derive more psychological satisfaction from pursuing the collective good than do others. These hard-core activists initiate collective action even though the costs of doing so are highest in the beginning and the marginal change in the probability of success attributable to any individual's efforts is insignificant.

Less dedicated activists join subsequently for two reasons. (1) As the number of participants increases, the marginal change in the probability of success increases, while the cost of participation decreases. Oberschall postulates an S-shaped relationship between the probability of success and the number of activists; up to a certain point, the marginal effectiveness of participation increases with the number of participants before decreasing beyond that point. Therefore the production or transformation function relating contributions to the likelihood of producing the collective good accelerates at low levels of cooperation and decelerates subsequently. An individual may discover that it is worthwhile to participate in collective action after others have cleared the way, even though it was unprofitable to do so before (cf. Oliver, Marwell, and Teixeira 1985). (2) Likewise, if the first wave of activists enjoys some early successes, then estimates of the probability of success for a given number of participants will be systematically upgraded. Past success at obtaining the collective good therefore has an effect on the dynamics of mobilization similar to that of successful political mobilization: both increase the prospect that future collective action will be fruitful.[3]

3. I would disagree with Oberschall, however, that a person participates when his chance of making a difference increases sufficiently; rather, it is the prospect of collec-

Finally, in the mobilization equation we have to take into consideration how the opposition to the movement deters participation. The price of participation may include not only time, effort, and money but also retaliation from those who oppose the cause. Opponents can threaten activists with economic sanctions (loss of jobs and financial credit), harassment, verbal threats, beatings, and other forms of violence. As stipulated in equation (7.2), the strength of this opposition is assumed to be proportional to the level of mobilization. In turn, the ability of the opposition to deter participation in collective action is equal to the product of its strength and a coefficient d. Therefore as the opposition grows, it becomes more risky for individuals to become involved.

One additional complication is that the authorities themselves often attempt to put down demonstrations and protests. An official crackdown on the protesters might be accomplished by passing measures designed to thwart collective action or by implementing a policy of mass arrests and imprisonment. Strictly speaking, such measures should not be entered into equation (7.1), because they are not "supplies" to the activists but instead are direct deterrents to participation in collective action.[4] One way to incorporate the weight of these official deterrents would be to introduce a second coefficient d_2 that was also a function of the level of mobilization; however, to keep matters simple, I will assume that the magnitude of the d coefficient takes into account the strength of the official opposition to the movement as well as the impact of popular opposition.[5]

By implication, the alleviation of repressive conditions may open the door to protest. As Peter Eisinger (1973) notes, "Official tolerance, signified by the unwillingness or even inability to suppress protest by force, may serve as the functional equivalent of license to protest. Such license represents an opportunity in the whole structure of opportuni-

---

tive success, i.e., the possibility of making a difference collectively, that creates obligations and incentives for an individual to contribute.

4. Sometimes, on the other hand, such crackdowns should be regarded as policies that widen the gulf between what the protesters are demanding and what the authorities are supplying. Wholesale repression, for example, does not merely punish active protesters but reduces the quality of life for all members of the group seeking reform. In this sense, mobilization has inspired a "negative" amount of supply.

5. For example, the deterrence posed by official sanctions might be equal to $-d_2M(t-1)$, while the effect of popular opposition equals $-d_1O(t-1)$. Therefore the combined impact of these two sources of opposition equals $-(d_1p + d_2)M(t-1)$. As long as $p \neq 0$, we can always find some value of d such that $dp = (d_1p + d_2)$.

ties: protest offers a chance to gain a hearing in public councils. The openness of the system, in other words, is conducive to protest" (27).

When all of these factors are combined, the level of mobilization in any period t equals:

$$M(t) = a + bS(t) + cM(t - 1) - dO(t - 1), \qquad (7.3)$$

where:

$M(t)$ and $M(t - 1)$ are the levels of mobilization in favor of change in periods t and $t - 1$, respectively;

$S(t)$ is the level of supply in period t;

$O(t - 1)$ is the level of opposition to change in period $t - 1$;

a is the size of the autonomous leadership;

b is the bandwagon rate due to successful collective action— "success" being defined by the level of supply $S(t)$; therefore $bS(t)$ is the number of additional people who become active as a result of this success;

c is the contagion rate due to successful mobilization in period $t - 1$; therefore $cM(t - 1)$ is the number of people who are active in period t because other people are active in period $t - 1$; and

d is the deterrent effect of the opposition.

SOME PROPERTIES OF THE SUPPLY-AND-DEMAND MODEL

The coefficients in the supply-and-demand model are treated as constants. Although this is unrealistic, because the various propensities in the model—to join, to oppose, to respond to collective action, etc.— are likely to evolve with the changing circumstances and stages of the conflict, it is nonetheless often safe to assume that the coefficients will be more or less constant within different stages of the social movement; therefore instead of making the model more complicated by introducing variable coefficients, we can carry out a separate analysis of each phase of the movement and make appropriate adjustments of the coefficients where this is necessary.

We should note, however, some of the ways that the coefficients are likely to vary in relation to other factors in the model. Keep in mind that these assumptions are only rules of thumb and need not hold up in every instance. Indeed, I will argue later that a group typically will have to conspire to break some of the rules in order to have any chance at initiating collective action.

Among the more important assumptions about how the coefficients will fluctuate are the following:

First, we should expect that the bandwagon rate will vary with the level of supply: when few or no concessions are made to the movement, the rate of jumping on the bandwagon is low; but when the level of supply increases, so does the bandwagon rate. This simply assumes that people will not be enticed by the success of the movement until that success is noteworthy. While small successes remove some of the uncertainty associated with the prospects of collective action, important victories provide assurance that political activism will pay dividends.

Second, the contagion rate is likely to be related to the level of mobilization: people will join at a faster rate when more people are already in the movement. This reflects the higher cost of joining the movement in its early stages when there is neither safety in numbers nor attractive prospects for success. When this assumption holds, it makes starting the movement all the harder, because although the potential for collective action exists—in the sense that there are many people willing to participate at some point in the future—there may not be enough early starters available to activate this potential.

Third, because the contagion rate is based at least in part on prospective calculations of the probability of success, contagion will also tend to depend on the eventual ability of the movement to wrest concessions from the government. A friendly government gives hope and encouragement to the activists by opening the door to reform. It may also stimulate expansion of a social movement by clamping down on reactionary groups which deter those who are supportive of the cause from active participation (Jenkins 1983, 548). On the other hand, if the targets of political pressure—whether businesses, local governments, or the federal government—are unsympathetic and unresponsive to the protests and demands of the aggrieved group, then members of this group will be less motivated to participate in collective action or, given involvement, less eager to persevere. In the absence of periodic reinforcement, participants increasingly will come to believe that their efforts are wasted and as a result will choose to minimize their expenditures (of time, energy, and money) on the campaign. Similarly, those who are participating out of an obligation to their friends are more likely to be relieved of that obligation if it becomes apparent that collective action is ineffectual. Even those participants who are involved for the sheer fun of it will find their interest waning in the long run and their energy and curiosity shifting to more novel, alternative forms of recreational activity.

And fourth, we should expect that the rate of responsiveness will in many cases be low or negligible when the level of mobilization is low and will increase only when the movement is able to apply sustained pressure. Slight pressure, in other words, tends to be discounted; only when the movement is too big to be ignored does it finally win concessions. One implication of this is that the movement usually gets very little boost from the government in its early stages; rather, it has to rely on its own resources if it wishes to survive.[6]

In addition to these variations, the absolute levels of the bandwagon and contagion rates will depend on the degree to which those seeking change are motivated by effective leaders and connected by organizations, associations, and other social networks. As I explained in chapter 3, regular social exchange is conducive to the development of mutual obligations, trust, commitment, and sympathy. Individuals who belong to a close-knit community are better able to coordinate their preferences and choices and to take advantage of opportunities to supply themselves with public goods.

Therefore we should expect that as the degree of organization in a group increases, so will the bandwagon and contagion effects in response to successful collective action and successful political mobilization. The organizers of collective action will be able to work through these established social groups in recruiting activists to the cause. Current participants in the movement will have ties to those who have yet to join and will be able to persuade or pressure them to cooperate. The strength of commitments in close-knit communities is such that individuals will participate earlier than they would in circumstances where such trust, solidarity, and obligation are absent.

Social organization is also conducive to increasing the determination and resilience of activists. People who know each other and who have a history of successful collaboration are less likely to become frustrated at the earliest sign of failure. Camaraderie and friendship will shore up the spirits of individual participants and increase their durability in a cause, even when that cause may appear out of reach.

All of the variables and parameters in the model are admittedly difficult to operationalize beyond specifying the components that might enter into measuring them. Questions of precise measurement will be

6. McNall (1988) is only one of many students of social movements who has made this observation: "For a group to achieve power or success, large numbers of people must be mobilized over extended periods of time. Success is seldom instantaneous, which means that some group of people, usually a bureaucratic staff, must act in the collective's name during setbacks or lulls in the drive for power. It must find ways to cut through the diversity of interests represented by the membership to find programs and ideas around which the group can rally. It is normally the leadership which develops new strategy and methods of creative escalation, for there must be a sense of going forward" (229).

set aside here, since my primary intent is to use the model to provide an abstract representation of the dynamics of collective action.

ANALYSIS OF THE SUPPLY-AND-DEMAND MODEL

The outcome of efforts to organize collective action will depend on the parameters of the system and on the initial level of mobilization. In principle, there will be some level of mobilization, M^*, which if attained will leave the system in a steady state. That is, if the system reaches M^*, the level of mobilization will remain constant in all subsequent time periods barring future changes to the parameters of the system.

To determine the equilibrium point, we substitute equations (7.1) and (7.2) into equation (7.3) and after separating the constant terms from the coefficients of the equation, set both $M(t)$ and $M(t - 1)$ to some constant value M^*:

$$\begin{aligned}
M(t) &= a + b[i + r_1 M(t - 1) - r_2 p M(t - 1)] \\
&\quad + cM(t - 1) - dpM(t - 1) \\
&= (a + bi) + (br_1 - br_2 p + c - dp)M(t - 1). \\
M^* &= (a + bi) + [b(r_1 - r_2 p) + c - dp]M^*.
\end{aligned}$$

Therefore M^* equals:

$$\frac{a + bi}{1 - (bR + c - dp)}, \tag{7.4}$$

where

$$R = (r_1 - r_2 p).$$

First examine the numerator of the equilibrium. The a term represents the constant level of mobilization independent of supply (i.e., the number of die-hard activists), while bi is the product of the bandwagon rate and the independent or constant level of supply.

The two components of the numerator therefore underscore our assumption about the critical role that leadership plays in the initiation of collective action. If the agents of both supply and demand are entirely responsive or reactive (a and $i = 0$), there will be no energizing force to start the system in motion. The system will remain in equilibrium at a zero level of mobilization.

Note as well that the initial push can originate from either the demand or the supply side of the system, or both sources may contribute jointly. An activist administration can in effect create demand by focusing the nation's attention on various social problems in the course of trying to ameliorate them. The election of Kennedy, for instance, created a spirit of hope and optimism among liberal forces in the country. Kennedy, in turn, focused national attention on the need for public virtue in domestic affairs when his administration launched a government attack on such domestic concerns as poverty, crime, urban blight, education, and other socioeconomic problems (Charles R. Morris 1984). The women's movement, for example, was given a boost when Kennedy established the President's Commission on the Status of Women in 1961. The resulting 1963 report detailed how women did not enjoy the same rights and opportunities as men. As a consequence of this report, analogous state commissions were formed to focus on the problem. These commissions brought politically active women together, drew attention to the concerns and demands of women, and created expectations that appropriate government action would be taken in response (Freeman 1975, 52).

On the other hand, a hostile regime can depress collective action by taking initiatives opposed to the interests of the protesters, or by expeditiously removing or eliminating the leaders of the movement. In South Africa, for example, black opposition to the government has been contained because new leaders of potential movements "get cut down so fast. A student leader lasts for three to six months. The police are on them very fast. They go to jail, or they go to exile" (Lelyveld 1985, 186). Either way, organized protest is dealt a severe blow.

While either the salutary or detrimental effect of government initiative is manifest in the bi term in the numerator, the contribution of "responsiveness" is traced through the R term in the denominator. The R coefficient equals net government responsiveness to both proponents and opponents of change. The value of R can be positive, negative, or 0 depending on whether the government favors the activists, their opponents, or neither. Assume for the moment that the denominator has a positive value (i.e., $1 + dp > bR + c$). The more responsive the government becomes to the proponents of change, the smaller the divisor will be in the expression for M^*, and hence the larger M^* will be. Conversely, increased responsiveness to the opposition dampens political mobilization. Overall, therefore, the model suggests correctly that the most fertile periods of liberal activism will coincide with liberal administrations which both initiate and respond favorably to demands for social change. By so doing, liberal administrations supply social reforms that fuel political activism that in turn stimulates further supply.

Examination of the denominator also shows, as we might expect, that bandwagon and contagion effects increase the magnitude of collective action and are directly related to the equilibrium value, while the rate of countermobilization and the capacity of the opposition to deter participation reduce M^*. This merely underscores the tug-of-war between advocates of change and their detractors that is represented by the model. Both sides marshal their forces in an effort to gain the attention and favor of the authorities. The opposition, however, also tries to directly deter political activism by employing threats, intimidation, and other means to raise the cost of participation.

What of the cases where $(1 + dp) \leq (bR + c)$? When $(1 + dp) = (bR + c)$, the denominator of $M^* = 0$; consequently, the equilibrium point is undefined. When $(1 + dp) < (bR + c)$, the equilibrium is negative (assuming $a + bi$ is positive). For reasons that I will explain in greater detail below, in neither case will the level of mobilization settle down to an equilibrium point; in both cases $M(t)$ in the long run will skyrocket without bound.

By examining the equilibrium, we quickly see why collective action is so difficult to sustain in the absence of periodic successes. In the model, success propels the movement at the same time that it retards the onset of frustration among the activists. When the activists fail to extract concessions from the government or the groups they are pressuring, the only factors preventing the campaign from collapsing ($M \leq 0$) are the commitment and tenacity of the hard-core activists, a, and the contagion, c, of the collective action itself, since M^* equals:

$$\frac{a}{(1 + dp + br_2p) - c}$$

when i and r_1 are negligible. A further problem is that the contagion of the movement is also likely to weaken unless contributors are rewarded with at least periodic successes. As we shall see later (in chapter 8), during the major Albany and Birmingham campaigns of the civil rights movement, the intransigence of the local community leaders devastated the former campaign and seriously threatened the viability of the latter.

THE TIME PATH OF THE SYSTEM

The actual time path of the system (whether the level of mobilization oscillates, increases monotonically to equilibrium, dampens down, etc.) depends on the relative values of the various coefficients in the model. After the supply equation is substituted into the demand equation, the system is reduced to a standard first-order difference equation of the form:

$$M(t + 1) = AM(t) + B, \tag{7.5}$$

$$\text{where } A = (bR + c - dp), \tag{7.6}$$

$$\text{and } B = (a + bi). \tag{7.7}$$

We can develop some appreciation of the dynamics of the model by playing out the first few values of $M(t)$ for $t = 0, 1, 2$.
At $t = 0$:

$$M(1) = AM(0) + B.$$

At $t = 1$:

$$M(2) = A(AM(0) + B) + B = A^2 M(0) + AB + B$$
$$= A^2 M(0) + B(1 + A).$$

At $t = 2$:

$$M(3) = A(A^2 M(0) + AB + B) + B$$
$$= A^3 M(0) + A^2 B + AB + B$$
$$= A^3 M(0) + B(1 + A + A^2).$$

In general, for any t:

$$M(t) = A^t M(0) + B(1 + A + A^2 + \ldots + A^{t-1}). \tag{7.8}$$

The expression in the parentheses is a geometric series that in the limit, as $t \to \infty$, converges to

$$\frac{1 - A^t}{1 - A} = \frac{1}{1 - A}$$

when $|A| < 1$. When $A = 1$, however, the series reduces to $tA = t$, which does not converge in the limit. Likewise, if $|A| > 1$ or if $A = -1$, the series again diverges as t increases. (For a proof of this result, see Thomas and Finney 1979, 754–55.)

The long-term behavior of $M(t)$ clearly depends on the A term in the solution. If $A = 1$, $M(t) = M(0) + Bt$ will diverge monotonically either to positive infinity (when $B > 0$) or to negative infinity (when $B < 0$), or remain constant at $M(0)$ (when $B = 0$).

If $0 < A < 1$, A^t will converge to zero and

$$M(t) = A^t M(0) + B \frac{(1 - A^t)}{1 - A}$$

will converge along a monotonic path from $M(0)$ to

$$\frac{B}{1 - A}.$$

Therefore if $M(0)$ is greater than M^*, the time path of $M(t)$ will decline; while if $M(0)$ is less than M^*, the time path will rise. (Of course if $M(0)$ already equals M^*, the level of mobilization will stay the same.)

If $A > 1$, A^t will increase monotonically without bound as will the solution sequence $M(t)$.

If A is negative, A^t oscillates between negative and positive values depending on whether t is odd or even. When $0 > A > -1$, this oscillation will dampen down to zero in the limit and, as a result, $M(t)$ will again settle into the equilibrium value $B/(1 - A)$.

However, if $A = -1$, A^t will oscillate between -1 (when t is odd) and $+1$ (when t is even), and $M(t)$ will oscillate evenly, or "within bounds," about the equilibrium value without ever reaching it. When $A < -1$, A^t and by implication $M(t)$ will oscillate along a divergent path. (A summary of the determinants of each path is provided in Goldberg 1958, 84–85.)

The path of $M(t)$ therefore will be determined by the sequence A^t and $M(0)$, the initial level of mobilization. First consider the elements of the A term in our model, regrouped into three components for easier interpretation:

$$A = bR + c - dp,$$

or

bandwagon rate $+$ contagion rate $-$ deterrent effect of opposition $\times$ government respon- siveness $\times$ rate of counter- mobilization.

The first component bR reflects the relationship between the government's responsiveness to demand and the activists' responsiveness to supply. Assume for the moment that the contagion rate, c, and the combined forces dampening political mobilization, dp, equal zero, so that $M(t) = bRM(t - 1) + (a + bi)$. To appreciate what separates a stable from an unstable system, consider how the system behaves when bR equals 1. If bR equals 1 and if there is no independent demand or supply (both a and i equal 0), the level of mobilization inspired by supply will remain constant across time periods: $M(t)$ for all t will equal $M(0)$. But if either a or i is not zero, then the level of mobilization in any period *t* will equal the level of mobilization in the preceding period *plus* some additional amount (*a* + *bi*). As figure 7.1 illustrates, barring the intervention of mitigating forces, this is an extremely volatile system. Once an initial demand is made, or a policy is enacted, the forces of supply and demand feed off each other in an insatiable parasitic fashion: the more that is supplied, the more that is demanded, and the more that is then supplied, and so forth until supply and demand spiral to impossible heights. Only a model, but not a real political system, can accommodate such escalation.

Clearly anytime *bR* gets as large as unity, the level of mobilization will be unstable insofar as it will never reach equilibrium unless it begins at equilibrium. On the other hand, consider how the level of mobilization fluctuates when the relationship between the bandwagon effect and responsiveness is slightly less than perfect (*bR* approaches 1). In this circumstance, depicted in figure 7.2, the system does possess an equilibrium:

$$\frac{a + bi}{(1 - bR)}.$$

Since *A* is now a positive fraction, (0 < *bR* < 1), the level of mobilization will rise monotonically (as long as (*a* + *bi*) > 0) but gradually dampen down to the equilibrium point as *t* increases.

Even though collective action levels off, this can still be a happy state of affairs for the activists if most of their demands are being satisfied (i.e., if responsiveness is high). When that is the case, the concessions forced by collective action stimulate continued moderate re-

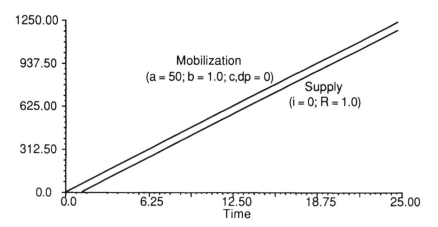

FIGURE 7.1. Mobilization and Supply Move in Harmony But Without Limit

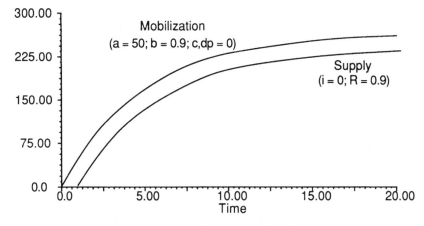

FIGURE 7.2. Mobilization and Supply Fuel Each Other But Approach Equilibria

cruitment to the movement; although the campaign does not take off, it turns out that large-scale mass mobilization is not crucial for the attainment of the greater portion of the activists' goals because of the responsiveness of the government.

On the other hand, consider the situation in which the government shows no initiative in addressing the activists' concerns and is very unresponsive (i and R close to zero), so that significant concessions are granted only if the activists successfully mount a large and sustained campaign. More realistically, assume that i equals zero and that R varies according to the extensiveness of collective action, so that it is zero when there is inchoate public activism and much larger when public pressure becomes overwhelming.

Here the activists face some problems. When $R = 0$, then $bR = 0$; assuming that the initial level of mobilization equals a (the number of leaders), and still assuming that the contagion rate and the factors that deter mobilization are negligible, then:

$$
\begin{aligned}
M(1) &= a + b[i + RM(0)] \\
&= a + bi + bRa \\
&= a + 0 + 0 \\
&= a.
\end{aligned}
$$

Therefore when both i and R equal 0, there will be no expansion of collective action beyond the initial core of activists. This is obviously a catch-22: people refrain from joining in the protests until they can see some tangible success, but any chance of success is ruled out unless people initially enlist in the campaign. This fits Aldon Morris's (1984,

282–83) argument that in the early stages of a social movement, the activists are largely left to their own devices, and they will sink or swim depending on the strength of their indigenous organizational and financial resources. Outside assistance from sympathetic and supportive third parties tends to be conditional upon the ability of the movement to launch and sustain itself. The movement is therefore caught in a bind, since it has to prove its mettle before it can attract external aid, but remains ineffective until more powerful outside interests contribute their resources. Therefore a weakly organized movement will probably cave in quickly if it meets any resistance from the opposition.

Obviously, to escape this self-defeating trap, there will have to be some people who are willing to participate irrespective of the past success of collective action. Simply stated, the only way that the level of mobilization can increase without the benefit of periodic concessions is if there is an element of recruitment that is independent of this factor. The link between the rates of success and recruitment has to be broken.

Return now to the complete model, in which c and dp do not equal 0, and consider the second major component of the A coefficient. The coefficient c represents the effect of the current level of mobilization on the level of mobilization in the subsequent time period, or the "self-stimulating," contagious aspect of collective action. As I mentioned earlier, this new mobilization can be as success-oriented as the mobilization that is a direct function of past achievements. This may be true even among those who enlist because they cannot withstand the social pressure exerted by those who are committed to the cause, or because they want to conform to what others are doing. The main difference may be that the new mobilization is based not on a *retrospective* recognition of past success but rather on a *prospective* analysis of the likelihood of future success; each individual decides to join when he calculates that the prospects are satisfactory given the existing level of participation. Ignorance may be of some assistance. Former civil rights activist Mary King (1987), for example, recalls that her naïveté was conducive to participation. Had she known about the slim prospects of the movement, she may have quit much earlier; instead by "not comprehending the obstacles from within or without," she remained "undaunted" (26).

Therefore even if the government is unresponsive, new recruitment that feeds on itself rather than on the success of the movement can make collective action possible. Not, however, if the deterrents exceed the stimulants to collective action (i.e., $dp > bR + c$). If this holds, the level of mobilization will oscillate over time. If $dp - (bR +$

c) is greater than 1 (making $A < -1$), $M(t)$ will oscillate along a divergent path: collective action will be initiated but will then be swiftly quashed, as illustrated in figure 7.3. If, alternatively, dp exceeds ($bR + c$) by less than 1, (making $-1 < A < 0$), $M(t)$ will oscillate but will dampen down to a low equilibrium level. (See figure 7.4.)

Strong opposition can therefore keep the level of mobilization down, even if the movement is adequately organized. But note that the equilibrium resulting from this balance of forces is likely to be extremely fragile. Only if the authorities maintain repression indefinitely will the movement remain underground. As soon as there is a relaxation of sanctions, there will be a burst of political activism. Therefore opponents of the movement will also have an interest in dismantling the organizational apparatus of the movement (i.e., reducing the values of b and c).

There will also be occasions (discussed in chapters 3 and 6) when attempts to deter political activism will actually have a stimulative effect. In these cases, d assumes a negative value, thereby augmenting the forces that promote participation in the movement. When d reverses sign, the opposition injects new life into a dying movement by attempting to suppress it. For example, if the movement is already unraveling because $0 < dp - (bR + c) < 1$, additional attempts to suppress it instead *reduce* the size of dp and promote higher levels of mobilization.

As long as ($bR + c$) is greater than dp, A will be positive and the level of mobilization will increase over time. This result is obvious: in

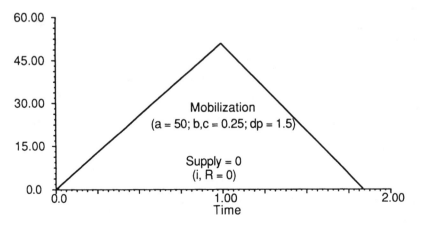

FIGURE 7.3. Mobilization is Quashed by Strong Opposition

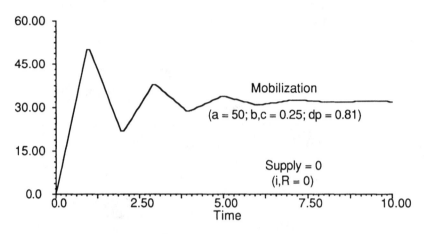

FIGURE 7.4. Mobilization Dampens in the Face of Opposition

order for collective action to expand, people have to be joining at a rate faster than the rate at which they are dropping out. The rate of enlistment will depend on the organizational strength of the movement—as reflected in b and c—and the degree of government responsiveness R to the movement's demands. When $(bR + c)$ exceeds dp by less than 1, $M(t)$ will asymptotically approach equilibrium (as in figure 7.2). If $(bR + c) - dp = 1$, then $A = 1$, and $M(t)$ will diverge upward (as in figure 7.1) as long as $B = (a + bi)$ is positive. If, in the extreme case, $(bR + c) - dp > 1$, then $A > 1$, and A^t will increase exponentially over time. Consequently $M(t)$ will again diverge upward without bound (see figure 7.5).

What is more uncertain are the practical implications of this result. In the game-theoretical analysis of collective action, I noted that people want to share in a winning affair, but that in general they prefer not to see their time, energy, and money squandered and their lives and limbs endangered in a foolhardy venture. The results from the dynamic model show that this demise can be averted if people join for reasons other than the past success of the campaign and, moreover, are sufficiently resolute to delay frustration long enough to turn around its fortunes.

The contagion rate, however, is not independent of the long-term fate of the movement. As I explained earlier, if sustained collective action does not bring dividends, then activists are likely to become frustrated and reluctant to continue; therefore the contagion of the movement will diminish unless participants are periodically reinforced with favorable outcomes. Should the authorities remain obstinate (i.e.,

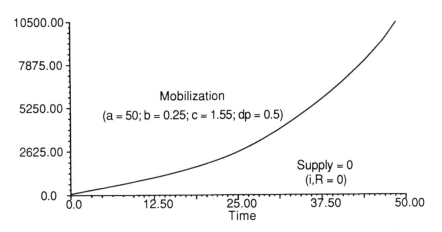

FIGURE 7.5. Mobilization Climbs Without Bound Despite No Supply

if R does not increase significantly), the movement will collapse follow-ing a brief flurry of activity during which hopes are high concerning the possibility of success. For example, the failure of the populist movement in the late nineteenth century has been attributed to the organizational weakness of the Farmer's Alliance. Alliance members believed that their goals could be easily reached through the electoral system. They thought their problems would be solved if they put into office candidates who were responsive to their demands and sympa-thetic to their problems. The Alliance failed, according to McNall (1988), because it did not develop a strong organizational structure and therefore was ill-equipped to endure a long-term struggle. If the move-ment had prevailed as quickly as many of its members anticipated, this weakness would not have materialized. "But it would be the lack of an organizational structure that would prove to be the undoing of the farmers' movement, when the material gains they sought were not immediately forthcoming" (187). The speed with which the farmers' alliances were created, the weak commitments that were required of their members, and the absence of a bonding ideology made it easy for farmers to abandon the movement when other avenues of political par-ticipation seemed more promising.

Another practical matter that may prevent contagion from sustain-ing collective action is that the size of the contagion rate will probably vary with the level of mobilization. Before the contagion effect "kicks in," the number of initial activists may have to exceed a particular threshold. This prerequisite makes the leaders of collective action even more important to the overall outcome of the campaign. If followers are not willing to join until the movement reaches a particular size, but are willing to participate in great numbers once this threshold is attained, then the activation of the contagion effect depends on whether the size of the leadership is large enough to tip this process in motion.

SUMMARY OF DEDUCTIONS FROM THE SUPPLY-AND-DEMAND MODEL

In sum, my analysis of the supply-and-demand model has produced the following deductions:

1. A steadfast leadership is crucial for the initiation of collective action. The importance of a hard core of leaders who are not easily deterred by the tough going at the start of a campaign is magnified even further when the authorities resist change and refuse to be intimidated unless the activists are able to place considerable pressure on them. Leaders in such cases may constitute the critical mass needed to stimulate participation among the rank and file. It follows that opponents of collective action have a strong interest in removing such pivotal individuals from the process.

2. Administrations that are favorable to change and reform can paradoxically foster political protest by drawing attention to social ills and expressing concern for the interests of hitherto neglected groups. Individuals will be more likely to participate in collective action if they are given openings in the political process. Sympathetic administrations therefore have the potential to promote a cycle of protest and reform.

3. A movement will not expand beyond its initial size if the government is unresponsive unless the willingness of activists to join the movement despite its lack of success exceeds the strength of the opposition forces. Stated simply, when collective action can claim few if any victories in its early stages, it will be sustained only if existing participants are willing to persevere while new participants are motivated to join for reasons other than the past successfulness of the cause.

What we have to realize, however, is that in practice both the contagion and bandwagon rates are likely to be correlated with the successfulness of the political campaign. Participation that is motivated by social pressure will slacken if the cause appears to be out of reach, because people will not feel obligated to expend their resources on such an effort; on the other hand, if victory is within grasp and held to be contingent on successful organization, the social pressure on the individual to join will be considerable.

By the same token, if people are conforming because they wish to be part of a memorable event, the successfulness of the campaign will obviously have a bearing on their evaluation of its significance; few people want to invest in a flash-in-the-pan campaign. Thus, because the remedies suggested by the model for effete activism are difficult to manufacture in practice, we should bet against the long-term viability of collective action when it is not punctuated by intermittent accomplishments. Not many will live by Pascal's adage that "It is not necessary to hope in order to undertake. Nor to succeed in order to persevere."

4. Movements succeed by marshaling the community resources of the group as well as enlisting the aid of outside allies. If the harmony between supply and demand bR combined with the contagion rate c exceeds the opposition forces dp, then the level of mobilization will climb monotonically and converge to the equilibrium value if $(bR + c) - dp < 1$, or diverge upward if $(bR + c) - dp \geq 1$. The factors promoting mobilization therefore have to be sufficiently offset by the factors retarding mobilization if the supply and demand system is to enjoy stability.

5. On the other hand, a combination of official repression and effective mass countermobilization can either discourage or completely suppress collective action. If the dampening forces outweigh the stimulating forces in the system, the level of mobilization will oscillate. Whether this oscillation will settle down to an equilibrium again depends on the size of $A = bR + c - dp$. If $A > -1$, the level of mobilization will dampen down to M^*; otherwise $(A \leq -1)$, it will oscillate but diverge within or without bounds. In either case collective action will collapse or diminish following a brief initial surge.

Although repression always works in principle, if the movement is supported by strong organizations and community relationships, repression will have to be maintained or there will be an explosion of political protest. For this reason, opponents of the cause have an interest in preventing the formation of political and social organizations or disrupting those that exist, just as they have an incentive to neutralize the leaders or potential leaders of the movement.[7]

ANALYZING THE ORIGINS OF THE CIVIL RIGHTS MOVEMENT

The supply-and-demand model helps us to understand how the civil rights movement was initiated. When we dissect the origins of the

---

7. Ironically, Israel's attempt to repress the *intifada,* or Palestinian uprising, through mass imprisonment has helped to foster the development of community bonds among political activists. In the course of Israel's occupation of the West Bank and

movement, we discover several important developments that were instrumental in first framing and then resolving the coordination problem that characterizes public-spirited collective action. First, the growth and development of indigenous black institutions and organizations laid the foundation for the movement. Second, the movement was encouraged by small but significant concessions made by the federal government. And third, the cost of political participation in the movement was marginally lowered as opposition to political activism weakened.

Better organization increased the solidarity of blacks and made it easier for them to coordinate their preferences and choices; increased government responsiveness gave blacks hope and optimism that change could be accomplished; and weaker social control gave them the freedom to implement their political strategy. These developments readily translate, in terms of our model, into higher recruitment rates (b and c), greater responsiveness (R) by the authorities to proponents of change, and weaker opposition (dp) to social reform. The combination of these changes was sufficient to stimulate political activism and lay the foundation for the movement that emerged in the 1950s.

CHANGES IN THE STRENGTH OF THE OPPOSITION

Prior to the 1930s, the repression of the southern black population was so severe and all-encompassing that the cost of protest was prohibitive. Because political, economic, and police power was concentrated in their hands, white supremacists possessed a variety of means to ensure that blacks toed the line. Uncooperative blacks could be arbitrarily fired, denied credit, arrested and imprisoned without due process, and beaten and killed by mobs—all with impunity. So long as the strength of the opposition forces exceeded the combined strength of the forces stimulating collective action ($bR + c < dp$), A was negative in this period; consequently attempts to mobilize were either suppressed to an

---

Gaza prior to the *intifada*, about forty thousand went through Israel's security prisons. "Rather than serving as a deterrent and a punitive framework for breaking the PLO's strongest cadres, Israel's prisons were transformed into higher 'academies,' as the inmates called them, for reflection and education, ideological and spiritual rehabilitation, and experiments with new political constructs. In many cases these stints in prison framed the outlook and tempered the character of men who were then earmarked for leadership. . . . In effect, the 40,000 'academy graduates' were a whole new class of Palestinian society. They had shared an indelible experience and were bound to one another by unusually strong ties of trust and friendship—stronger, it turned out, than the loyalties among members of any political faction" (Ya'ari 1989, 26–27).

insignificant level ($-1 < A < 0$) or deterred completely ($A \leq -1$), as illustrated in figures 7.3 and 7.4.

The seeds of the civil rights movement were sown in the depression and New Deal years of the thirties. As blacks moved out of the rural South and into the cities in pursuit of industrial employment, their numbers became geographically concentrated and they began to acquire the financial resources needed to develop and nurture the indigenous institutions and organizations that were essential to the movement. The segregation of blacks in the cities also reduced their susceptibility to racial violence and oppression and allowed them breathing room to prepare a challenge to the social order (McAdam 1982, 94–98). As blacks grew in political strength, repression was alleviated. McAdam found that the number of blacks lynched in the South declined as black political fortunes rose between 1930 and 1955. "The suggestion is that the growing political power of blacks nationally increased the South's fear of federal intervention and thus restrained the use of extreme control measures. In turn, this restraint created a more favorable context in which blacks could mobilize" (1988, 701).

It was in this earlier generation that the forerunners of the modern movement organized the network of civil rights activists, benefactors, and supporters who would spearhead the drive for social change in the 1950s. The issue of racial equality was elevated to the national agenda during this period, and public opinion began to turn slowly against the racism that infected the nation's minds and institutions.

The scientific and intellectual communities also greatly abetted the cause of racial equality in the 1930s by discrediting prevailing ideas about the inferiority of blacks. Many scientists felt impelled to denounce racial theories at this time because of the parallels between these theories and the racial ideas then emanating from Nazi Germany. While numerous leading researchers had for decades combated doctrines that reinforced and legitimated white supremacy, many others within the academy required the gruesome spectacle of Nazism to awaken them to the inconsistency between the ideal of equality and the reality of racial prejudice and intolerance in the United States (Sitkoff 1978, 190–96). Thus, in a classic demonstration of people's need for cognitive consistency, scientists realized that they could not in good conscience attack Nazism while subscribing to racial beliefs that smacked of the same notions of Aryan supremacy.

In this new intellectual climate, social scientists focused instead on the deficiencies in whites that accounted for their racial prejudice; in so doing, they turned the tables on previous investigators who sought evidence for the inferiority of blacks. Studies revealed that prejudiced individuals were more inclined to be insecure, frustrated, poorly educated, of low socioeconomic status, ignorant, and parochial. But in the spirit of the times, which emphasized the primacy of cultural forces on individual development, researchers held that these subjects were nonetheless redeemable through education and increased social interaction with blacks (ibid., 196–97).

COORDINATING PREFERENCES: LEADERSHIP AND ORGANIZATIONS

Organizing, lobbying, and protesting on behalf of civil rights and racial equality gathered momentum in the thirties despite the dampening effects of the depression. "Forsaking accommodation, more blacks than ever before marched, struck, boycotted, lobbied, and rallied against racial discrimination. Established groups adapted, found new allies and sources of support, augmented their rapport with Afro-Americans outside the 'Talented Tenth' and acted and spoke in an increasingly radical manner. New militant organizations prodded those more conservative to greater aggressiveness and amplified the volume and visibility of the whole movement for human rights" (Sitkoff 1978, 244). Protests were mounted in various locations around the country against discrimination in public accommodations, labor unions, and voter registration laws, and against separate schools, segregated school cafeterias and fraternities, separate professional baseball leagues, discriminatory employment practices and salaries, racial stereotyping in Hollywood movies, racial inequality in housing and education, and discrimination in the administration of justice.

A number of groups contributed to the development of racial consciousness, black pride, and political awareness in the black community, the most conspicuous of which was the NAACP. The NAACP applied steady pressure on Congress and the executive to place the race issue on the national agenda; association lawyers plotted out a legal strategy to gradually strike down Jim Crow practices. A major accomplishment of the NAACP was to make racism an issue in American politics. By publicizing discrimination in the work place and in labor unions, lobbying for federal antilynching legislation, and condemning the disenfranchisement of blacks, the NAACP worked on the conscience of the nation and steadily gained support from both blacks and whites in the northern states.

Despite few victories between 1930 and 1950, civil rights activists during this period nevertheless forged a strong and viable coalition of dedicated supporters who would remain persistent advocates of the interests of blacks in the years to come. Consequently the nascent movement was able to grow *despite* its mediocre record of success.[8] The NAACP grew significantly in terms of membership and financial contributions; new civil rights organizations sprouted in northern cities; and the civil rights coalition expanded to include labor groups, professional associations, women's groups, university and school organizations, and large numbers of white clergymen. During this period, the social networks connecting the black community were also greatly fortified. In addition to the multiplication of NAACP chapters, enrollment in black colleges increased sharply, the black churches grew in size and strength, black labor unions were organized, and a black press was developed.

The black church in particular became the hub of the civil rights movement. As blacks migrated to the cities and as the socioeconomic status of the black community increased, the urban churches gradually took on a new character. Congregations became on average better educated, the financial base of the church expanded, and the church multiplied its programs and activities and adopted a more active political stance. The church was an established social institution whose traditions and infrastructure could be adapted for political purposes. It supplied the movement with a respected, articulate, and charismatic corps of clergymen leaders who were relatively independent of the white community. In addition, the church provided a convenient, organized pool of manpower for collective action and a reliable source of financial support for political activity (Aldon Morris 1984, 4).

The church served as a community center and a sanctuary for the local black population, a place where blacks could establish and fortify social ties, express their artistic and musical abilities, engage in song and prayer, and debate the important social and political issues affecting the black community. Moreover, there was a common culture connecting the multitude of churches in the South and the North. "Most of their congregations sang the same songs, were inspired by similar sermons, and recognized the importance of cooperation and of giving financially to their church and other worthy causes" (ibid., 11).

An even more important element of the church network was the linkages among black ministers in different communities. Friendships, professional association meetings, and civic conferences kept ministers in contact with each other and established a line of communication

---

8. However, as I indicate in the following section, government responsiveness to those calling for reform was also beginning to improve at this time.

across all social sectors and walks of life in the black community. This facilitated rapid mobilization of the black masses for political demonstrations and other forms of direct action when the time called for it.

With the formation of the Southern Christian Leadership Conference (SCLC), local community groups throughout the South were connected formally by a national organization. Formerly isolated protest groups were thus united under a single banner; the resulting social and communication networks made it easier to share campaign experiences and information and reassured local activists that they were operating within a larger national movement. Affiliation with SCLC therefore increased the confidence of local units by making them aware that there were similar groups elsewhere engaged in the same struggle as they were (ibid., 95).

Changes in Government Responsiveness

Organizational growth and increased political assertiveness in the black community after 1930 went hand in hand with the friendlier treatment that blacks were accorded by both the executive and judicial branches of government. The courts made concessions in response to black protests (Piven and Cloward 1977, 207). The Supreme Court, in particular, boosted the morale of civil rights activists by providing a number of favorable opinions during this period. The Court not only heard more civil rights cases after 1930 but rendered decisions that were favorable to blacks in a much higher proportion of them. Less than half of the fifty-three decisions handed down between 1876 and 1930 advanced civil rights, while over 90 percent of the seventy-five cases adjudicated between 1930 and 1955 were so decided (McAdam 1982, 84).

Although Roosevelt did not come into office with a reputation for being supportive of racial equality—indeed, for that reason he was spurned by black voters in 1932—it was his administration that responded, however hesitantly, to the plight of black Americans and in so doing played a key role in reinforcing and stimulating the forces of social reform in the depression years. Through government-sponsored conferences and studies, directives, executive orders, and proposed legislation, the administration displayed a willingness to offer the New Deal on equitable terms to both black and white Americans. Such actions signaled a change in the tone of the federal government on the race issue and encouraged supporters of racial equality to press their demands in order to capitalize on the government's newfound responsiveness. As Sitkoff (1978) explains, the New Deal did little to redress the inferior economic and social position of blacks in American society. Nevertheless, the Roosevelt administration effectively disturbed the status quo "by substantively and symbolically assisting blacks to an unprecedented extent, by making explicit as never before the federal government's recognition and responsibility for the plight of Afro-Americans, and by creating a reform atmosphere that made possible a major campaign for civil rights" (59).

Prior to the Roosevelt administration, there was little sympathy at the national political level for the problems of the black community. Blacks accurately perceived the futility of collective action in this period. The improvement in the political climate during the Roosevelt years gave blacks the incentive to articulate their concerns and develop plans to deal with their troubles. "Each concession, however rhetorical, conferred legitimacy on the goals of the struggle and gave reason for hope that the goals could be reached, with the result that protest was stimulated all the more" (Piven and Cloward 1977, 206).

The greater responsiveness of the federal government was in no small part attributable to the power that blacks were gaining at the polls. The black vote in the thirties was viewed increasingly by both parties as being up for grabs. At the same time the number of blacks on the voter rolls was rising sharply because of concerted voter registration drives in both the North and the South. Black leaders and newspapers instructed black voters to forsake their longstanding attachment to the party of Lincoln, which had begun to take their support for granted, and to cast their ballots according to their assessment of the present-day platforms of the two major parties (Sitkoff 1978, 91–94).

By the midterm elections in 1934, Democratic candidates in areas that contained sizable black electorates were making sincere and frequently successful attempts to capture the black vote. By 1936 the president was reaping the rewards of his administration's New Deal programs. He fortified his support in the black community by running an effective campaign in which he showcased blacks in high-level positions, promoted the good works of his tireless wife on civil rights issues, recruited prominent black spokesmen to address black forums on his behalf, and disassociated himself from the racist southern component of his party. In marked contrast to the election results only four years earlier, when over two-thirds of the black vote went to Al Smith, this time around Roosevelt garnered over three-quarters of the black vote. Politicians and pundits hailed the black electorate as a volatile swing vote that potentially constituted the balance of power in American elections. Both major parties devoted greater attention in their campaign strategies to the black electorate—the Democrats in their effort to retain the black vote in their camp, the Republicans in their hope to recapture it to theirs (ibid., 96–97).

As McAdam (1982) puts it, government attentiveness to the problems of blacks in the thirties and forties, albeit carefully circumscribed, "triggered a growing sense of political efficacy among certain segments of the black community. . . . The result, throughout the period, was an accelerating cycle of black action and federal response, with a growing sense of political efficacy an important psychological by-product of the process" (110).

In sum, the government in this period had little inclination to initiate reform, but it was willing to react to outside pressure. Therefore what is significant about this early period in the movement is that civil rights leaders were able to successfully capitalize on the increased responsiveness of the government by mobilizing the rank and file and publicizing their demands. Recruitment into the movement was greatly facilitated by the development and fortification of indigenous black institutions. Because the black community was better organized than it had ever been in the past, it possessed the resources necessary to build and sustain the movement during this period. Although the few substantive gains that were made in this period encouraged further political activity, it was mainly the cohesion, strength, and solidarity of the black community that accounted for its participation and tenacity in the protracted struggle. Consistent with my model, civil rights activists had to mobilize largely in anticipation of concessions from the government rather than in response to them.

8 | *Strategies of Collective Action*

Nothing succeeds as planned.
Joseph Heller, *Good As Gold*

We can draw several corollary inferences from the model of collective action developed in chapter 7.

1. First, we can surmise what strategies will be employed by the activists and the authorities. Since it is easier to mobilize people when they have some hope of achieving their goals, we can expect the leaders of collective action to try to persuade their followers that the demands of the group will not fall on deaf ears. The leaders will emphasize to the rank and file that they will prevail in the conflict if they persevere and work together. An abiding faith among the activists that they will succeed keeps frustration down while increasing the contagiousness of the movement. In the course of the Russian Revolution, for instance, "when the terminal point was distant the revolutionary movement was small; it was a secret society. When the chances of revolution increased—the secret society expanded into a real revolutionary party and mass movement" (Gross 1958, 356).

Participation in the assurance game depends on the belief that the movement has sufficient resources to be able to win concessions from the opposition. Sooner or later, however, collective action will have to produce real dividends, since the activists will not be able to suspend their disappointment indefinitely; without periodic reinforcement, the contagious influence of the movement will decline as each activist perceives a diminution in the benefits of participation.

A sympathetic government or a government that is perceived to be responsive to popular demands will obviously encourage collective action. This relationship is confirmed in Jenkins and Perrow's (1977) research on the farm workers movement in the 1960s, Nelkin and Pollack's (1981) analysis of popular protest in West Germany against nuclear power, Gale's (1986) research on the contemporary environmental movement, and McAdam's (1982) study of the civil rights movement (see McAdam 1988). Similarly, White (1988) notes that, in premodern Japan, protest was believed to enjoy greater prospects of success—and protesters were therefore encouraged—because there existed a "culturally recognized obligation of the government to rule with *jinsei* ('benevolently'). The notion of *jinsei* did not obligate the government to be kind but only to maintain conditions under which the populace could endure, in exchange for which the people were obligated to offer up taxes" (41).

By the same token, if those in power are antagonistic to the movement, we can expect them to try to quash the demonstrations by convincing the activists that they will not capitulate to their demands. To show they mean business, the authorities will step up their arrests of protesters, pass laws that restrict the tactics available to them, and use other maneuvers that increase the cost of political activism.

The confrontation of these strategies will often result in a battle of wills in which each side attempts to outlast the other. Consider, for example, the civil rights demonstrations that took place in the downtown centers of southern cities. Since these protests deterred residents from patronizing local businesses, the longer the protesters could sustain their actions, the more pressure they exerted on store owners to seek a resolution to the conflict in order to prevent further disruptions. Meanwhile, the managers of local businesses knew that they could discourage the protesters by denying them the satisfaction of any concessions, however trivial. Theater managers in Durham, North Carolina, used this strategy to foil a desegregation campaign in 1961. As one participant recalled:

> the movement started a picket line, a boycott, of all the theaters, which were all segregated except for the Negro theaters. . . . The theater picketing continues, then, throughout all of the next school year, a year and a half, and after that . . . it became quite obvious that the theater managers were quite entrenched in it [segregation] and demoralization set into the movement. Since it was composed mostly of youth, of high school kids by and large, it was unrealistic to expect that they would continue to be enthused about this. So this died off. (Blumberg 1968, 478)

Therefore in this case the opposition prevailed because it resisted the pressure long enough for the activists to become discouraged. Keep in mind, however, that even when stonewalling works, and the political activists quit the campaign because they are frustrated by their lack of success, the original grievance that motivated their actions remains. In all probability the same grievance will stimulate renewed protests in the future. "Protests are terminated," Blumberg writes, ". . . either by success or by waning enthusiasm. This latter form of termination, such as was reported with picketing the theaters, is usually temporary and the establishments involved are incorporated among the objects of later major protests" (479). The notion that there is an *accumulation* of demands that must be satisfied before protest is dampened will be explored in greater detail in chapter 9.

2. Since it is crucial to establish the viability of collective action, the leaders of a movement are also likely to provide inflated estimates of the sizes of their organizations and the anticipated or actual attendance at rallies, marches, and demonstrations. Crowd estimates, for example, were inflated by organizers of a 1989 Washington, D.C., rally in support of the right to an abortion. "The United States Park Police estimated that 300,000 people marched from the Washington Monument to the Capitol . . . some organizers contended that the crowd was twice as large" (Toner 1989, 1). Inflated membership and attendance figures serve notice to the authorities that the movement is a potent force which enjoys considerable popular support. Because supply is a function of the level of mobilization, misperception of the size of the movement may prompt greater concessions than would have been provided if the level of support for the movement had been assessed correctly.

According to Luker (1984, 141–44), an important factor behind the 1973 *Roe* v. *Wade* decision was the prochoice movement's ability to mount a much larger campaign in support of *Roe* than the prolife movement mounted in opposition. Amicus briefs in favor of Roe were submitted by a great number of respected groups and organizations. The Court was given the impression that the prochoice movement far outnumbered the prolife constituency, which was thought to be dominated by middle-class male Catholics. "Individual pro-life activists had testified before state legislatures and taken stands in professional meetings, but the pro-life forces had so far been largely unable to present demonstrations of massive support of the kind that characterized the pro-choice movement" (143). The Court, however, did not anticipate that its decision would activate the substantial amount of latent opposition to abortion prevailing in the country.

Oftentimes the press will inadvertently assist a cause by overreporting the number of participants at marches and rallies. Typically, reporters will confuse spectators and even opponents present at these events with the actual protesters. Organizers of civil rights demonstrations capitalized on the reporters' errors by scheduling their rallies at times of the day when it was certain that a larger number of onlookers would be present. For example, there were occasions during the Birmingham protests, according to SCLC leader Wyatt Walker, when "we weren't marching but 12, 14, 16, 18. But the papers were reporting 1,400" (Fairclough 1987, 121).

Exaggerating the size of a movement also encourages participation by those who would contribute to the cause if they did not believe that the inchoate movement was too ineffectual to have an impact on society. The level of mobilization in any period is partly determined by the level of mobilization in the preceding period; therefore inflated estimates of the size of the movement will increase the number of people attracted to the movement in subsequent periods. This is how a widespread expectation that an upcoming rally will attract a large number of supporters can amount to a self-fulfilling prophecy. An individual will attend because he wants to be a part of a memorable and successful historical event; but it is actually his participation and the participation of hundreds or thousands of other like-minded individuals which ensure that the rally is both successful and memorable.

In some instances the most effective organizing strategy is to keep people in the dark about the number of participants. Populist organizers of local farmers' alliances were instructed to encourage people to sign up but to conceal from the group the actual number of people who had already committed themselves. As soon as a few people had signed up, the organizer was supposed to announce to the gathering that there was a sufficient number to form an alliance (McNall 1988, 232). Presumably both concealment of the total number and the pronouncement that an organization was viable were intended to create the impression that more people were enthusiastic about the proposal than may have been the case.

3. In addition to trumpeting the potency of collective action, the leaders of a movement will try to get some concrete victories under their belts as quickly as possible. Doing so establishes a level of proficiency and success that reinforces their followers and makes the movement attractive to others. Concrete successes spur a bandwagon of new participants (since $M(t)$ is partly a function of $S(t)$). In addition, concessions establish the responsiveness of the authorities to political pressure, which tends to sustain the rate of contagion.

Popkin (1979), for example, stresses that peasants could be more effectively organized behind the pursuit of local, small-scale goals that impinged upon their lives and generated immediate benefits.

This suggests that an important way to increase the peasants' estimate of success and, therefore, the probability of contribution is to decrease the scope of the project for which he is being recruited—and thus shorten the interval before benefits are received. . . . Peasants in the late 1960s still laughed about the early attempts by young Trotskyites and Communists to organize them for a national revolution, for industrialization, or even for a world revolution! (262)

Frequently within local civil rights campaigns, the first targets selected by activists for picketing or demonstrations were those that were susceptible to political pressure. Occasionally it appears that this strategy was chanced upon without extensive planning. In the Durham protest cited above, a participant tried to explain the logic of the movement:

The long-range objective is to desegregate the town, to do whatever they can to eradicate the inequities that the Negro might be enduring. This comprises a vast number of things of which [a particular establishment targeted for protests] is one small part. But it was a vulnerable part, so they went after it—more because it was possible than because it was a significant step in some master plan. (Blumberg 1968, 487)

More systematic were the efforts of the younger civil rights organizations to gain credibility in the black community by instigating effective protests. In its early years, for example, CORE lacked an effective national policy to attract attention to itself as a potent frontline civil rights organization. The Journey of Reconciliation in 1947, a precursor to the freedom rides of the 1960s, was intended as a first step toward correcting this image problem. While the journey did not bring about the desegregation of the bus lines, it drew a spotlight to CORE's activities and lent credibility and respectability to its novel direct action methods.

The desire to gain greater credibility also led CORE to claim indirect credit for the success of the 1955 Montgomery bus boycott. In its publication, the *CORE-lator*, the bus boycott was described as a "CORE-TYPE PROTEST," and in subsequent fundraising letters, the Montgomery campaign was used to highlight the potential effectiveness of CORE techniques throughout the South (Meier and Rudwick 1975, 76).

It was not until CORE initiated the freedom rides, however, that the organization was pushed to the front ranks of the movement; as a result, fund-raising became easier and more productive, and the organization was able to almost double its staff between 1963 and 1964. The size and number of CORE chapters also increased dramatically, although the number of active members in the largest chapter still rarely exceeded one hundred. But even though the number of hardcore activists in CORE remained small, there was an impressive increase in the number of sympathizers who were willing to participate in the campaigns initiated by the organization. By sustaining picket lines, lending their energy to rallies and demonstrations, and participating in marches and blockades, these active sympathizers gave an immeasurable boost to the effectiveness of CORE's direct action tactics (ibid., 227).

4. Since it is important to build a record of success, there will be an evolution of tactical strategies over the course of the movement. Tactics that work in forcing the opposition to supply concessions will become popular, while those that prove ineffective will be abandoned. Each innovative tactic will lose its appeal within a movement once its effectiveness is reduced by the tactical countermaneuvers of the opposition. Leaders of collective action must therefore devise a continuing series of novel tactics in order to retain their followers and maintain the leverage of the movement. During the civil rights movement, several innovative tactics, such as the bus boycott, the sit-in, and the freedom ride, grabbed the spotlight at different times. After a new tactic was introduced, the following months of activity in the civil rights movement tended to be dominated by copycat campaigns in other locales around the country (McAdam 1983).

The popularity of various tactics used over the course of the civil rights movement rose and fell according to their successfulness in gaining media attention, provoking southern authorities, and extracting meaningful concessions. As each tactic was introduced, it tended to catch the opposition (and the public) by surprise and consequently enjoyed its greatest success immediately; as the opposition developed an effective strategy to respond to the new tactic, civil rights activists gradually abandoned that tactic in favor of a new one.

5. Although unresponsive authorities hamper efforts to organize collective action, political activists who are able nonetheless to organize protests and win concessions from the authorities will soften the opposition and make subsequent campaigns easier to conduct. This is because the threshold level of mobilization which must be reached before concessions are made is gradually lowered when it becomes apparent to

the authorities that resistance only forestalls the inevitable and harms their interests in the interim.

Protest groups therefore benefit by acquiring a reputation for toughness and endurance. In discussing the art of commitment among nations, Schelling (1966) notes the importance of persuading the other side in a conflict that one actually has the intentions one claims to have: "To fight abroad is a military act, but to *persuade* enemies or allies that one would fight abroad, under circumstances of great cost and risk, requires more than a military capability. It requires projecting intentions. It requires *having* those intentions, even deliberately acquiring them, and communicating them persuasively to make other countries behave" (36). Obviously the ability to make credible threats is also very important for any group trying to exert pressure on the government or some other party. The group has to convey that it is resilient and capable of persevering until the other side is ready to concede.

Therefore if the activists can provide evidence from past confrontations that the movement enjoys high rates of recruitment to its campaigns (demonstrating that *b* and *c* are large), then the authorities will recognize that there is a substantial potential for collective action and be more responsive. Success therefore breeds success. When we examine the bus boycott, for instance, we find that its effectiveness required excellent organization and leadership and almost complete cooperation in the black community. All those requirements were in place in Montgomery in 1955, but even so, large numbers of individuals had to endure long periods of inconvenience and sometimes hardship before the boycott succeeded. However, the privations suffered by the first black communities to initiate boycotts (Montgomery and Tallahassee) made it easier for the movement to organize subsequent boycotts. Interpreting the early boycotts as an indication of the determination of blacks, city officials became more inclined to make concessions and bring about a quick resolution of the conflict.

As in the case of bus boycotts, sit-ins became more effective over time because early successes paved the way for subsequent victories; businesses made concessions to avoid replaying the conflicts they witnessed in neighboring communities. As I pointed out in chapter 5, the proven effectiveness of direct action tactics in general in the early 1960s encouraged civil rights activists to tackle projects that they would not have contemplated in an earlier period, and to do so with considerable success.

THE ALBANY AND BIRMINGHAM CAMPAIGNS

Many of the principles of collective action outlined in this chapter and the last were on display in two of the major campaigns of the civil rights movement: the Albany, Georgia, protests in 1961–62 and the Birmingham protests in 1963. Both campaigns proved to be a contest of wills between the activists and the local authorities. The contrasting outcomes of the two campaigns demonstrate the importance of a steadfast leadership, extensive community organization, and a carefully conceived battle plan which consists of realistic and attainable goals.

Albany

The Albany campaign proved that without the prospect of success, enthusiasm for collective action will be ephemeral. During the early demonstrations initiated by SNCC, large numbers of townspeople overcame their fears of arrest and imprisonment long enough to join the protests, but they quickly developed second thoughts when they found themselves stuck in dirty, crowded jails. Their unease grew worse when it became apparent that the local authorities were not going to cave in easily and that SNCC did not have sufficient funds to bail them out.

Reluctantly SNCC summoned the aid of Martin Luther King, Jr., and SCLC to raise money from around the country for the protesters and to draw nationwide attention to the serious confrontation taking place in Albany. SNCC quickly became so frustrated by SCLC's takeover of the campaign that its workers were torn between leaving town or, alternatively, persuading King and SCLC to depart. Such tension between SNCC and King once again highlights the element of credit claiming that could never be completely eliminated from the movement. Even while out of town, King would be telephoned for his assessment of the Albany crisis at a time when SNCC leaders felt that they deserved to be receiving greater attention (Branch 1988, 614). The rivalry between the two organizations did not go unnoticed by the Albany authorities, who refused to make concessions to the protesters (Aldon Morris 1984, 239–46).

After King arrived, he immediately got himself arrested and declared that he would refuse bail and remain in jail until segregation was abolished. As a result, the morale of hundreds of followers who had been imprisoned earlier was suddenly rejuvenated. King, however, left jail prematurely and deflated the movement when he mistakenly believed that city officials had conceded and agreed to desegregate buses, parks, theaters, and lunch counters, when they had agreed only to eliminate segregated bus terminals and to entertain further desegregation at a later date.

Deeply embarrassed and concerned that the capitulation of the Albany movement would call into question the viability of nonviolent tactics, King vowed to resume the protests until the demands of the movement were met. Unfortunately, King's plan was derailed by a federal court injunction against further demonstrations and protests in the city, which he chose to obey because he wished to maintain good relations with the same federal courts that had often aided the civil rights cause with favorable decisions. SNCC and many of King's followers were dismayed by his decision to obey the injunction, and there was an attempt to carry on the protests in his absence. Without King's charismatic leadership, however, the movement was short-lived and "simply lost its momentum" (Oates 1982, 195).

In their retrospective analysis of the reasons behind the failure of the Albany movement, King and his SCLC colleagues concluded that they had not sufficiently focused on the achievement of particular goals. By not winning small victories at each step of the way, they were unable to maintain the determination and conviction of their followers. Instead, King noted, "Our protest was so vague that we got nothing, and the people were left very depressed and in despair" (Oates 1982, 189).

While King and his charges lost heart, city officials and the police did all they could to dampen the movement. The Albany police for the most part acted cordially and lawfully toward the demonstrators. By refraining from the use of force, they denied the national media a sensational story and the activists a passionate issue to rally around. By refusing to negotiate, city officials discouraged the protesters from continuing.

Birmingham

To make up for the Albany debacle, King and his troops sought redemption in Birmingham. By this time, King had begun to question whether the strategy of nonviolence in itself would be able to win concessions in the South; he was more convinced than ever that federal intervention was essential if blacks were ever going to achieve equal status in this country. For this reason, the demonstrations in Birmingham, while ostensibly directed at the local merchants and officials, was also packaged for consumption in Washington and the rest of the country.

Birmingham was ripe for protest in the late 1950s, but the black community lacked leadership. The most prominent black townspeople, who were the most obvious candidates for leadership, were all vulnerable to retribution from those in authority. Any black business leader would lose his operating license if he tried to organize a campaign against segregation; any black person who showed an inclination to take charge was subjected to reprisals and harassment from the police and the local Ku Klux Klan. Under the circumstances, as Ed Gardner, an old-time resident, reflected poignantly, the only hope was to find a leader who was invulnerable to such pressures, someone with nothing to lose "but his life" (Raines 1977, 140).

SCLC was determined to step into the breach by providing the necessary leadership for the community. The Birmingham movement was much better planned than the Albany movement in terms of scheduling, finances, strategy, goals, and training. A sign of this planning was SCLC executive director Wyatt Walker's elaborate calculations of the likelihood of success in Birmingham:

> They must be prepared to put upwards of a thousand people in jail
> at one time, maybe more. They had to keep the average jailgoer in-
> side at least five or six days at a time before bailing out. Walker
> projected various bail costs to the SCLC against jail costs to the city.
> Given the estimated value of the weekly Negro shopping power, he
> calculated the dollar and percentage losses to the downtown mer-
> chants from the boycott at various degrees of success. (Branch 1988,
> 690)

In addition, King had alerted allies and supporters around the country of SCLC's need for financial support in its forthcoming campaign in Birmingham; an official in New York would keep in close contact and wire funds to SCLC as they were needed to bail protesters out of jail.

SCLC's strategy was to disrupt business as usual at the stores in downtown Birmingham through boycotts and continual sit-ins, the aim being to exert both moral and economic pressure on the stores to desegregate their facilities and adopt certain fair employment hiring practices.

But SCLC had trouble obtaining the full support of black residents in Birmingham. Some detractors were fairly comfortable with their standing in the city and thought King a troublemaker; others, on the contrary, resented the strategy of nonviolence preached by King and instead wished to take more aggressive measures against their white oppressors. A third group had been second-class citizens for so long that they had become apathetic and resigned to their station in life.

To remedy this situation, King made a successful personal appeal to local black leaders to use their influence to galvanize local support in the community behind the Birmingham campaign—which, he argued, represented a critical juncture in the entire civil rights movement. King and SCLC also toiled to minimize conflict within the black community by holding meetings with all local business, professional, and religious leaders. It was during these meetings that internal disagreements and doubts were ironed out, opposition was tempered, and group solidarity was increased. Ministers in Birmingham who were reluctant to support the demonstrations were embarrassed into action by a lecture delivered by King in which he pointed out that their privileges carried social responsibilities. "If you can't stand up with your own people," he chastised them, "you are not fit to be a leader!" (Aldon Morris 1984, 263).

Mass cohesion and commitment to the movement were fortified by song, prayer, and continual meetings. Song was a particularly effective tonic in this campaign as in others, in part, I am sure, because it was an overt method by which people could reassure each other of their continued commitment to the movement. There were, of course, also lessons conveyed in the songs. For example, a typical song exhorting absolute commitment was entitled "Ninety-Nine and a Half Won't Do," a transparent reference to the inadequacy of anything less than a total, 100 percent effort on behalf of the campaign (ibid., 256). The regular meetings also served a didactic purpose. In separate sessions at the Negro churches, King persuaded the young radicals in the community to join the demonstrations and prepared them for the confrontations they would have with the Birmingham police by training them in the way of nonviolent protest.

The unification of the community behind the campaign was essential. Because Bull Connor was determined to round up the demonstrators as quickly as they surfaced, King needed a large pool of recruits to ensure that new volunteers would be available to maintain the picket lines and sit-ins in place of those who were jailed. The goal was to sustain a high level of protest while those who had been thrown in jail could be bailed out and sent back into the fray.

Despite careful planning, however, SCLC, just a week after the campaign had begun, learned that its fund of bail money had been depleted and that it could no longer get its people out of the jails. To compound this problem, King had committed himself to being arrested at this juncture and would therefore be unavailable to tap his connections around the country for additional contributions during the crisis. After some debate among his colleagues, King decided he had to keep his word to his followers. He was arrested as scheduled and was placed in solitary confinement, where he wrote, on bits and scraps of paper, the famous "Letter from Birmingham Jail."

When King emerged from prison, his worst fear, that the movement had lost its energy and momentum, was confirmed. "To his dismay . . . the demonstrations had dwindled to mostly small-scale picket lines and sit-ins involving only a dozen volunteers a day. . . . [I]t was clearer to King's advisers that they must escalate the pressure before serious negotiations could begin. Something had to be done to stimulate recruiting, to get people marching again" (Oates 1982, 231).

But at that stage in the campaign, the pool of volunteers had run dry. The people with the strongest motivation to protest had been the first to be imprisoned in Birmingham. Attempts to round up more demonstrators for a march to City Hall produced fewer volunteers than hoped for. Wyatt Walker faced the dismal facts: "We had scraped the bottom of the barrel of adults who would go [to jail]. . . . We needed some new something" (ibid., 232).

In the nick of time, SCLC's younger charges, headed by James Bevel, capitalized on their ties to the high school and recruited hundreds of students to take up the cause. This move was criticized by some, but whether it was expedient or calculated, it was clearly a masterly stroke. The high school students, and the grade school children who came with them, obviously did not appreciate—at least initially—the danger of the situation; they were immune to economic reprisals from the white community, and the police were unlikely to treat them as roughly as they treated the adult protesters. The children, in essence, were the ideal recruits, since they were enthralled by the whole spectacle of the campaign and eager to follow their elders in relentless droves.

The first wave of youthful protesters were quick to "display their energy and enthusiasm." "Singing 'We Shall Overcome' and chanting slogans, the demonstrators filed out of the church in groups, taking different routes toward City Hall. Most were quickly arrested and they piled into paddy wagons or school buses in an almost festive mood" (Lewis 1964, 179).

The thousands of enthusiastic youngsters replenished the movement. They packed the downtown streets, and as quickly as they were arrested, they were reinforced the next day by a fresh battalion of students. Each new contingent of demonstrators was larger than the last. When the Birmingham jails were filled to capacity, there were still thousands of protestors out on the streets keeping the campaign alive. Only then, when it was apparent that business as usual could no longer be conducted in downtown Birmingham and that the federal government would no longer remain on the sidelines, did the business community relent and go to the negotiating table.

MODELING THE ALBANY AND BIRMINGHAM CAMPAIGNS

We can understand the contrasting outcomes of the Albany and Birmingham campaigns in terms of the differential success each had in mobilizing the local community. Success in each instance required the maintenance of high levels of mobilization through sustained and vigorous demonstrations. By disrupting city business, the protesters in theory would force local officials to negotiate and make concessions.

As we have seen, however, the Albany campaign was marked throughout by waverings in the enthusiasm of the protesters, cagey maneuvers by the local authorities, and strategic errors on the part of the civil rights leadership. Ultimately fatigue and frustration brought the campaign to an unceremonious conclusion. The Birmingham campaign also had moments when it appeared that the local authorities would weather the storm and prevail, but in the end the activists proved to have greater resilience than their opponents.

Our simple supply-and-demand model can shed some light on the dynamics of the two campaigns.

I assume as before that both government initiative (i) and government responsiveness to the protests (r_1) are either (1) very small, so that large-scale mobilization is necessary to obtain significant concessions, or (2) equal to zero unless the demonstrators prove they can sustain a high degree of pressure, in which case responsiveness increases. Under the second assumption, a high level of mobilization must be maintained over several time periods before local authorities will make any concessions. For this reason, oscillating time paths or declining levels of mobilization over time will not wring concessions from the authorities.

Because the government does not supply concessions in either scenario unless it is forced to do so—and therefore does little to encourage the movement—we can for all intents and purposes set i and r_1 equal to zero and examine the time path of the level of mobilization, given assumptions about the remaining parameters. The reduced equation:

$$M(t) = a + (c - br_2p - dp)M(t - 1) \qquad (8.1)$$

has the corresponding equilibrium:

$$M^* = \frac{a}{1 - (c - br_2p - dp)},$$

or

$$M^* = \frac{a}{1 - A} \text{ where } A = (c - br_2p - dp). \qquad (8.2)$$

Whether or not collective action develops therefore depends on the size of the contagion factor relative to the dampening effect of (1) policies that are contrary to the aims of the movement and (2) threats posed by the local police and opponents of the movement. If c exceeds $(br_2p + dp)$, collective action will expand, but if the reverse is true, or if the two forces are approximately equal, the movement will die one of several possible deaths (see figures 8.1 and 8.2).

In Albany, the level of activism started out strong but was countered effectively by the concerted efforts of city officials and the local police, the latter efficiently rounding up the demonstrators and killing the movement through kindness. Neither long-term nor short-term goals could be accomplished. The activists could not force city officials

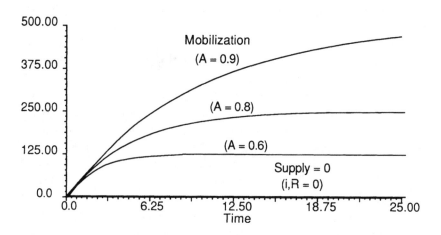

FIGURE 8.1. Mobilization Climbs Despite Unresponsive Authorities

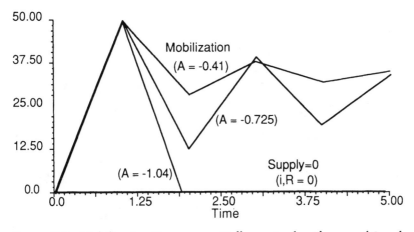

FIGURE 8.2. Mobilization Dampens or Collapses in the Absence of Supply

to negotiate an end to all forms of racial segregation, and they were not able to fill the jails and exact such a great financial cost on the city that the officials were forced to seek a solution to the problem.

"Filling the jails" was a very specific short-term goal that in principle should have focused the energies of the activists on a manageable task. If this goal had been successfully accomplished, it would have been instrumental in attaining the ultimate goal of desegregation. However, the Albany police chief Laurie Pritchett was well aware that King might attempt this Gandhian strategy. Therefore he arranged for those arrested to be transported to jails outside of the city, which effectively transformed the Albany jail into "a bottomless pit" (Barkan 1984, 550).

Under the circumstances, allowing oneself to be arrested and sent to jail became a fairly ritualistic (i.e., meaningless) activity, insofar as it had a negligible effect on the city. In other words, no amount of coordination by the activists could be deemed successful; no matter how many of them went to prison, there would still be room for more, and there would be no negotiations. The Albany campaign succeeded, an NAACP official observed wryly, "only if the goal was to go to jail" (Miller 1968, 139). Not surprisingly, then, there was a marked decrease in the willingness of activists to be arrested, and the number of participants in the Albany demonstrations steadily declined. Few people wanted to invest their resources in a venture that appeared destined to fail. One student expressed the view of many: "The young people are not interested in peaceful demonstrations in the street. That only means arrest with no bail money. The people here have been going to jail for over two years now. They are tired of going to jail" (Barkan 1984, 558).

As long as change is believed to be imminent, frustration in a social movement will be minimized. This may make the difference between an expanding and a contracting movement, for if the opposition is strong and local authorities are unresponsive to the activists' demands, then the fate of the campaign will depend on the magnitude of the contagion rate and the resilience of the activists. The opposition will therefore be intent on putting a damper on the optimism of the protesters. Should it become apparent to the activists that they are in for a protracted struggle with little chance of being victorious, the onset of frustration may ensure the collapse of the movement.

Because of the lack of success, frustration grew in Albany; even King's efforts were insufficient to sustain the tremendous enthusiasm that was present at the first rally he addressed. Despair eroded the rate of recruitment and reduced the size of the local population that was prepared to be mobilized. When c diminishes, so does the equilibrium M^*. If c declines to the point where $-1 < A < 0$, the level of mobilization dwindles over time to a very low equilibrium value along a damped oscillatory path (as in figure 8.2). In effect, the activists are gradually worn down by those who oppose the movement, including the local authorities. The trajectory forecasted by the model roughly corresponds to the path taken by the Albany campaign. While the Albany activists began with spirit and determination, they ended up bickering among themselves. Protests that drew large numbers of supporters at the start of the campaign attracted few by its conclusion. When King and SCLC finally left the city, the Albany movement came to a complete halt, demonstrating once more the vital role that leadership plays in sustaining collective action.[1]

In addition to being more unified and better organized than the Albany protests, the Birmingham campaign pursued more specific purposes; businesses were targeted for economic boycotts, sit-ins, and picketing, whereas in Albany the diffuse and overly ambitious goal had been the elimination of all forms of racial discrimination. Blacks also held greater purchasing power in Birmingham, so the boycott was a more potent instrument of protest; even though a large majority of the

---

1. King was sufficiently frustrated by the stagnation and internal factionalization of the civil rights movement after the Albany campaign that he contemplated retiring to a lucrative position with a private foundation that would have paid him $100,000 a year to give lectures around the country.

black community joined the Albany boycott, it was not able to place sufficient pressure on merchants to exact concessions to its demands.

The Birmingham campaign was designed to proceed in several stages. Economic boycotts, sit-ins, and pickets would initiate the movement, to be followed by mass marches and demonstrations, and then by "D" day, when protesters would get themselves arrested and jailed. In spite of the careful precampaign planning and organizing by SCLC, a considerable proportion of the local black community was recruited to the movement only after it was already underway. In this regard, the movement was highly contagious. Wyatt Walker of SCLC noted the difference in motivation between early and late participants in the movement when he observed that "there's two kinds of people. People who are committed to the movement and people who get committed by the movement. And the largest proportion of the people in Birmingham including most of the black pastors, they got committed by the movement" (Aldon Morris 1984, 264).

This predominance of latecomers in collective endeavors is to be expected, given the way that costs and benefits tend to vary with the strength of a movement. As the number of participants increases, there is a corresponding increase in the social pressure on remaining members of the community to become involved, while at the same time the movement becomes more attractive to those who are willing to participate if the cause provides them with expressive and psychological benefits.

However, as the Albany experience revealed, the presence of a large number of followers in a movement makes collective action volatile and difficult to sustain. Despite being better organized than the Albany campaign, the Birmingham demonstrations almost suffered the same fate and might have if not for certain propitious tactics in the second half of the campaign. We should therefore dissect the Birmingham campaign into two parts. In the first part, the campaign started with great enthusiasm but quickly began to grind to a halt; as in Albany, frustration and imprisonment rapidly reduced the ranks of the activists. The movement tottered ($br_2p + dp > c$), when it could not attain any of its objectives. The jailing of King in Birmingham, like his voluntary departure from Albany, almost killed the movement by creating a void in the leadership ranks.

But what happened in the second part was a modification of the parameters of the conflict. The recruitment of student volunteers brought to the movement energetic activists who would not be easily frustrated or deterred. Furthermore, the ability of the local authorities to quell demonstrations through mass imprisonment was reduced as the jails rapidly filled to capacity.

The higher recruitment rate (c) combined with the constraint on the deterrents (d) to participation allowed the movement to take off. If A is close to 1 (but < 1), the level of mobilization will rise sharply (as in figure 8.1) toward a high equilibrium value, since $M^* = a/1 - A$ (assuming still that i and $r_1 = 0$). Despite the efforts of city officials to dampen the campaign, demand steadily increased with each additional wave of student volunteers. Attempts to intimidate the protesters added fuel to the fire. It was the ability of the demonstrators to mount a campaign and sustain their pressure on the Birmingham community that was responsible for the eventual accord between the city's civic leaders and the black community.

9 | *The Rise and Fall of Collective Action*

It was the best of times, it was the worst of times.
Charles Dickens

With the momentous victory in Birmingham under its belt, the civil rights movement picked up momentum across the nation. New participants were inspired to join the struggle for racial equality; veterans of the movement rededicated themselves and devoted more of their time to the cause; money suddenly poured in to the major organizations spearheading the movement from sympathetic businesses, labor unions, churches, student groups, and individuals; demonstrations and protests broke out in countless cities as civil rights leaders issued demands for equality in a growing number of realms.

Public opinion grew increasingly supportive of this new phase of the movement. The disturbing images transmitted from Birmingham by the national media had convinced white northerners of the depth of the racial conflict in the South and the intransigence of local officials. Surveys conducted in this period showed that civil rights had become the nation's most important problem in the minds of millions of Americans, that the proportion of Americans who thought the pace of change in race relations was too fast was declining, and that support was growing for measures guaranteeing voting rights, access to housing, and desegregated schools and public accommodations. "White moderates," Meier (1970) writes, ". . . had become so committed to Civil Rights that they clamored for the chance to pay the money to enable them to risk their lives" (481).

But as the scope of the civil rights movement changed, so too did its style and tone. While in the wake of the successful Birmingham campaign the new mood within the movement was hopeful and optimistic, it was also becoming marked with impatience and anger. According to a national poll (*Newsweek*, 29 July 1963), the feeling among black leaders was that they had waited long enough to be included as equals in American society, endured enough humiliation, violence, and frustration, and tolerated enough token concessions and piecemeal improvements; it was time, in their view, for sweeping and immediate changes.

The major civil rights organizations recognized the new temper and spirit of the movement and competed among themselves for the additional manpower and financial resources that were now available. The practical consequence of this infighting was to reinforce and further the radicalizing trend of the movement's rank and file. Even the traditionally more moderate and temperate NAACP and Urban League, which in the past had been ambivalent about the wisdom of disruptive protests, now endorsed the use of bold direct action strategies.

The civil rights leadership realized that it could stay at the forefront of the movement only if it adopted a more aggressive and insistent posture. (King: "There go my people. I must catch them, for I am their leader.") Moreover, the leadership feared that a go-slow strategy would quickly dampen the newfound enthusiasm, optimism, and energy of the rank and file. It was believed that unless the surge in mass participation was rewarded with tangible improvements in the status of blacks, there would be widespread disillusionment with the efficacy of collective action and wholesale withdrawal from the movement. Individual blacks would again seek to cope with their problems as best they could in their own idiosyncratic ways. To ensure that this would not occur, "the civil rights organizations demanded as much as they could as quickly as possible. In tandem, the NAACP, CORE, SNCC, and SCLC schooled their followers in the politics of disorder, planning even more provocative demonstrations" (Sitkoff 1981, 148).

The changing nature of the demand for remedies for the racial problem is of course only one side of the supply-and-demand equation. Of equal importance to the viability of the civil rights movement in this period was the awakening in midterm, after two years in the doldrums, of the Kennedy administration to the need for federal intervention on the race issue. Kennedy had tried to walk a fine line on the race issue in order to hold both northern blacks and southern whites within his electoral coalition. He appointed blacks to positions of responsibility in his administration, endorsed in the abstract the goal of racial equality, made himself accessible to the leaders of civil rights organizations, and promoted equal opportunity hiring practices within the federal government.

Yet Kennedy also appointed to the federal bench archconservatives who were hostile to the goal of racial equality. Moreover, the actions of his administration on the more contentious issues, e.g., the problem of segregated transportation lines and discriminatory housing practices, were cautious and circumspect; they were designed to placate blacks and to achieve peace and stability without unduly ruffling the feathers of southern whites. Kennedy favored the use of executive orders and litigation to promote social equality. In his long-term rationale, legislative resistance to civil rights measures could be overcome when blacks secured their right to vote and possessed significant electoral and political power.

Only the continued disruption and turmoil created by the civil rights movement in the South forced the administration to face the race issue squarely. Civil rights leaders understood these dynamics. "We put on pressure and create a crisis," explained James Farmer, "and then they react" (Piven and Cloward 1977, 235). A month after the discord in Birmingham, following further turmoil in Alabama over the desegregation of the University of Alabama, President Kennedy delivered a historic national address imploring Americans to recognize the shameful conditions under which blacks were forced to live in the United States. The President noted that blacks were being denied not only their political rights but also an equal opportunity to enjoy the same quality of life as white Americans: compared to whites, blacks were more likely to be unemployed, had a shorter life expectancy, earned on average only a fraction of the income that whites earned, and were likely to hold less desirable occupations. Under the circumstances, the President asked rhetorically, what white man would be willing to exchange places with the Negro?

Kennedy's unequivocal speech in support of racial equality marked a turning point in his administration's stance on civil rights. By increasing its commitment to the goal of racial equality, the administration gave further encouragement to the civil rights movement. Protests and demonstrations were initiated across the nation that summer, capped by the unforgettable March on Washington. Perhaps the highlight of the movement, the march attracted a quarter of a million supporters and symbolized all that was admirable and noble about the civil rights cause. To most observers, it appeared as if the civil rights movement was never more united or more influential. Subsequent events seemed to bear this out as in the following two years the movement experienced its greatest successes when Congress passed the 1964 Civil Rights Act and the 1965 Voting Rights Act. In the afterglow of these victories, discussions took place between civil rights leaders and President Johnson about the next phase of the movement.

No one could be faulted for thinking that there were additional reforms on the horizon. Yet ironically, at the height of its success, the civil rights movement began to come apart at the seams. After 1965, the number of protests and civil actions sponsored by the movement suddenly plummeted (McAdam 1982, 121). Martin Luther King, Jr., muttered, "There is no more civil rights movement. President Johnson signed it out of existence when he signed the voting rights bill." In this final phase, disagreement arose within the ranks about the best strategy to adopt to make further progress. The unity of purpose, spirit, and ideals that had characterized the movement suddenly belonged to the past. New ideas were in short supply. Direct action tactics that had served the movement brilliantly began to appear outdated and unsuited to a new generation of problems. Nonviolence and patience gave way to civil unrest and riots in cities across the nation. How to explain the "apparent paradox of these unprecedented outbursts of black violence, disorder, and frustration exploding just at the peak of optimism?" (Woodward 1974, 191).

Changes in the Assurance Game

I shall discuss these changes in the fortunes of the civil rights movement in terms of the game-theoretic and dynamic models developed in the previous chapters. My basic point in this chapter is that the program of the civil rights movement which gave the movement consensus, unity, and purpose in the 1950s and early 1960s disintegrated in the mid-sixties and precipitated the fragmentation of a broad coalition of activists. As the demands of the movement were met, civil rights activists found themselves divided, some satisfied by the results, others frustrated and disappointed, and still others angered by the way the movement veered in the final years. All of these reactions weakened the momentum of the movement and in the end broke it apart.

In chapter 6 I argued that social movements in general, and the civil rights movement in particular, can be usefully modeled as *n*-person assurance games. Unlike in the prisoner's dilemma, the players in the assurance game prefer involvement to staying on the sidelines, so long as enough others also participate to give collective action a reasonable chance to succeed. This additional proviso is crucial because it ensures that a collective action problem—albeit of a different form than the prisoner's dilemma—still exists; thus, we still have reason to believe that collective action in pursuit of such goals as freedom, justice, morality, and equality will be rare events that will occur only under the right combination (or "coordination") of circumstances.

Of course not all members of the aggrieved group naturally see their situation as a problem of coordination. In point of fact, the structure of the game has to be established by the participants themselves and will change with the changing fortunes of the movement. While social networks provide the avenues for recruitment of new members into the movement, they act largely as conduits for reaching prospective candidates. Participants must also have symbolic or ideological reasons for sustained devotion to a collective endeavor. Without an ideology to provide activists with an explanation for their current predicament, to outline a course of action, and to justify the prescriptions of the movement, collective action will remain fragmented, stalled, and directionless; leaders of the cause will be unable to generate enough passion and commitment among its supporters for collective action to succeed.

For example, an important development in the gay rights movement was the explicit rejection of the notion that there was anything abnormal or immoral about homosexuality. So long as the morality of homosexuality remained debatable, homosexuals were not only subject to public ridicule but were also themselves ashamed to be homosexuals. Consequently, many homosexuals could not fully embrace the movement because they were not convinced that their cause was just. By persuading homosexuals to remove personal doubts about the morality of the cause, a new generation of militant leaders in the movement increased the vigor of homosexual political activism accordingly.

At the turn of the twentieth century, it is probably safe to say, the situation facing black Americans could not even be characterized as a prisoner's dilemma, let alone as a coordination problem in which involvement was preferred to inaction. The forces of society—government, police, businessmen, employers, white supremacists—were so strongly united against blacks that mass protest was both futile and dangerous. Before there were any collective action problems of the sort epitomized by the prisoner's dilemma, civil rights leaders had to sell a program for social change that demonstrated the benefits of community action. Prospective civil rights activists had to come to believe that collective action was an effective means to achieve their goals.

A psychological change, however, had to occur not only within the aggrieved minority population but also among the authoritative elements in the political system—in particular the executive, Congress, and the Courts. It is unproductive for activists to delude themselves into thinking that collective action can instigate changes in the status quo if the other elements of the equation—namely, the agencies capable of supplying the public good—are completely unsympathetic to the notion of reform. What this means is that successful collective action does not depend solely on the potential activists' ability to believe in themselves but also on the alignment of other critical actors in the political process.

The development of group solidarity, mutual obligations and commitments, and a program for social change effectively transforms the game situation facing potential activists. Not only is the potential and power of collective action recognized, but individuals eschew, or are deterred from, free riding when presented with the opportunity to contribute. Selective social and psychological incentives therefore turn the prisoner's dilemma into an assurance problem in which each person prefers cooperation to abstention so long as others also cooperate.

Once collective action has been successfully initiated, why does it then collapse? A possible reason is that collective action is not as profitable as the activists anticipated it would be when they made their decisions to join. Believing himself to be a party to a losing or failing effort, each activist chooses to bail out. For each activist the prerequisite for participation in the assurance game is that there is a sufficient number of collaborators to ensure that collective action will be effective. Should coordination occur, yet not force concessions from the opposition, it is likely to be short-lived because each activist prefers to refrain if political activism does not pay dividends. Failure to extract concessions may mean that collective action is futile irrespective of the number involved, or that this particular instance of collective action is undersized and impotent.

In practice there is also likely to be a bandwagon effect during the evacuation process: because the timetable for the success of the movement is seldom agreed upon, people will become flustered and frustrated at different points in time. The activists who are the first to throw in the towel may set off a chain reaction, since the remaining activists will have to reevaluate the probability that they will be successful in light of the defection in their ranks. Such a reassessment may cause yet other activists to conclude that the prospects of success have been lowered sufficiently to prompt them to withdraw as well. New withdrawals precipitate another round of recalculations and perhaps a new wave of withdrawals, and so on until few if any activists are left to carry on the struggle.

The scenario just described is a blueprint for failure, or more precisely, for how a limited setback can sow the seeds of a more monumental failure. It does not, however, describe the downfall of the civil rights movement, because that movement's decline was immediately preceded not by failure but by its greatest triumphs. If success breeds success, as it did in the heyday of the movement, why did it ultimately spawn failure in the late 1960s?

SATISFACTION AND THE EXHAUSTION OF IDEAS

The major reason can be traced to the changing structure of the game facing political activists as their aspirations are satisfied. A situation takes on the features of an assurance game when a group of activists recognize the collective as well as individual benefits of collaborating in collective action. This occurs when there is agreement that there are outstanding problems to be addressed and that collective political pressure is an effective way to correct them.

As the goals of collective action are achieved, the usefulness of political activism is correspondingly diminished. At the start of the movement, when little or nothing has been accomplished, the value of coordination is at a maximum: history is waiting to be made; but as the demands of the movement are gradually answered with social and legislative changes, the residual demands take on less importance. Many in the rank and file sincerely believe that most of their work has been done and that (presumably) others can provide the finishing touches. In other words, the marginal utility of further collaboration and collective action is reduced with each successful campaign waged by the activists.

In order to prevent stagnation and complacency from setting in, movement leaders must recharge the rank and file with new plans and goals that inspire further contributions of money, time, and effort. Activists devoid of a sense of purpose quickly become "tired radicals"— to use Leuchtenberg's (1958) appellation for the effete proponents of Progressivism at the end of that course of political reform. In the case of Progressivism, the movement "faded in the 1920's in part because it had succeeded too well. Women's suffrage had been a long-time goal, and prohibition and immigration restriction . . . were important aims of the prewar progressives" (126–27).

Therefore the breakdown of the assurance game may be attributable simply to the exhaustion of ideas. This does not mean that civil rights activists could not conceive of further goals beyond the 1964 and 1965 Civil Rights and Voting Rights Acts, but only that they had difficulty developing and planning new political campaigns around them. Throughout the civil rights struggle, the movement's leaders had initiated bold new tactics such as the freedom rides, sit-ins, and boycotts at strategic moments to reinvigorate the movement and foil the counterstrategies of the southern authorities. But once-effective tactics suddenly appeared antiquated as the demands of the civil rights movement were satisfied. A prime example of this occurred in 1966, after James Meredith was shot and wounded while marching from Memphis to Jackson on a one-man mission to encourage blacks to exercise their right to vote. When King hurried to Mississippi to organize another march on Meredith's behalf, there were many in the procession who openly questioned the relevance of marching, especially when it appeared more productive to go from door to door to try to persuade blacks to register to vote.

It might even be said that nonviolent direct action ended with the voting rights battle. "After the Selma campaign," Sitkoff (1981) writes,

> the leading organizations of the movement had floundered in their search for new programs. Everyone agreed on the need to move beyond the traditional civil-rights agenda, but no one developed a viable strategy for solving the complex problems of inadequate housing, dead-end jobs, no jobs, and inferior schooling. A sense of irrelevancy particularly rankled the dedicated activists in CORE and SNCC. They considered themselves the cutting edge of the movement, yet they now stood still. (209)

DISAPPOINTMENT AND BACKLASH

In general, two other developments can halt the continued progress of a social movement. One is disappointment and the other is known colloquially as "backlash." By "disappointment," I am referring not to the unhappiness that results from failing to achieve one's goals but to the discontent that surfaces when the fruits of one's labor do not live up to expectations. More broadly, in the realm of political activism, where striving and achieving are often tightly fused, the source of disappointment can be as closely associated with the experience of collective action as with its products.

Hirschman (1982) makes this point forcefully in his analysis of private and public action, which I referred to earlier in my discussion of the impetus behind public-spirited collective action. In "rebounding" from private to public life, citizens, according to Hirschman, are prone to exaggerate the benefits and underestimate the costs of political participation. Once engaged, they realize that their new activity takes up considerably more of their time than they had originally budgeted.

Therefore, almost from the start, political activists discover that they are paying significant opportunity costs for their participation. Equally devastating is learning that on the opposite side of the ledger, the benefits of participation diminish steadily over time. This will occur, Hirschman claims, whether or not the aims of collective action are reached: "Take nonfulfillment first. Prolonged but largely unsuccessful advocacy of a cause will often bring discouragement and eventual abandonment of a struggle sensed as futile. Another possibility is that nominally success is achieved, but that in triumph the cause turns out to be far less attractive than had been anticipated" (93–94).

Hirschman adds that there is also a special quality about public activism that makes it almost inherently disappointing no matter what its outcome. Because it is motivated by high ideals and good intentions, public action almost never lives up to one's expectations. For example, Degler (1980) writes that "to listen to advocates of woman suffrage in the decade or so before the ratification of the Nineteenth Amendment in 1920, one would have thought that the millenium would result once women were permitted to vote" (328). In that case and countless others, the actual consequences of reform were considerably more sobering. The original goals of collective action are often diluted or sidetracked, coalitions with strange bedfellows are formed for strategic reasons, compromises are made in the belief that some gain is better than none at all, and participants are seen to be using collective action as a shroud for personal gain and glory.

All of these turns for the worse mean that "the spell that transformed costs into benefits will be broken and the more usual kind of cost accounting will reassert itself. Along with openings for corruption, opportunities for free rides will suddenly seem attractive" (Hirschman 1982, 126).

Perceived unfairness in the distribution of credit following the Montgomery boycott, for example, contributed to the demise of the Montgomery Improvement Association. "E. D. Nixon . . . became openly hostile to King's manner and importance. . . . King himself suffered a corresponding letdown. He was fearful of the bombs, saddened by the backsliding on bus integration, hurt by criticisms within the MIA that he traveled too much and received too much attention, and depressed by the carping disunity among the MIA leadership" (Branch 1988, 200–201).

In short, disappointment occurs when the accomplishments of collective action seem inadequate, incomplete, or compromised. There may be a "public face of victory," but it masks a "private face of disillusionment"—to use Hodgson's (1976, 184) characterization of the final phase of the civil rights movement.

On the other hand, if the goals of collective action are seen as excessive, inordinate, or unreasonable, there will be a backlash or reaction against the movement. Here I am referring specifically to supporters within the movement who have a clear idea about the goals they wish to achieve through collective action. To go beyond those goals constitutes a distortion, a vulgarization of the original intent and spirit of the movement. Such "excess" transforms the collective good into a collective "bad."

Therefore a backlash occurs within the movement when people have had more than their fill of social change and reform. Whereas the undersupply of change generates frustration and a sense of futility, the oversupply of change, or rather the supply of undesired change, produces an aversive response. Both symptoms, however, if left unattended, promote defection.

The Decline of the Civil Rights Movement

The combination of these four factors—satisfaction, the exhaustion of ideas, disappointment, and backlash—goes far toward explaining the demise of the civil rights movement at the height of its power.

The achievement of the right to vote gave blacks access to conventional electoral channels and reduced their involvement in the various direct action forms of political participation that had been the hallmark of the civil rights movement. The creation of new opportunities in government, business, industry, federally sponsored programs, and education also drained leaders and followers from the movement. Not only did one form of voice (participating in elections and in government) replace another (protesting) but as a result, protest became less legitimate and justifiable in the eyes of the American public. If change could be accomplished through the electoral process and other mainstream avenues, the reasoning went, it was no longer necessary to resort to disruptive street tactics.

As I suggested above, by the late sixties, the dimensions of the race problem had changed significantly. Segregated lunch counters, bus terminals, hotels, schools, and public accommodations and blatant violations of the right of blacks to register and vote were relatively easily identified problems. These problems had correspondingly straightforward legislative solutions that could be effectively enforced. On the other hand, the new generation of problems concerning housing discrimination, de facto neighborhood segregation, white flight to the suburbs, job discrimination, high rates of adult illiteracy, and so forth, were more difficult to eradicate because they did not lend themselves to solutions by simple legislative decree.

Problems such as housing and job discrimination are insidious and difficult to detect and punish. De facto segregation in neighborhoods results from preferences that reflect deep-seated attitudes about the racial, ethnic, and socioeconomic groups that one wishes to live among and associate with; people cannot be prevented by law from moving out of and into the neighborhoods of their choice. Similarly, the deeply rooted social and economic problems facing the average black individual as a result of an impoverished childhood and an inferior education did not lend themselves to the mass protests, marches, and demonstrations that were so instrumental in terminating Jim Crow practices. As Woodward (1967) put it, "They were not amenable to romantic crusades and the evangelical approach" (34). These problems, on the contrary, can only be solved in the long run by changing individuals, through investment in education and job training in the case of blacks, and in the case of whites through education and social contact to reduce latent prejudices that have persisted in American society for generations.

CORE leader James Farmer (1985) recognized that the civil rights movement would have to adapt to this new phase if it was going to survive. While President Johnson was working to get the voting rights bill through Congress, he met with Farmer to discuss how he might help to achieve the future goals of the movement. Farmer took the opportunity to express his concern that millions of blacks who had received an improper education lacked the skills necessary to take advantage of their new opportunities. If there was ever going to be real equality between the races, Farmer offered, there would have to be a determined effort to defeat illiteracy in this country. In fact, he continued, civil rights veterans were now ready to quit their direct action campaigns in order to tackle this new challenge: "We have in the movement thousands of volunteers with intelligence, dedication, and boundless energies, who don't consider sitting-in, freedom riding, and going to jail to be the most meaningful things in the world any longer. They're standing by now, waiting for direction" (295).

But Farmer's view proved to be only one among many. Disagreement over the direction that subsequent collective action should take contributed significantly to the demise of the civil rights movement following its greatest successes. The civil rights movement encompassed a variety of organizations holding very different ideas about the best way to bring about social change. Mainstream organizations like the Urban League and the NAACP pursued legal changes and social programs benefiting blacks by lobbying and working for the election of sympathetic politicians; militant groups such as SNCC, SCLC, and CORE eschewed these conventional methods and pressed for the continued use of more unorthodox direct action tactics.

The coalition between the more radical groups and the older civil rights organizations did not materialize until the historic March on Washington in 1963, when each faction agreed to compromise to some degree on the tactics it would adopt to achieve its goals; in essence, the Urban League and the NAACP volunteered greater participation in direct action, while the more radical groups agreed to temper their demands and methods so as not to alienate white liberal supporters from the movement.

The unification of the major civil rights organizations contributed significantly to the eventual passage of the civil rights acts of 1964 and 1965. In addition to exerting concerted pressure on the administration and Congress, the civil rights coalition, especially through its mass demonstrations and protests, attracted the spotlight of the media and tilted public opinion toward both awareness and acceptance of the need for social change.

Ironically, the passage of the historic civil rights acts laid the foundation for the eventual demise of the civil rights coalition. To the more radical elements within the coalition, the legislative gains appeared to be mostly formalistic, since the new laws did not suddenly transform the economic status of most blacks. Moreover, the imperfect enforcement of the new legislation revealed with special clarity the contrast between law and practice, theory and reality. Black radicals therefore increasingly railed against what they believed to be the movement's paper successes—legislative victories that provided symbolic satisfaction but did little to alleviate the immediate problems suffered disproportionately by the black community, such as unemployment, poverty, unsatisfactory housing, inadequate medical care, and illiteracy. "Now on the very eve of those triumphs," Woodward (1974) writes, "the triumphs themselves suddenly appeared quaint and anachronistic" (193).

One consequence of this internal dissension was that in the second half of the 1960s, the major organizations coordinating the civil rights movement (NAACP, CORE, SNCC, and SCLC) assumed a proportionately smaller role in initiating political activism. According to McAdam's (1982) analysis, the four major civil rights groups initiated three-quarters of all organized events taking place between 1961 and 1965, but only one-third of the events occurring in 1970 (183).

Thus, by 1966 a major schism had developed in the civil rights movement between the mainstream "integrationist" faction that sought continued progress through political channels and a more radical faction that increasingly scorned the nonviolent tactics of the traditional black leadership. Radical activists, who were already uncomfortable about moderating their activities in the interests of the broader coalition, took the sluggishness of political and economic change as a signal that more drastic measures were necessary. This new phase, which extended from the mid to late 1960s, was marked by "the rise of militant-racial leaders and organizations outbidding each other in their extreme demands and militant rhetoric and turning against the moderate leadership" (Oberschall 1973, 207–8).

Whether or not it was an inevitable outgrowth of the civil rights movement, "Black Power" proved to be both an organizational and a public relations disaster. The concept was extremely unpopular to most Americans. While it garnered a good deal of media coverage, it alienated white Americans (especially wealthy benefactors of civil rights causes), moderate blacks, and traditional allies of the civil rights movement in Congress and the administration. Charles R. Sims, the founder of the southern black vigilante group, Deacons for Defense and Justice, noted bluntly that the idea of Black Power repulsed many white supporters: "a lot of civil rights volunteer workers *quit* and you can't blame 'em. How can you work with a son of a bitch that every time you look up he's throwin' up his fist talkin' 'bout Black Power" (Raines 1977, 422).

Moreover, the promotion of black separatism hastened the perception among those in the mainstream of the movement that the cause was getting out of hand and going too far. By this point the accomplishments of the civil rights movement had added up. "One new civil rights bill then followed another," Woodward (1967) recounts, "each bolder and more aggressive than the last: 1957, 1960, 1964, 1965" (30). "Sweeping, comprehensive statutes, they promised the oppressed emancipation from the bonds of segregation and discrimination; protection of civil rights; restoration of the franchise and political rights; and broadened opportunities for education and economic advancement" (ibid.). Surveying these changes, white allies were increasingly heard to ask, "What *more* do they want?" (ibid., 33).

"They" wanted to export the spirit of reform to other parts of the country, but the civil rights movement proved not to travel well outside of the South. Recruitment to the cause was troublesome because the North did not have anything comparable to the tightly knit black organizations in the South—especially the church—that had provided the movement with a highly adaptable, ready-made social network. While the major civil rights groups tried to establish similar networks in northern cities, they had little success coordinating and channeling the discontent in the urban ghettos into coherent political action.

Significantly, by moving north the civil rights movement broadened the base of opposition forces by incurring the wrath of groups that had hitherto either abstractly supported or been indifferent toward the change in race relations. The expansion of the opposition made it difficult for either political party to wholeheartedly embrace the civil rights issue without facing the loss of key constituents (and not just southerners) in forthcoming elections.

Another factor that hurt the civil rights movement was the Vietnam War. After 1965, the Vietnam War supplanted civil rights as the most important problem facing the country in the eyes of the American public. The war not only diverted public attention from civil rights problems, but it also drained away considerable manpower that had been available to the civil rights movement.

Furthermore, the overlap between antiwar and civil rights protesters and the eventual open denunciation of the war by key civil rights leaders, including Martin Luther King, Jr. (in 1966), disrupted the harmonious relationship between the Johnson administration and the civil rights movement. Because the civil rights leaders would not support Johnson's actions in Vietnam, the President became much less agreeable to new programs and directions they were proposing for the civil rights movement.

Problems have a way of snowballing. At the psychological and emotional level, the declining success of activism depressed the spirits and self-confidence of activists and reduced their desire to engage in protest activity. Goldman (1970, 242, 249) presents data showing that between the mid and late 1960s the proportion of blacks who reported a willingness to participate in marches, picketing, sit-ins, and economic boycotts, and to go to jail in the course of these activities, had decreased by around 10 percent. Thus, whereas in the first half of the decade, the civil rights workers' success built upon itself and set in motion a popular bandwagon, a string of failures in the political arena sent the process tottering in the opposite direction. These dynamics are consistent with my assumption that people will not join just any cause that they sympathize with but only those efforts that they believe have a chance to succeed. Since people require different likelihoods of success before they participate, we see causes like the civil rights movement accumulating and unraveling over time according to their achievements and failures.

With the civil rights movement reeling, the final blow was delivered when the Johnson administration gave way to the Nixon presidency. Nixon capitalized on the backlash that was developing in the country over the changes and turmoil of the 1960s. Antiwar protests and urban and campus unrest had created a new law and order issue for politicians. While the Kennedy and Johnson administrations were crucial to the long-term success of the civil rights movement, the election of Nixon in 1968 was a major factor in its rapid demise. As strained as the relationship between the civil rights leadership and the executive branch had become as a consequence of Johnson's policies in Vietnam, they were virtually severed when Nixon took office. It was clear from the election returns that Nixon owed larger debts to the South than to blacks, who had voted almost unanimously (97 percent) for Humphrey. It was, according to Daniel Patrick Moynihan, the start of "a period of benign neglect" of racial problems in the country.

Whereas Johnson had tried to rush his Great Society programs through Congress, hoping to capitalize on a short-lived electoral mandate, Nixon's goal was to cool down demands on the federal government. He gave clear signals that his administration would be less responsive (if not unresponsive) to the problems of black Americans. He nominated southern conservatives to the Supreme Court, became inaccessible to black politicians, focused attention on law and order issues and away from civil rights, and backed away from enforcement of the civil rights and voting rights acts.

To recapitulate, many veteran activists were co-opted into mainstream politics following achievement of the major goals of the movement; conversely, radicals disenchanted with the same results defected from the movement and sought alternative means of protest. As the movement traveled north to combat housing discrimination, de facto segregation, and employment problems, it had difficulty recruiting new supporters and was accused of going "too far" and "too fast" by many of its former allies. The turn to Black Power further alienated past supporters, and the close association between the civil rights and anti-war movements left civil rights leaders estranged from the Johnson administration. In the end, the accomplishments of the movement turned the country's attention away from the civil rights issue. Vietnam and law and order issues grabbed the spotlight. Although the civil rights movement had been immensely successful in defeating segregation in the South, it could not galvanize support for a new generation of social and economic problems.

THE DYNAMICS OF RISE AND DECLINE

To capture the dynamics of the rise and fall of collective action, we need to add to our model a term that measures the difference between the aspirations and the achievements of the activists. When this difference is great, members of the aggrieved group have a strong incentive to engage in collective action; when it is small, the motivation is appropriately reduced. Therefore consider that in every time period there are some new problems that emerge, or, more subjectively, are identified or defined by political leaders and targeted for solution. In conjunction with these problems, demands are formulated which accumulate if unmet and dissipate if satisfied. These are not necessarily all of the problems and demands of the group; rather, we should think of a subset of the group's grievances which for one reason or another (e.g., because they have clear solutions, because there is group agreement about how to address the problem, because they are highly symbolic) are capable of inspiring and sustaining collective action. Therefore, as in the previous version of this model, political leaders play a central role in the organization of collective action. By articulating the demands of the movement, political leaders give direction and a sense of purpose to the rank and file.

If D represents the constant or basic amount of demand that is formulated in every time period and $S(t)$ is the level of supply in period t, then in the course of T periods, the difference between the amount supplied and the amount demanded equals:

$$\sum_{t=1}^{T}(S - D).$$

Intuitively, if this sum is negative, political activism should be stimulated, and if it is positive, activism should be dampened. A group that has been neglected for a long time will require more concessions before it is placated than a group that has been catered to within the political process.

(I should note here that there of course need not be any constant amount of demand added in each period; it is merely a simple initial assumption in the model. Later I will consider how the dynamics of the model are affected if the number of demands formulated per period diminishes with time. In the case of the civil rights movement, I will argue that the inability of leaders of the movement to formulate new demands which could inspire collective action helped to precipitate the rapid decline of the movement.)

These additional features can be straightforwardly added to the model developed in chapter 7 by adjusting the mobilization equation to take into account the degree to which total supply has kept pace with accumulated demand:

$$M(t) = a + b[S(t) - \sum_{t=1}^{T}(S - D)]$$

$$+ c[M(t - 1) - \frac{1}{R}\sum_{t=1}^{T}(S - D)] - dO(t - 1). \quad (9.1)$$

$$S(t) = i + r_1 M(t - 1) - r_2 O(t - 1). \quad (9.2)$$

$$O(t) = pM(t). \quad (9.3)$$

where:

$M(t)$ and $M(t - 1)$ are the levels of mobilization in favor of change in periods t and $t - 1$, respectively;

$S(t)$ is the level of supply in period t;

$O(t)$ and $O(t - 1)$ are the levels of opposition to change in periods t and $t - 1$, respectively;

a is the size of the autonomous leadership;

b is the size of the bandwagon rate due to successful collective action—"success" being defined by the level of supply $S(t)$; therefore $bS(t)$ is the number of additional people who become active as a result of this success;

c is the size of the contagion rate due to successful mobilization in period $t - 1$; therefore $cM(t - 1)$ is the number of people who become active in period t because other people are active in period $t - 1$;

d is the strength of the deterrents to participation in collective action;

p is the opposition's rate of countermobilization;

i is the amount of government initiative per period;

r_1 is the rate of government responsiveness to the proponents of change;

r_2 is the rate of government responsiveness to the opponents of change;

$\sum_{t=1}^{T}(S - D)$ is the difference between total supply and total demand over T time periods; and

$1/R$ is an adjustment factor which makes the units of supply commensurate with the units of mobilization; $R = (r_1 - r_2 p)$.

Here as before, participation in collective action is stimulated by the level of supply in the current period and the level of mobilization in the preceding period, except that now $S(t)$ and $M(t - 1)$ are either discounted or augmented by the amount of excess supply or demand accumulated over the course of T periods.

If demand outstrips supply, the difference (a negative number),

$$\sum_{t=1}^{T}(S - D) < 0$$

is *subtracted* from the current level of supply $S(t)$ and the previous level of mobilization $M(t - 1)$; the totals are then multiplied by b and c, respectively, to give an additional boost to the current level of mobilization. But notice that if the level of mobilization escalates and is met by a correspondingly stepped-up level of supply which exceeds the basic demand per period, the accumulated difference between total supply and total demand shrinks, and with it the stimulus to future collective action. As the authorities compensate for their past neglect, and the activists reach their goals, people become satisfied and have less reason and motivation to agitate for change. Or people may become so deeply disappointed with the results they have achieved that they will be either turned off by political activism or motivated to express themselves through alternative channels. Both developments slow the momentum behind collective action.

If mobilization and supply continue to fuel each other, accumulated supply may eventually exceed the storehouse of demands that constitutes the basis for collective action. When this occurs, the supply-and-demand process begins to unravel. The surplus dampens the stimulative effect of both current supply and previous mobilization on mobilization in the current period. When the two expressions in parentheses

$$[S(t) - \sum_{t=1}^{T}(S - D)]$$

and

$$[M(t - 1) - \frac{1}{R} \sum_{t=1}^{T}(S - D)]$$

turn negative, the bandwagon and contagion processes become bandwagons *in reverse* as people defect from the movement. People withdraw because they believe the movement is going beyond its original goals.

Of course there remains the question of why demand skyrockets and then collapses with equal suddenness. As people get their fill of social change, why doesn't the level of activism instead dampen down to some stable, moderate level without for all intents and purposes being eliminated?

The main reason, I will show, is that governments tend to be unresponsive to social movements until they have reached major proportions. Movements, in turn, tend to have only a limited store of ideas, demands, and goals that are capable of sustaining individual participation in collective action. Consequently when the government finally responds favorably to popular pressure, the concessions it makes quickly remove the impetus behind the movement, causing participants to suffer from the series of responses just outlined that are each detrimental to further collective action. After the basic demands of the group, $\sum_{t=1}^{T} D$, have been answered, the movement loses its momentum unless its leaders can develop new projects that are amenable to large-scale political activism. Barring new goals that enjoy a consensus among the rank and file, the movement founders. Activists withdraw because they are either satisfied or disappointed with their achievements, or because they are unhappy with the new direction taken by factions within the movement.

These results will become more apparent as we examine the dynamics of the supply-and-demand model under varying assumptions about the responsiveness of the government and the relative strengths of the proponents and opponents of change.

When we substitute equation (9.3) into equation (9.1) and expand, we obtain:

$$M(t) = a + bS(t) - b\sum_{t=1}^{T} S + b\sum_{t=1}^{T} D + cM(t - 1) - \frac{c}{R}\sum_{t=1}^{T} S$$
$$+ \frac{c}{R}\sum_{t=1}^{T} D - dpM(t - 1)$$

$$= (a + bTD - \frac{ci}{R} + \frac{cTD}{R}) - (b + \frac{c}{R}) \sum_{t=1}^{T-1} S - dpM(t - 1). \quad (9.4)$$

The summation sign can be eliminated by writing out the equation for two successive time periods, $M(t)$ and $M(t - 1)$, and taking their difference to produce a standard second-order difference equation.

$$M(t) - M(t - 1) = [\frac{cD}{R} + bD] - dpM(t - 1) + dpM(t - 2)$$

$$- (b + \frac{c}{R})S(t - 1). \quad (9.5)$$

Substituting for S in the mobilization equation gives us:

$$M(t) - M(t - 1) = (b + \frac{c}{R})(D - i) - dpM(t - 1)$$

$$- (bR + c - dp)M(t - 2), \quad (9.6)$$

or

$$M(t) = (b + \frac{c}{R})(D - i) + (1 - dp)M(t - 1)$$

$$- (bR + c - dp)M(t - 2). \quad (9.7)$$

Consider first the equilibrium level of mobilization. Setting all of the M values in equation (9.6) to some constant M^* and solving, we obtain:

$$0 = (b + \frac{c}{R}) (D - i) - (bR + c) M^*,$$

or

$$M^* = \frac{D - i}{R}. \quad (9.8)$$

The prerequisite for the existence of an equilibrium is therefore extremely simple: R cannot equal 0.

As previously, the equilibrium value represents the level at which political mobilization will stabilize (if it is reached). Notice, however, that the equilibrium is now explicitly tied to the degree to which the demands of the aggrieved group have been satisfied. The numerator, $(D - i)$, is the difference between the amount of demand generated per period and the per period or basic level of supply as a result of government initiative. Therefore if the government addresses the concerns of the group in a timely manner, there will be no accumulation of demand

and by implication no incentive for the group to resort to collective action.

The same result will be achieved if the group runs out of demands after its initial goals have been reached, in which case M^* will equal $-i/R$. As long as $i \geq 0$, collective action will collapse. Therefore a movement cannot be sustained unless its leaders continually replenish its agenda for change. A satisfied movement is quickly relegated to the pages of history. This may be why leaders are harder to locate for one-shot lumpy goods. As Frohlich, Oppenheimer, and Young (1971) point out, "Durable collective goods raise problems for such a leader since they limit his activities to a 'one-shot' enterprise. If he has promised to provide bridges, for example, and the bridges are supplied, the leader must turn to new programs or vacate the leadership role" (55).

At the other extreme, if the group's problems have not been completely met by government initiative ($D \neq i$) and on balance government responsiveness is either 0 or favors those who oppose change (i.e., $R \leq 0$), the equilibrium level of mobilization will in the first case be unbounded at positive infinity and in the second case be negative. Technically, of course, no equilibrium will exist when the denominator, R, equals 0.

Finally, note that in this version of the model a favorable government response to the proponents of change stimulates a bandwagon effect but nevertheless lowers the equilibrium level of mobilization. This is because supply satisfies the demands of the protesters at the same time that it fuels additional mobilization; subsequent mobilization therefore tapers off as the group's demands are met. In the initial version of the model presented in chapter 7, supply fueled both additional mobilization and additional demand, so that it was impossible for the level of mobilization to outstrip the number of outstanding demands.

Even when there is a high equilibrium level of mobilization (because R is small), collective action may remain dormant or "latent" for a lengthy period. This is because in the mobilization equation, the term representing accumulated demand is multiplied by the bandwagon and contagion coefficients. If these coefficients are equal to 0, the level of mobilization will not increase beyond its initial level, while if they are positive but negligible, mobilization will increase at an extremely slow rate. Recall that the strength of the bandwagon and contagion rates depends especially on the availability of effective leaders and on the extent to which the group is connected by social and political organizations. All told then, weak leadership and anemic organization may prevent the group from effectively pressing its demands in the political arena. Here the model departs from more conventional "frustration-aggression" premises which hold that people take to the streets in increasing numbers as their basic demands are left unmet: the more a group is denied, in other words, the more assertive it becomes.

In my view, the dynamics of the frustration-aggression model are too smooth and continuous: neglect leads automatically to discontent and then to collective action. There really are no collective action problems of the sort that we have been reviewing and trying to resolve. Conversely, by treating accumulated demand as an underlying factor, we acknowledge that the long-term frustration of wants and desires creates the potential for political activism, yet also recognize that additional coordination problems must still be surmounted before collective action is manifest.

Moreover, the separate treatment of political demand and organizational strength in the model helps to account for the apparently sudden and unexpected "explosion" of political activism. All seems relatively quiet and normal at one moment, and then the underlying demand is successfully organized and coordinated by political entrepreneurs and released into the political process. A marked increase in b and c will provoke new mobilization that is proportional not just to the current level of supply (b times $S(t)$) and the previous level of mobilization (c times $M(t - 1)$), but to these levels of supply and mobilization *plus* the accumulated amount of demand that has not been delivered over the course of preceding time periods. For example, figure 9.1 traces the time path of political mobilization over twenty-five periods when b and c equal .01, while figure 9.2 shows how the trajectory of this path moves steeply upward when b and c are raised to .5.

Therefore when there is considerable backed-up demand and, in the extreme case, the b and c rates increase dramatically from 0 or near 0 to some large number, the level of mobilization will leap sharply above previous levels. It will seem as if a group, after being dormant and locked out of the political process for an extended period, suddenly chooses to pour out all of its past and present grievances. I hasten to add, however, that I suspect such cases will be rare. The organizational process is more likely to take place gradually over an extended period, although there may be some critical event—e.g., an arrest, a killing, a funeral—that suddenly coordinates demands and makes the movement appear to be more spontaneous than it actually is.

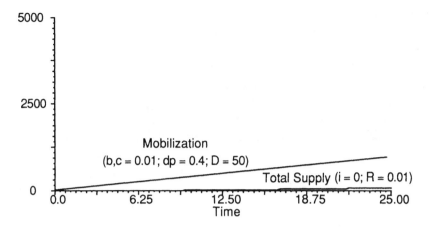

FIGURE 9.1. Mobilization Increases Slowly with Weak Organization

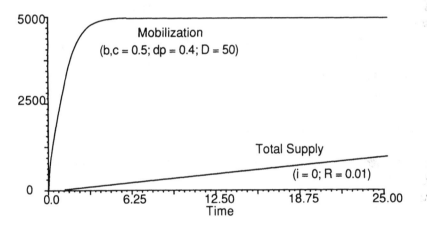

FIGURE 9.2. Mobilization Increases Rapidly with Strong Organization

Consider more closely what it means for the level of mobilization to reach equilibrium. Put in the most neutral terms, when the system is in equilibrium, the level of mobilization is neither increasing nor decreasing but maintaining a steady state; specifically, this steady state is maintained because the level of supply per period equals the level of demand generated per period. What we have to bear in mind is that even though at equilibrium the *present* rates of supply and demand are in harmony, this does not imply that *total* supply has necessarily caught up with *total* demand. At the point where the system attains equilibrium, total supply may have caught up with total demand, or it may continue to lag behind. Consequently the level of mobilization can attain equilibrium at any point from a very high level (when there is a backlog of unmet past demand) to 0 (when total demand has been completely satisfied) to a negative value—in practice unrealizable—(when there has been an oversupply of the collective good).

So that this point can be better appreciated, I provide below two contrasting illustrations of the process by which the level of mobilization attains stability. In the first example, basic demand, D, greatly exceeds government initiatives, i, b equals .1, c equals .3, R equals .1, and dp equals .2. Under these assumptions, the level of mobilization increases sharply at first and then continues to grow but at a progressively slower rate before ultimately flattening out at the equilibrium value when $S(t)$ equals D. (See figure 9.3.) Notice that despite having settled into a steady state, mobilization has increased substantially since the opening period; consequently there is a stable state in the model but not necessarily a happy or stable state of political affairs in reality. Although collective action has leveled, it has become a relatively permanent presence in the society because of the government's sluggish response to the group's overall demands. In essence the group has determined that it can extract sufficient (per period) concessions from the government only by maintaining a high level of mobilization.

Compare these results to the second example, which begins where the first example ends, with $M = 400$. If we increase the rate of government responsiveness (from .1 to .4), as well as the level of govern-

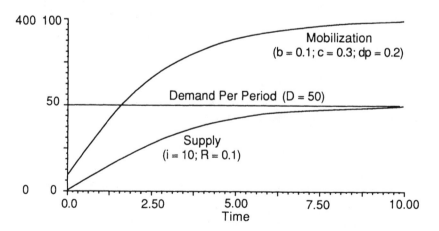

FIGURE 9.3. Mobilization Climbs Until Supply Equals Demand Generated Per Period. The outer vertical scale is for $M(t)$, while the inner scale is for $S(t)$ and D.

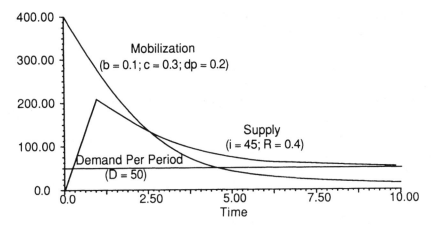

FIGURE 9.4. Mobilization Plummets as Government Initiative and Responsiveness Increase

ment initiative (from 10 to 45), while leaving all else equal, we see that the level of mobilization declines steadily. (See figure 9.4.) The drop-off occurs because the level of supply is so high initially that it satisfies not only current basic demand but also a portion of the demand that has accumulated over past periods. As this backed-up demand is gradually dissipated, the level of mobilization adjusts downward until it reaches equilibrium when supply equals the basic amount demanded per period.

As these examples illustrate, the system can attain equilibrium at considerably varying levels, all of which technically represent stability but which in reality can represent significantly different substantive results. Under the first set of assumptions made above, collective action gains in strength before stabilizing at a high equilibrium value. In contrast, under the second set of assumptions the high rates of government initiative and responsiveness prompt steady demobilization.

As shown above in equation (9.8), the equilibrium level of mobilization depends on the two sources of government output and on the basic amount of demand per period. Government initiative, i, is a negative term in the numerator of the equilibrium formula, while the responsiveness coefficient is in the denominator. Therefore the effect of increasing either term, ceteris paribus, is to lower the equilibrium point. In other words, the equilibrium value can be lowered to any given level by increasing either (1) government initiative in addressing and resolving the activists' grievances or (2) government responsiveness to the activists' demands. For example, one way to reduce mobilization to zero is by setting the amount of initiative equal to the basic level of demand; alternatively, if basic demand exceeds government initiative, the equilibrium value can still be reduced as close to zero as desired by increasing the responsiveness factor. (The equilibrium value $\rightarrow 0$ as $R \rightarrow \infty$.) While superficially it appears that there is little to choose between the two methods—either will lower the point at which the system will stabilize—it turns out that they have quite different impacts on the time path or dynamics of the system. Indeed, how the coefficients representing the two forms of supply are adjusted can make the difference between whether the system will eventually stabilize or will fall out of kilter and remain disequilibrated.

THE TIME PATH OF POLITICAL MOBILIZATION

Technically the time path that political mobilization will follow is determined by the roots of the characteristic equation associated with the model.

This characteristic equation, a quadratic,

$$m^2 - (1 - dp)m + (bR + c - dp) = 0 \tag{9.9}$$

has the standard solution

$$m_1, m_2 = \frac{(1 - dp) \pm \sqrt{(1 - dp)^2 - 4(bR + c - dp)}}{2}. \tag{9.10}$$

Notice that i, the degree of government initiative, is nowhere to be found in the quadratic formula and therefore plays no role in the time path of the system. Consequently fluctuations in i will not have ramifications for the dynamics of mobilization, in contrast to changes in R, which may affect the time path as well as, by implication, whether or not the system will attain equilibrium.

Some reflection makes this result less surprising than it may at first appear. While collective action is stimulated by both sources of supply, only one source—that which is the result of government responsiveness—is in turn affected by the stepped-up mobilization. There is no reciprocal linkage between government initiative and mobilization; hence we refer to such supply as "autonomous." When i is changed, this simply alters the level of mobilization by some constant amount without altering the path (oscillatory, monotonic, or constant) of $M(t)$. (As we shall see shortly, it was the lack of government initiative on the race issue that contributed to the crisis atmosphere in the early 1960s.)

SOLUTION OF THE GENERAL EQUATION

Although I will not go into the details of why (the reader is referred to Goldberg 1958, 134–43), the two root m_1 and m_2 enter into the solution of the mobilization equation (9.7) as follows:

$$M(t) = k_1 m_1{}^t + k_2 m_2 t + \frac{D - i}{R}, \qquad (9.11)$$

where k_1 and k_2 are arbitrary constants that are determined by the first two starting values of the system; and

$$\frac{D - i}{R}$$

is a familiar constant, the equilibrium point M^* of the system. The parameters of the model (b, c, d, p, and R) therefore determine, as specified by equation (9.10), the roots of the characteristic equation (9.9). In turn, these roots determine the time path of political mobilization according to equation (9.11).

Intuitively we can draw several conclusions about how the dynamics of the system will be affected by the roots m_1 and m_2. First, since both roots are raised to the power t, if they are positive but less than 1, both $k_1 m_1{}^t$ and $k_2 m_2{}^t$ will decrease in size over time and approach 0 in the limit; consequently $M(t)$ will follow a monotonic path to the equilibrium point M^*.

If both roots are positive, but one is greater than 1, then the solution function will contain an explosive component. A root greater than unity, taken to increasingly higher powers, will increase without bound. As a result, $M(t)$ will not stabilize but instead diverge.

A negative root adds an oscillatory term to the time path of mobilization, since a negative number taken to an even power (time periods 2, 4, 6, . . .) results in a positive product, while a negative number raised to an odd power (time periods 1, 3, 5, . . .) remains an odd number. If the absolute value of this root is less than 1, the oscillation will be damped over time and converge on 0; if its absolute value is greater than 1, the oscillation will increase in amplitude over time and the time path will be divergent.

Given any two roots, it can be shown that the root with the largest absolute value will have the dominant effect on the time path of the system. To illustrate, if $0 < m_1 < 1$ and $m_2 > 1$, the $m_1{}^t$ term in the solution will approach 0 in the limit, while the $m_2{}^t$ term will grow without bound. The net result is an unbounded time path for the level of mobilization. In general, since any root less than 1 in absolute value leads to a convergent path (either damped oscillatory or monotonic), while any root greater than 1 in absolute value leads to a divergent path (oscillatory or monotonic), any solution containing a mixture of these two types of roots will be divergent, because the convergent component of the solution will eventually vanish, leaving only the divergent component.

A slight complication occurs when the number under the square root sign in the quadratic formula is negative. When $(1 - dp)^2 < 4(bR + c - dp)$, the roots of the system are complex numbers.

Complex roots give rise to the following solution equation:

$$M(t) = k_1 \mu^t \cos(t\theta + k_2). \qquad (9.12)$$

For our purposes, all we need to note about this complicated expression is that it involves the product of a constant (k_1), a "modulus" (μ), and a cosine function that oscillates evenly between -1 and $+1$. Because there is a cosine function in the solution, the time path of $M(t)$ will always oscillate; whether $M(t)$ will eventually stabilize depends essentially on the size of μ. If μ is greater than one, the time path of mobilization will diverge (that is, it will cut an increasingly broad swath); however, if μ is less than one, the level of mobilization will dampen down to a stable equilibrium. It can be shown easily (see Goldberg 1958, 172) that the modulus equals the third coefficient of the characteristic equation (9.9); in our particular model, this means that $\mu = (bR + c - dp)$.

STABILITY CONDITIONS OF THE MODEL

A basic theorem in the theory of linear difference equations states that the roots of the general characteristic equation $m^2 + Bm + C = 0$ will be less than one in absolute value (thus ensuring a stable system) if the coefficients of the equation satisfy three necessary and sufficient conditions:

(i) $1 + B + C > 0$.
(ii) $1 - B + C > 0$.
(iii) $1 - C > 0$.

Substituting the coefficients of equation (9.9) into the first inequality gives us:

(i) $bR + c > 0$. $\qquad (9.13)$

This means that the sum of the factors stimulating mobilization—the contagion rate plus the product of the bandwagon rate and the rate of government responsiveness—must be greater than zero. On the assumption that $b, c > 0$, this inequality will hold as long as R is greater than or equal to zero. If, on the contrary, R is negative and $(bR + c) \leq 0$, then one of the roots will be equal to or greater than 1, while the other root will be less than or equal to $-dp$. The first root drives the level of mobilization upwards without bound (collective action expands as demands are left unmet), while the second root dampens political mobilization. If the deterrents to the movement (opposition combined with repression) are sufficiently potent that the second root has the largest absolute value of the two roots, the level of mobilization will rise but then eventually collapse. The speed of the demise varies directly with the strength of the deterrents.

If, conversely, the absolute value of the first root is larger, then $M(t)$ will increase at a pace that is directly related to the size of the positive root. In practice, however, when $R \leq 0$, the rates of recruitment will often be correspondingly small because the prospects of success are so poor; therefore collective action may remain inchoate indefinitely even though the level of mobilization is increasing slowly over time.

The second prerequisite for a stable equilibrium is:

$$\text{(ii)} \quad bR + c > 2(dp - 1). \tag{9.14}$$

If (9.13) holds, (9.14) is violated only when dp is sufficiently large (dp must at least be > 1). This means that the root with the largest absolute value will be < -1. Again, depending on the strength of the opposition, this implies that the movement will be brought down either immediately or in the long-run.

The third and final condition for a stable system is:

$$\text{(iii)} \quad bR + c < 1 + dp. \tag{9.15}$$

This condition stipulates that the forces stimulating political mobilization cannot be excessive. When this inequality is violated, the level of mobilization oscillates along an unbounded path. There are two primary substantive interpretations of this result. If the government is hostile (R is negative), collective action disbands without achieving any of its goals because political activism is self-defeating: political mobilization stimulates supply that runs contrary to the interests of the group. On the other hand, if R is positive, the level of mobilization climbs rapidly and collapses when the goals of the movement are met and exceeded. In other words, mobilization fuels and in turn is fueled by a high level of supply, but when total supply outstrips total demand, the level of mobilization suddenly "peaks out" and plummets to zero and below, where we no longer provide a substantive interpretation of the results beyond saying that collective action has collapsed.

In effect, the system is thrown out of kilter—overheated—but is then sharply overcorrected. The response of the authorities is sufficiently great that participants in the movement get all that they require and more in order to prompt them to bail out of the movement. The cooling mechanism in the system doesn't bring demand down to some manageable level and set it on an even keel; it douses it completely.

THE PATH OF THE CIVIL RIGHTS MOVEMENT

I stated earlier that in the first part of the twentieth century through the twenties and thirties, mass collective action was precluded by heavy resistance in the country at large and indifference and hostility at all levels of government. These obstacles to collective action were compounded by weak organization and a pessimistic if not hopeless attitude in the black community. In terms of the model parameters, b and c—the two propensities to participate in collective action—were small; the overall rate of responsiveness, $R = (r_1 - r_2 p)$, was zero or negative; while dp, the term reflecting the rate and strength of resistance, was large. Given that either of the first two stability conditions was not met, so long as dp was sufficiently large, the root with the largest absolute value was negative. Thus, attempts to initiate collective action were immediately snuffed out; the time path of mobilization rose briefly but then dropped to zero and below.

These various barriers were gradually overcome between the mid-thirties and the mid-fifties, when a number of social and political changes created the necessary conditions for action on the "Negro problem" in America. Scholarship was contradicting racist stereotypes and ideas about blacks; the war against fascism abroad focused American attention on the shortcomings of their own putative democratic society; the migration of blacks into northern cities increased their political power; the war economy upgraded the economic standing of blacks; cities provided more protective enclaves; black churches and colleges became more effective centers for the organization of collective action; all three branches of government began to give more weight to black concerns and grievances—all these developments stepped up the rate of recruitment to the civil rights movement by marginally increasing R, reducing dp, and increasing b and c. This is familiar territory and no more need be said.

Turn now to the new parameter added to the model in this chapter. As defined earlier this parameter, $\sum_{t=1}^{T}(S - D)$ represents the difference between the programmatic aspirations and actual accomplishments of the civil rights movement aggregated over the course of T time periods. During these decades, the black community's demands for social change accumulated and greatly exceeded the degree of actual reform. To the extent that the status of blacks was improved in the early postwar years, this scarcely dented the total amount of change being sought and served mainly to encourage still greater efforts to achieve additional reforms on the road to complete social and political equality.

The long-standing refusal of the local and national governments to initiate or respond to pressure for social reform on the race issue permitted this buildup of demand. If, contrary to fact, the amount of initiative per period (i) had kept pace with the amount of demand generated per period (D), or if the rate of responsiveness had been much greater, $\sum_{t=1}^{T}(S - D)$ would have been close to zero, and there would have been little incentive for blacks to organize protest actions. Rather than taking off as it did, the time path of mobilization would have simply stabilized at a relatively low equilibrium. The scenario modeled in figure 9.4, for example, shows how the level of mobilization, $M(t)$, decreases when both government initiative and responsiveness are sufficient to meet the demands of the group.

But events unfolded otherwise. For years the federal government had procrastinated and stood by, creating commissions to study the race problem while blacks were being beaten, lynched, and denied due process and basic individual rights and liberties. Though Truman's Commission on Civil Rights reported that it had been "shocked" and "ashamed" by its findings on the treatment of blacks in this country, it was still up to Congress to take remedial action, but Congress refused to do so (Sundquist 1968, 222). In 1953, weak civil rights bills authorizing investigative commissions and more ambitious legislation outlawing segregation in interstate transportation and discriminatory employment practices stalled at various stages in the legislative process.

Civil rights legislation was completely shunted aside in the first three years of Eisenhower's administration. The new administration saw little profit in expending energy in an area that had proven so fruitless in the Truman presidency; moreover it preferred not to disrupt its working relationship with southern Democrats (ibid., 223). Eisenhower also believed that the power and authority of the federal government should be constrained. His public pronouncements concerning civil rights reflected his conviction that social customs best evolve at their own pace rather than at an "artificial" rate mandated by new laws. He endorsed Sumner's dictum that "stateways do not change folkways." "I believe in programs accomplished through the intelligence of people and through the cooperation of people more than law, if we can get it that way" (Sundquist 1968, 224).

It was not until his 1957 State of the Union address that Eisenhower strongly endorsed a four-part civil rights bill, which after being weakened by amendments became the Civil Rights Act of 1957. While the 1957 act broadened voting rights, it did not provide any federal authority to deal with southern resistance to school desegregation, which was the major civil rights problem at that time. Southern officials were using their wits to devise legitimate means to sidestep the Supreme Court edict, resorting in many instances to closing schools down rather than allowing them to be integrated. Eisenhower found it necessary to order federal troops into Little Rock, Arkansas, to enforce the integration of a high school. Civil rights proponents cited the 1957 act as evidence that only anemic civil rights legislation would be able to sneak through the Senate without being filibustered.

Ironically, a secondary provision of the 1957 act that created a Civil Rights Commission proved to be the most potent aspect of the law. What the commission did was document and publicize the widespread abuses of voting rights in the South that the 1957 act was unable to remedy. Because blacks were being systematically excluded from registering, the commission recommended that the federal government be empowered to register voters in those counties where discrimination had been certified (Sundquist 1968, 244). Nonetheless, Eisenhower continued to procrastinate and, in place of the commission's assertive recommendation, he offered a second "moderate" civil rights bill that provided additional measures to ensure fair federal election procedures. This bill passed in 1960 and, like the 1957 Civil Rights Act, was hailed as a victory for the southerners, since it again forestalled meaningful federal action in several areas of concern, including desegregation of public schools and public facilities.

Matters came to a head in the early 1960s, when an increasingly restless, growing civil rights movement escalated its pressure on local communities and the federal government to provide concessions or risk the danger of explosive civil disturbances in cities throughout the country. By the time the government finally developed the resolve to confront the race issue squarely, black demands for equality had become so forceful and their anger and frustration so apparent that the government no longer held a viable option to pursue an ameliorative and moderate strategy of social change. "It had become urgent," Hodgson (1976) writes, "to take action effective enough and swift enough to meet the mounting surge of black impatience" (158). Similarly, Sitkoff (1981) comments on the pressing need for decisive governmental action to steady the nation at this juncture: "The President . . . had to dampen the explosive potential for widespread racial violence and to maintain the confidence of the mass of blacks in government" (156).

Kennedy himself voiced the same dire conclusion, that "events in Birmingham and elsewhere have so increased the cries for equality that no city or state or legislative body can prudently choose to ignore them." The answer lay not in "repressive police action" or "token moves or talk." Rather, the President admonished, "It is a time to act in the Congress, in your state and local legislative body, and, above all, in all our daily lives" (Sitkoff 1981, 158). The administration's reasoning went as follows:

> If the uprising would not die down among the Negro masses, and could not be dampened by Negro leaders, how could they avoid a nightmarish string of Birminghams? President Kennedy toyed briefly with legislating "a reasonable limitation of the right to demonstration," but switched quickly to the idea of civil rights legislation. All his aides recognized that legislation on some of the basic Negro demands offered the advantage of "biting the bullet"—of getting past the dilemma with one difficult but sweeping move. (Branch 1988, 808)

Thus cornered by the circumstances, the administration responded by sponsoring a sweeping new civil rights bill that included provisions for desegregating public accommodations and schools, eliminating discriminatory practices in federally funded programs and facilities, studying and implementing methods for reducing racial strife, and promoting economic opportunities for blacks.

Formal racial equality—at the polling place, in public accommodations, and in public schools—was something that white America on the whole was prepared to support and, as Hodgson (1976, 180) puts it, willing to "give" to blacks. Considering the general intransigence in the country on the issue of civil rights only a few short years earlier, this was itself an impressive development. The irony here is that while the core of the civil rights movement was united in demanding formal equality for blacks, there were already at this time more radical elements within the movement who were clamoring for something beyond equality of political rights—not formal but actual equality between the conditions of their lives and those of the white majority. At this juncture in the civil rights movement, these activists were running out of patience with the sluggishness of the political process because reforms had come haltingly when they had been made at all.

The delicacy of the situation at this stage stems from the historical path of the civil rights movement. Because the national government was slow to respond to the race issue, civil rights activists had to organize largely without the benefit of political sponsorship. This meant that they could not rely on their past success at squeezing concessions from the government as a way to attract greater support for their efforts; instead, the growth of the movement had to rely heavily on dedication, determination, and an idealistic and perhaps unrealistic optimism about their ability to transform the American political system and society.

In other words, when government responsiveness, R, is small, the movement cannot expand on the basis of its success. Consequently collective action is viable only if (1) the rates of recruitment to the movement, b and c, are sufficiently large; and (2) the participants are not easily frustrated by their lack of success. Rapid recruitment combined with a low rate of responsiveness, however, forewarns of possible trouble. It means that the rate of mobilization is high, grievances have accumulated, and the governmental response is inadequate. Under the circumstances, the only way that significant concessions can be wrested from the government is by sustaining high levels of mobilization and pressure.

It was thus in this context of increasing social turmoil that the Kennedy and Johnson administrations worked in concert with an activist Congress and "brought to a harvest a generation's backlog of ideas and social legislation" (Schlesinger 1965, 18). C. Vann Woodward (1967) traces the debt even further into the past, seeing it as "a period of restitution, an effort to fulfill promises a century old, the redemption of a historic commitment" (34).

As noteworthy as the *degree* of change was the *pace* of change. "Things did change," Hodgson (1976) writes, "and with remarkable speed.

> The federal government did move to positions that would have been unthinkably radical only a few years before. The poverty program is an example. The billions of federal money poured into compensa-

tory education add up to another. The standard President Johnson proposed . . . was not mere equality of opportunity but equality of condition: "not equality as a right and a theory, but equality as a fact and a result." The clear implication of that standard was that, to reach that result, the federal government and the other institutions of society must go beyond equality in their treatment of a historically disadvantaged minority. They must accept the principle of compensation. (181)

This explosion of supply and demand can be explained as follows. As collective action escalates, there are only two ways for the government to alleviate the (manifested) political pressure that has accumulated in the system. These are (1) to drastically step up the level of repression, or (2) to provide concessions through some combination of initiative and responsiveness.

Repression, under the circumstances, is akin to putting a lid on a boiling pot. The popular protest may be cowed but the underlying grievances will remain and will eventually spark renewed activity in the future (when the protesters become better organized or when the weight of repression is lifted).

When the federal government instead responded favorably to the civil rights movement in the mid-1960s with a torrent of progressive legislation, this immediately stimulated the movement to further activity, but then dampened and stopped its momentum. We would anticipate the first part of this outcome in light of the assumptions of our model. If the movement took off despite low government responsiveness, because the black community was sufficiently cohesive and organized to be mobilized, this means that the rates of recruitment to the movement, b and c, were large enough to initiate and sustain collective action. Obviously the best way to combat a low rate of responsiveness is to generate a high level of mobilization, because $S(t)$ is a function of $M(t - 1)$. As the political pressure escalated, the government made concessions to the movement. These concessions in turn fueled further political mobilization, which induced even further concessions. The question is why didn't this process continue indefinitely?

From the properties of our model of political mobilization, we can deduce that this spiraling process can be sustained only if the movement continually generates new goals for itself. If, for example, new demands are constantly added at a rate of D per period, it is possible that the movement will maintain a high level of mobilization in pursuit of one generation of goals after another. Fresh demands therefore fore-

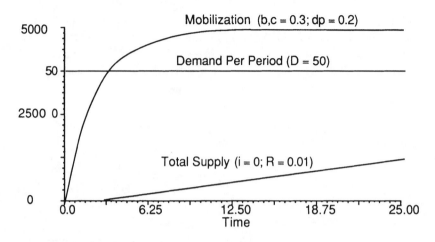

FIGURE 9.5. Mobilization is Sustained by Constant New Demands. The outer vertical scale is for M(t) and ΣS, while the inner scale is for Dw^t.

stall the letdown inevitably associated with the achievement of the movement's goals. Figure 9.5, for example, shows how a continually replenished reservoir of demands is capable of supporting a high level of political mobilization. The movement regularly forces concessions from the authorities, but there are always new demands to pursue.

But this is clearly an unrealistic scenario. Most mass movements are focused on a small number of goals, if not a single objective, such as passing a law, amending the constitution, winning the right to vote, ending a war, ousting a dictator, and so on. Once the central goals of the movement have been fulfilled, it is difficult for the leaders of the movement to generate new goals that have the same magnitude and carry the same urgency as those just accomplished. The absence of new goals in the movement promotes the decline of collective action.

The key factor in this process therefore is the value of D. As we saw in figure 9.5, if D is a positive constant, it is conceivable that the movement will persist even if the authorities are responsive, because it will be continually motivated by new goals. But what happens if we assume that demand dissipates over time? In particular, what if the level of demand added per period equals Dw^t, where w is some constant and t indexes the period of time ($t = 1, 2, 3, \ldots$). If w equals 1, then demand is the same constant D that we have assumed in the analysis to this point. If w is greater than 1, the level of demand added per period increases over time. Finally, if w is less than 1, the level of demand generated declines in each succeeding period and eventually shrinks to zero.

Allowing demand to vary over time in this fashion does not change the solution of equation (9.7), but it does alter the equilibrium of the system, M^*, in a straightforward manner. It can be easily shown that M^* now equals:

$$\frac{Dw^t - i}{R}$$

instead of $(D - i)/R$.

Obviously if w is greater than 1, our system of political mobilization and supply can have no equilibrium: w^t and therefore Dw^t and M^* will increase without bound. On the other hand, if w is less than 1, an equilibrium will exist, but it will diminish over time. M^* will be at a maximum when $t = 1$ and will become progressively smaller as t increases because $w^t \to 0$ as $t \to \infty$. Therefore at "large" values of t, M^* will equal $-i/R$.

More importantly, fluctuations in M^* over time carry interesting implications for the dynamics of supply and political mobilization. For the simulation illustrated in figure 9.6, the parameters of the model are identical to the parameters underlying the process traced in figure 9.5, except that demand per period now equals Dw^t (where $w = .9999$). As in the previous simulation, political mobilization and supply reinforce each other initially and both climb upward. However, unlike the previous simulation, as total supply begins to reduce the reservoir of total demand, the level of mobilization begins to drop precipitously. (If in addition the rate of responsiveness increases at this stage, the descent will be even more rapid.) Without the stimulus of future plans

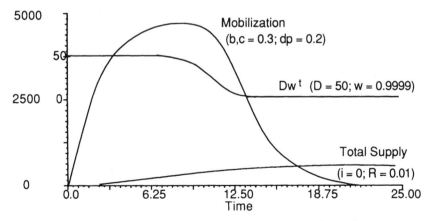

FIGURE 9.6. Mobilization Declines as Demands Are Satisfied. The outer vertical scale is for M(t) and ΣS, while the inner scale is for Dw^t.

and projects, participants in the movement grow complacent if not disappointed with their accomplishments.

In sum, the movement succeeds only when it is able to apply considerable pressure on the government. For the variety of reasons I have discussed throughout the book, this is a very difficult prerequisite to fulfill because many of the incentives to contribute to collective action are directly related to its prospects of success. Nevertheless, a movement that climbs this hurdle and consequently wins substantial concessions must then regenerate itself with a new sense of purpose. More often than not, a successful movement declines because it has accomplished the significant elements of its agenda and there are no further plans on the horizon that can stimulate another round of activism. Unfortunately the demise of the movement is also frequently accompanied by a corresponding decline in government responsiveness to the concerns of the group. The government, in other words, reverts to its earlier practice of ignoring calls for reform until there is another crescendo of demand.

Such an interpretation can be placed on the path of the civil rights movement in the 1960s. Even though the movement continued to make substantial gains through the early sixties, discontent rose within its ranks. The leaders of the movement were running out of powerful ideas to hold the attention and dedication of the rank and file. Activists reflected on their accomplishments and were either satisfied with the impressive legal reforms they had helped to bring about or, conversely, dismayed by the negligible changes in the day-to-day circumstances of blacks. Others viewed the radicalization of the movement as a disturbing departure from its original intent. Together these factors prompted the movement's sudden demise.

Once extinguished, the civil rights movement could not be restarted. The fragmenting of the civil rights coalition and the falling out between the movement's leaders and the White House hurt the recruitment rate of the movement, reduced government responsiveness, and magnified the level of frustration among activists. Fewer people were willing to participate in a new round of activism because they were tired, devoted their available energies to antiwar protests, did not share in the more radical philosophy and goals of the ascendant leadership, or had lost faith in a less responsive government. Lastly, popular resistance to the new goals was heightened, so that the dampening effects of political opposition were more pronounced.

There is potentially great irony in this outcome. Although the movement has succeeded in accomplishing its original objectives, its subsequent demise, combined with the public backlash against the rapid pace of social change, create the conditions for another extended period in which the problems of the aggrieved group are given less than adequate attention. New demands are once again allowed to accumulate, and collective pressure is permitted to build before the government is inclined to respond.

10 | *Conclusion*

The story is told. I think I now see the judicious reader putting on his spectacles to look for the moral.

Charlotte Brontë, *Shirley*

By the time the civil rights movement had run its course, it had permanently changed the nature of social relations in this country. So great was its impact that some writers marked the movement's demise in the late 1960s as the end of the "Second American Revolution."

For centuries the race problem had been the shame of the nation. Blacks remained a subjugated caste in a country that prided itself on its egalitarian tradition. Despite glimmers of hope during Reconstruction that this contradiction between ideal and reality would be erased, almost a century later, black Americans continued to be segregated from the rest of society and denied their political rights. Clearly white America was not about to extend its hand to bring blacks into the social, political, and economic mainstream without a struggle.

To win their rights, blacks had to organize and press their demands for reform. World War II and all the changes it wrought played a major part in providing the impetus for the black revolt, which sputtered and stalled before finally taking hold—if we can ever pinpoint such things—in that dramatic moment when seamstress and NAACP veteran Rosa Parks refused to give up her seat to a white passenger on a local bus, the incident that sparked the Montgomery bus boycott. She had, in the felicitous phrase of Martin Luther King, Jr., simply been "captured by the zeitgeist—the spirit of the times."

The Montgomery campaign provided an auspicious beginning to the civil rights movement. Because it attracted nationwide attention, the boycott gave blacks throughout the country a model of social change built around the use of nonviolent collective action. James Forman ([1972] 1985) writes that "the boycott woke me to the real—not merely theoretical—possibility of building a nonviolent mass movement of Southern black people to fight segregation" (85). John Lewis recalls being enthralled as a youngster by news of the Montgomery boycott: "In the papers that we got in the public schools system in the library, I read *everything* about what was happening there, and it was really one of the most exciting, one of the most moving things to me to see just a few miles away the black folks of Montgomery stickin' together, refusing to ride segregated buses, walking the streets. It was a moving movement" (Raines 1977, 73).

However, the boycott was only the first act of a drama that would take a decade to unfold. Before it was over, this morality play would be replete with heroes and villains, examples of courage, selflessness, and sacrifice, but also of cruelty, brutality, and hatred, crisis points and turning points, moments of despair and defeat, exuberance and victory.

While all good stories deserve retelling, my intent has not been to recount the history of the civil rights movement. There already exist many excellent accounts detailing the personalities, politics, and events of that period. Instead I have used examples drawn from that and other movements throughout the book to illustrate a general model of the dynamics of public-spirited collective action. Therefore while my reference point for much of the discussion has been the civil rights movement, the arguments I made and the models I proposed pertain to the broader issue of mass political activism.

Two questions have guided this inquiry. First, what determines whether rational individuals will participate in public-spirited collective action? Second, how do individual decisions to join (or quit) a movement translate into collective outcomes?

To summarize, I argued that many of the choices facing participants in public-spirited collective action can be represented in game-theoretic terms. In the study of collective action in general, this in itself is not a new point of departure. Other analysts have commonly modeled instances of collective action as a prisoner's dilemma game. In this well-known game, it is in each player's self-interest not to cooperate with the other players irrespective of their cooperative or uncooperative behavior. Unfortunately, if each player acts selfishly, the collective outcome—mutual defection—is less desirable than if all had cooperated. Individual rationality defeats collective rationality.

Collective action in pursuit of public goods often constitutes a multiple-player prisoner's dilemma (or collective action) problem. Since noncontributors cannot be excluded from enjoying public goods to the same extent as contributors, no one has an incentive to contribute to the collective provision of the public good. Each individual instead prefers to let others supply the public good while he enjoys a free ride. Consequently collective action is difficult to initiate because people must be given some added incentive (a "selective incentive") to participate over and above the rewards they will derive from attaining the collective goal itself.

Public-spirited collective action, however, offers little in the way of direct tangible selective incentives. Rather, the most prominent benefits are usually social and psychological. Many people participate in causes out of a sense of obligation to their families, friends, and associates; they go along to get along, to repeat a trite but true aphorism. Because we frequently depend on others for our own well-being and comfort, our self-interest is often served by looking out for and caring for the interests of others. Decency, honesty, and fair play may be instrumental in satisfying many personal needs and interests in communities in which both good and bad faith are reciprocated in kind. For this reason, collective action is best examined within the context of ongoing social relationships and is more accurately modeled as an iterated game. One's best strategy must take into account the repeated exchanges and encounters that one will have with other members of the community. Consequently it can be in one's long-term interest to cooperate in collective endeavors if noncooperation results in damage to one's reputation, ostracism, or repudiation from the community.

We should note that opportunities for publicly validating one's social and political credentials and convictions do not appear very frequently in our lives. In our mundane affairs, we occasionally find ourselves in situations where we can play the Good Samaritan, come forth and perform a selfless deed for our fellow man, or be a minor hero in righting a small injustice. Whether we choose to do so in such circumstances reveals the kind of people we are, our virtues, our characters, and our moralities. But fairly or unfairly, these local dramas are not usually considered the litmus tests of our moral resolve. Those tests are administered in conjunction with the grand issues of our day involving the lives and fates of masses of people. Consequently one's ethical and political preferences can often be expressed only in the context of significant public, political, and social affairs.

The psychological benefits of participating in collective action are more difficult to specify. They pertain to the satisfaction people receive from being a part of a collective experience, especially when that experience has historic connotations. The civil rights movement was a great event, and one that many blacks as well as whites were sure not to miss. Political participation also instills feelings of efficacy, self-esteem, righteousness, and competence that are part and parcel of playing an active role in the affairs of society. Those who engage in political activism primarily to extract the psychological or expressive benefits may be behaving noninstrumentally in relation to the collective goals of the movement but instrumentally in a narrowly rational sense in relation to a variety of personal aspirations.

I argued that the promise of social and psychological benefits for cooperating in collective action alters the choices facing the potential activist. Instead of preferring to free ride regardless of how others behave, he prefers to act in conformity with others: if others cooperate, he wishes to cooperate; if they act selfishly, he wants to do the same. People in the civil rights movement did not choose free ridership; on the contrary, they preferred participation to inactivity under the right condition—the condition being, I argued, that enough others also participate to make collective action successful. For this reason I made the case that public-spirited collective action is better modeled as an assurance game in which people find it in their interest to personally participate when others do likewise. They still face many collective action problems, but these are of a kind different from those posed by the prisoner's dilemma.

A group that is trying to organize must be able to develop the prospects of collective action to a point where people feel obligated to cooperate and eager to participate in the cause. Social obligation is greatest in conjunction with movements that promise to reap benefits for the entire group. When collective action by a group can wrest concessions from the government or the opposition, then members of that group face a test of their character and resolve. But when collective action constitutes at best an ineffective symbolic protest, many will in good conscience refrain from participating.

By the same token, the participatory or expressive benefits of political activism will be trimmed when collective action garners few victories. Individuals who become involved for the collective and historic experience will withdraw disappointed unless they are periodically reinforced by gains made through collective action.

The conditional status of the rewards offered for political activism makes the organization of collective action challenging, even though people feel obligated or pressured by others not to free ride and even though they may derive considerable satisfaction from being involved in a cause. If collective action is to materialize under these circumstances, some group of leaders typically will have to step into the breach and build the movement to a point where others find it a worthy investment.

The game-theoretic analysis provided a simple schema for understanding the choices facing potential participants in collective action. The assurance problem highlighted the catch-22 facing groups that are trying to organize. In order to have any chance of winning concessions from the authorities, the group first has to organize and press its demands in the political arena; but the incentive for individuals to cooperate in an organized movement depends first on a demonstration that collective action is a worthwhile investment.

How do groups escape this catch-22? For this part of the analysis, I moved from games to a dynamic model using difference equations in order to model explicitly those factors that affect how the assurance problem (or game) confronting political activists will be played out. The model was used to explain a variety of disparate observations about collective action based on a small, consistent set of assumptions about the factors that motivate individuals to participate.

The model represents the assurance problem in terms of a supply-and-demand relationship between a group that is seeking social change and the authorities that are capable of providing it. According to the model, two principal factors inspire political activism: successful examples of collective action and successful past political mobilization. Both developments increase the prospects and therefore the attractiveness of collective action to those contemplating whether or not to participate.

The model also distinguishes the behavior of leaders from that of the followers in a social movement. Leaders become involved irrespective of the degree of success and the level of mobilization previously established by the movement. Followers, on the other hand, join collective action only in response to success and the existing level of mobilization. In other words, leaders act autonomously, while followers jump on the bandwagon, as well as respond to the contagion of the movement.

I made a number of deductions from this simple supply-and-demand model of collective action. These included a specification of the equilibrium level of political mobilization; the conditions under which the level of mobilization will stabilize at this equilibrium value; and the circumstances in which the level of mobilization will rise or decline monotonically, or oscillate, within or without bounds, over time.

Two conclusions pertaining to the initiation of collective action are of particular importance. First, "unconditional cooperators," whose actions are not contingent upon the actions of others, are usually needed to initiate collective action. Such individuals step into the breach and pay the heavy start-up costs, while everyone else waits for more favorable circumstances before contributing. Second, in the absence of immediate concessions, the movement will have to expand on the basis of factors other than its record of success. When there are few if any victories to publicize, nonparticipants are not able to jump on the bandwagon of success; instead, if the movement is to grow, they must join because of the contagiousness of the movement itself: in short, they must choose to participate because they think that enough other people are participating to make collective action worthwhile.

Moreover, participants cannot be too easily frustrated by their lack of success. A working assumption of the dynamic model is that the resilience of the protesters is directly correlated with the responsiveness of the authorities. What we saw, however, is that the linkage will have to be severed if the nascent movement is to survive beyond the initial period when resistance to political pressure is strongest. Unless the activists are sufficiently determined to weather the early storm, collective action will in all probability collapse.

The dynamics of collective action are such that we can expect a variety of strategies to be employed by political activists in their efforts to build and sustain a movement. Quick victories will be sought in order to buoy the spirits of the rank and file. The leaders of the movement will express optimism about the effectiveness of collective action; they will also exaggerate the degree of popular support behind the movement, the size of their organizations, and the number of participants at rallies and demonstrations in order to bolster perceptions of the movement's potential among both followers and the opposition. The more successful the movement is believed to be, the more attractive it becomes to potential supporters and the more attention it will receive from the authorities.

In addition to trying to intimidate the authorities, the leadership will portray them as being pliable and susceptible to political pressure. The message to the rank and file will be that coordination will be rewarded with significant concessions; collective action will not be a futile gesture.

Tactics that work will diffuse and be imitated by different branches of the movement. Moreover, tactics that are effective in one setting will prove increasingly effective in subsequent confrontations until unfriendly authorities learn new methods to counteract them. Before such countermeasures are developed, the authorities will realize that it is in their interest to avoid a protracted conflict in which they will ultimately be the losers.

For their part, unsympathetic authorities will try to stonewall the activists by avoiding negotiations with them and denying them the concessions that would breathe new life into the movement. They may try to repress key leaders within the movement and interfere with the development of political and social organizations.

The end result of these strategies is a contest of wills in which each side attempts to outlast the other. The activists try to sustain their pressure long enough to force the authorities to the bargaining table, while the authorities implement measures that increase the cost of participation and discourage the protesters from persisting.

In my analysis of the origins of the civil rights movement, I showed that political mobilization was facilitated by the development of strong organizations and effective leadership as well as the ability of forerunners of the movement to win both symbolic and substantive concessions from local authorities and the federal government.

Black organizations and institutions helped to coordinate the preferences and actions of those who supported the civil rights movement. The growth of these organizations, such as the church, black colleges, and civil rights groups, was facilitated by the large-scale migration of blacks, starting in the 1930s, from the rural South to southern cities and urban centers in the North in pursuit of industrial and wartime employment. The black population became geographically concentrated as a result and began to acquire the financial resources necessary to develop and nurture the indigenous institutions and organizations that were essential to the movement. The segregation of blacks in the cities reduced their susceptibility to racial violence and oppression and gave them the autonomy needed to undertake a challenge to the social order.

But spontaneous collaboration did not occur within the civil rights movement, nor is it likely to occur in any instance of collective action that demands a substantial investment from the participants. Before the civil rights movement was possible, black leaders, civil rights organizations, and other liberal elites such as the scientific and intellectual communities had the difficult task of defining, and often reformulating, the nature of the race problem in this country. Large segments of the black population that had been persuaded by the prevailing propaganda to blame themselves habitually for their inferior status had to be taught to locate the source of their problems within the institutions of society.

In general, absolute levels of economic deprivation, inequality of opportunity, government incompetence, or a variety of other indicators of social decline are not as important in generating social unrest as the manner in which people come to interpret these facts. This is because the health of a nation is measured against standards that people set according to their notion of what social conditions are conceivable or possible within the context of the times. Feelings of deprivation and dissatisfaction are thus a consequence of counterfactual images that people hold of the way society ought to be, or could be, with the right leadership or the proper system of organization. Naturally these standards of comparison have been appropriately modified as the conditions of living have been generally improved throughout the world during the modern era. The same material circumstances that have given rise in the twentieth century to feelings of outrage and injustice and ultimately to social movements and revolts would have been construed in earlier centuries as the height of comfort and privilege.

For this reason we ought to be highly skeptical about the possibility of discovering any constant combination of objective factors in a society which will predictably set off a chain of events leading up to a collective movement. Rather, we will have to consider not only the conditions of the society but also the symbolic interpretations and judgments that people at that time make of them (Boulding 1956). All this, of course, is just another way of saying that people tend to experience relative deprivation rather than any absolute level of deprivation measured against a constant reference point. James C. Davies (1962) has captured this idea neatly in discussing the importance people place on the contrast between their expectations for themselves and the actual quality of their lives; when the gap exceeds some tolerable threshold, people are driven to do something in order to redress the imbalance.

Under this assumption, collective action can be stimulated in quite a variety of different objective circumstances—even, paradoxically, when economic growth is on the rise; such "revolutions of rising expectations" occur when the rate of social and economic improvement is not fast enough in the minds of the citizens. Without suggesting that the momentous English, American, French, and Russian revolutions were attributable solely to this factor, Crane Brinton (1938) points out that each of the revolts occurred at a time when the material condition of life in the society was on the whole improving.

World War II not only had a structural impact, causing massive relocation of blacks in response to the demands of the war economy, it also had monumental psychological ramifications. The wartime economy raised the economic status and standard of living of blacks, and in the process elevated the expectations they had concerning the quality of their lives. The new life circumstances of blacks in the rapidly modernizing industrial cities were accompanied by a revised outlook on their place in American society. "Freed from the confines of a rigid caste system and subject to urban formative experiences, blacks developed new norms and beliefs. Aggression could be turned against one's oppressor rather than against one's self, more employment and educational opportunities could be secured, and political power could be mobilized" (Sitkoff 1981, 15). The country as a whole had undergone the collective experience of defending liberty and democracy against the forces of fascism and totalitarianism. The war had been more than a physical contest between opposing military forces, it had also been a propaganda war of competing ideals and ideologies. For the country in general, but especially for black Americans, the war experience heightened the contrast between the ideals of American society and the harsh realities—segregation, discrimination, mob violence, lynchings, and political disenfranchisement—that it offered to its black citizens.

In his fine study of the civil rights movement, McAdam (1982) explicitly partitions these two factors. The institutional changes in the black community, he writes, only created the "structural potential" for collective action. In other words, while preestablished organizations, associations, and social networks ease the task of mobilizing people for collective action, they do not ensure that people will actually take the initiative. For the movement to take off, members of the aggrieved group also have to share a belief that collective action is an effective method of addressing their problems (105–6).

However, optimism among civil rights activists about the effectiveness of collective action could not have been sustained indefinitely without a real increase in the federal government's responsiveness to the plight of blacks. Organization without access is a dead end. The lifeblood of collective action is its ability to extract concessions—symbolic as well as tangible—from the opposition or the government. The expressive benefits that political activists receive from simply voicing their demands are always short-lived in the absence of identifiable effects. Until the 1930s, Congress, the courts, and the administration were at best indifferent and at worst hostile to the interests and aspirations of black Americans. This situation did not change until civil rights organizations gained strength and the black population acquired electoral power as a consequence of their migration into northern cities. These developments, in conjunction with the liberally disposed FDR administration, gave blacks a degree of access to government that they had never before enjoyed.

The increased responsiveness of all three branches of the federal government in the 1930s and 1940s to black demands fueled the organizational efforts of the inchoate civil rights movement. As blacks saw their efforts paying dividends, they stepped up their pressure and broadened their demands for social change. The spiraling relationship between supply and demand peaked in the first half of the 1960s during the Johnson and Kennedy administrations. This was the heyday of the movement, when the federal government finally realized that it would have to take the initiative and intervene aggressively in the South, and when the civil rights movement attracted the sympathy and support of large segments of the population throughout the country. In this brief but brilliant phase, the civil rights movement captured both the support of large segments of the public and the sponsorship of the government.

But why did the movement collapse? Only because it succeeded too well. Successful collective action pays a stream of material, social, and psychological benefits to participants in the movement. As the goals of the movement are achieved, however, new and equally attractive—and equally feasible—goals have to be devised to ensure the continued contribution of current members. Unless the new generation of goals displays the same luster as the earlier goals, participation in the movement will no longer carry the same participatory benefits that accrue to those who take part in "historic" or memorable causes. Furthermore, if the new set of goals are not as practicable as the earlier ones, then supporters of the cause will feel less obligated to lend their time and energy to fighting for them. Most people are reluctant to participate in lost causes. Unfortunately, to tired radicals who are satisfied with their efforts or disappointed over the impact of their achievements, no new agenda may be sufficiently attractive for them to want to sustain their level of commitment and participation. Consequently in the latter stages of the movement, the benefits of cooperation become almost as obscure as they were in the initial period of collective action when little of consequence could be gained through collaboration.

Many of these problems arose at the close of the civil rights movement. The success of the movement produced contentment in some and frustration in others. There was renewed disagreement over the best strategy to further the cause. The movement ran short of ideas and projects that could involve mass participation; and it encountered a new set of problems that was even more resistant to resolution than legalized segregation and discrimination. Therefore it is no surprise that this new phase of the movement proved less compelling than the last. Problems with long-term solutions do not lend themselves to the short-term reinforcement schedule that is often required to nurture large-scale political activism. In the absence of such periodic rewards, the benefits of participation diminish, and the obligation to contribute weakens.

References

Adams, J. Stacy. 1965. "Inequality in Social Exchange." In *Advances in Experimental Social Psychology,* Vol. 3, ed. Leonard Berkowitz, 267–99. New York: Academic Press.

Amis, Kingsley. 1953. *Lucky Jim.* New York: Penguin.

Aptheker, Herbert. 1989. *Abolitionism: A Revolutionary Movement.* Boston: Twayne Publishers.

Axelrod, Robert. 1981. "The Emergence of Cooperation Among Egoists." *American Political Science Review* 75: 306–18.

————. 1984. *The Evolution of Cooperation.* New York: Basic Books.

Barkan, Steven E. 1984. "Legal Control of the Southern Civil Rights Movement." *American Sociological Review* 49: 552–65.

Barnes, Catharine A. 1983. *Journey From Jim Crow.* New York: Columbia University Press.

Barry, Brian. 1978. *Sociologists, Economists, and Democracy.* Chicago: University of Chicago Press.

Becker, Howard S. 1960. "Notes on the Concept of Commitment." *American Journal of Sociology* 66: 32–40.

Benn, Stanley I. 1979. "The Problematic Rationality of Political Participation." In *Philosophy, Politics, and Society,* 5th series, ed. Peter Laslett and James Fishkin. New Haven: Yale University Press.

Berger, Phil. 1990. "Tyson's Tactics in Ring Questioned." *New York Times,* 13 February, sec. B, p. 10.

Binder, David. 1989. "Leipzig: Where Indignation Has Transformed Politics." *New York Times,* 6 December, p. 11.

Blumberg, Herbert H. 1968. "Accounting for a Nonviolent Mass Demonstration." In *Nonviolent Direct Action,* ed. A. Paul Hare and Herbert H. Blumberg. Washington and Cleveland: Corpus Books.

Boulding, Kenneth E. 1956. *The Image: Knowledge in Life and Society.* Ann Arbor: University of Michigan Press.

Branch, Taylor. 1988. *Parting the Waters.* New York: Simon and Schuster.

Brinton, Crane. 1938. *The Anatomy of Revolution.* New York: Norton.

Brown, Roger. 1965. *Social Psychology.* New York: Free Press.

Burstein, Paul. 1979. "Public Opinion, Demonstrations, and the Passage of Antidiscrimination Legislation." *Public Opinion Quarterly* 43: 157–72.

Carson, Clayborne. 1981. *In Struggle: SNCC and the Black Awakening of the 1960s.* Cambridge: Harvard University Press.

Chafe, William H. 1980. *Civilities and Civil Rights.* New York: Oxford University Press.

———. 1982. "The Civil Rights Revolution, 1945–1960: The Gods Bring Threads to Webs Begun." In *Reshaping America: Society and Institutions, 1945–1960,* ed. Robert H. Bremner and Gary N. Reichard. Columbus: Ohio State University Press.

Chicago Tribune. 1987. "Strike Notes." 30 September, sec. 4, p. 6.

Cicero. 1971. *On the Good Life.* New York: Penguin Books.

Clark, Kenneth B. 1966. "The Civil Rights Movement: Momentum and Organizations." *Daedalus* 95: 239–67.

Colburn, David R. 1985. *Racial Change and Community Crisis.* New York: Columbia University Press.

Cook, Constance Ewing. 1984. "Participation in Public Interest Groups: Membership Motivations." *American Politics Quarterly* 12: 409–30.

Davies, James C. 1962. "Toward a Theory of Revolution." *American Sociological Review* 27: 5–18.

Dawes, Robyn M. 1980. "Social Dilemmas." *Annual Review of Psychology* 31:169–93.

Dawes, Robyn M. and John M. Orbell. 1982. "Cooperation in Social Dilemma Situations: Thinking About It Doesn't Help." *Research in Experimental Economics* 2: 167–73.

Degler, Carl. 1980. *At Odds.* Oxford: Oxford University Press.

D'Emilio, John. 1983. *Sexual Politics, Sexual Communities.* Chicago: University of Chicago Press.

DeNardo, James. 1985. *Power in Numbers.* Princeton: Princeton University Press.

Dillon, Morton L. 1974. *The Abolitionists.* De Kalb: Northern Illinois University Press.

Eisinger, Peter K. 1973. "The Conditions of Protest Behavior in American Cities." *American Political Science Review* 67: 11–28.

Elster, Jon. 1979. *Ulysses and the Sirens.* Cambridge: Cambridge University Press.

———. 1983. *Sour Grapes: Studies in the Subversion of Rationality.* Cambridge: Cambridge University Press.

———. 1985. "Rationality, Morality, and Collective Action." *Ethics* 96: 136–55.

———. 1989. *The Cement of Society.* Cambridge: Cambridge University Press.

Elster, Jon, ed. 1986. *Rational Choice.* New York: New York University Press.

Evans, Sara. 1979. *Personal Politics.* New York: Vintage Books.

Fager, Charles E. 1974. *Selma 1965.* New York: Charles Scribner's Sons.

Fairclough, Adam. 1987. *To Redeem the Soul of America*. Athens: University of Georgia Press.

Fantasia, Rick. 1988. *Cultures of Solidarity*. Berkeley: University of California Press.

Farmer, James. 1985. *Lay Bare the Heart: An Autobiography of the Civil Rights Movement*. New York: New American Library.

Filler, Louis. 1978. *Vanguards and Followers*. Chicago: Nelson-Hall.

Fireman, Bruce, and William A. Gamson. 1979. "Utilitarian Logic in the Resource Mobilization Perspective." In *The Dynamics of Social Movements*, ed. Mayer N. Zald and J. D. McCarthy, 8–44. Cambridge: Winthrop Publishers.

Fishman, Jacob R., and Frederic Solomon. 1968. "The Student Sit-In Movement." In *Nonviolent Direct Action*, ed. A. Paul Hare and Herbert Blumberg, 362–80. Washington, D.C.: Corpus Books.

Fitzgerald. Michael W. 1989. *The Union League Movement in the Deep South*. Baton Rouge: Louisiana State University Press.

Forman, James. [1972] 1985. *The Making of Black Revolutionaries*. Washington, D.C.: Open Hand Publishing.

Frank, Robert H. 1987. "If *Homo Economicus* Could Choose His Own Utility Function, Would He Want One With a Conscience?" *American Economic Review* 77: 593–604.

———. 1988. *Passions Within Reason*. New York: Norton.

Frazier, Franklin E. 1963. *The Negro Church in America*. New York: Schocken Books.

Freeman, Jo. 1975. *The Politics of Women's Liberation*. New York: David McKay Company.

Frohlich, Norman, Joe A. Oppenheimer, and Oran R. Young. 1971. *Political Leadership and Collective Goods*. Princeton: Princeton University Press.

Gale, Richard P. 1986. "Social Movements and the State: The Environmental Movement, Counter-Movement, and Governmental Agencies." *Sociological Perspectives* 29: 202–40.

Garrow, David J. 1978. *Protest at Selma*. New Haven: Yale University Press.

———. 1986. *Bearing the Cross*. New York: Vintage Books.

Genovese, Eugene D. 1974. *Roll, Jordan, Roll*. New York: Vintage Books.

Goffman, Erving. 1963. *Stigma*. Englewood Cliffs, N. J.: Prentice-Hall.

———. 1967. *Interaction Ritual*. New York: Anchor Books.

———. 1971. *Relations in Public*. New York: Basic Books.

Goldberg, Samuel. 1958. *Introduction to Difference Equations*. New York: John Wiley.

Goldman, Peter. 1970. *Report from Black America*. New York: Simon and Schuster.

Goode, William J. 1978. *The Celebration of Heroes*. Berkeley: University of California Press.

Granovetter, Mark. 1978. "Threshold Models of Collective Behavior." *American Journal of Sociology* 83: 1420–43.

Granovetter, Mark, and Roland Soong. 1983. "Threshold Models of Diffusion and Collective Behavior." *Journal of Mathematical Sociology* 9: 165–79.

Greene, Graham. 1985. *The Tenth Man.* New York: Simon and Schuster.

Gross, F. 1958. *The Seizure of Political Power in a Century of Revolutions.* New York: Philosophical Library.

Haberman, Clyde. 1987. "Sound and Fury, and Now the First Death." *New York Times,* 21 June, p. 12.

Hampton, Jean. 1987. "Free-Rider Problems in the Production of Collective Goods." *Economics and Philosophy* 3: 245–73.

Hardin, Russell. 1971. "Collective Action as an Agreeable *n*-Prisoners' Dilemma." *Behavioral Science* 16: 472–81.

———. 1982. *Collective Action.* Baltimore: Johns Hopkins University Press.

———. 1985. "Individual Sanctions, Collective Benefits." In *Paradoxes of Rationality and Cooperation: Prisoner's Dilemma and Newcomb's Problem,* ed. Richmond Campbell and Lanning Sowden, 339–54. Vancouver: University of British Columbia Press.

Harsanyi, John C. 1969. "Rational-Choice Models of Political Behavior vs. Functionalist and Conformist Theories." *World Politics* 21: 513–38.

Hechter, Michael. 1987. *Principles of Group Solidarity.* Berkeley: University of California Press.

Hill, Thomas E., Jr. 1979. "Symbolic Protest and Calculated Silence." *Philosophy and Public Affairs* 9: 83–102.

Hirschman, Albert O. 1982. *Shifting Involvements.* Princeton: Princeton University Press.

———. 1985. "Against Parsimony: Three Easy Ways of Complicating Some Categories of Economic Discourse." *Economics and Philosophy* 1:7–21.

Hodgson, Godfrey. 1976. *America in Our Time.* New York: Vintage Books.

Hofstadter, Douglas. 1985. "The Prisoner's Dilemma, Computer Tournaments, and the Evolution of Cooperation." In Douglas Hofstadter, *Metamagical Themas,* 715–34. New York: Basic Books.

Homans, George C. 1974. *Social Behavior: Its Elementary Forms.* New York: Harcourt Brace Jovanovich.

Hume, David. [1739–40] 1969. *A Treatise of Human Nature.* New York: Penguin Books.

Jacoway, Elizabeth, and David R. Colburn, ed. 1982. *Southern Businessmen and Desegregation.* Baton Rouge: Louisiana State University Press.

Janis, Irving. 1972. *Victims of Groupthink.* Boston: Houghton Mifflin.

Jenkins, J. Craig. 1983. "Resource Mobilization Theory and the Study of Social Movements." *Annual Review of Sociology* 9: 527–53.

Jenkins, J. Craig, and Charles Perrow. 1977. "Insurgency of the Powerless: Farm Workers' Movements, 1946–1972." *American Sociological Review* 42: 249–68.

Kennedy, David M. 1970. *Birth Control in America: The Career of Margaret Sanger.* New Haven: Yale University Press.

King, Martin Luther, Jr. 1965. "Behind the Selma March." *Saturday Review,* 3 April, pp. 16–17 and 57.

King, Mary. 1987. *Freedom Song.* New York: William Morrow and Company.

Klehr, Harvey. 1984. *The Heyday of American Communism: The Depression Decade.* New York: Basic Books.

Klosko, George. 1987. "The Principle of Fairness and Political Obligation." *Ethics* 97: 353–62.

Kolata, Gina. 1990. "Under Pressures and Stigma, More Doctors Shun Abortion." *New York Times,* 8 January, pp. 1, 11.

Krebs, Dennis. 1982. "Psychological Approaches to Altruism: An Evaluation." *Ethics* 92: 447–58.

Kreps, David M., Paul Milgrom, John Roberts, and Robert Wilson. 1982. "Rational Cooperation in the Finitely Repeated Prisoners' Dilemma." *Journal of Economic Theory* 27: 245–52.

Kreps, David M., and Robert Wilson. 1982. "Reputation and Imperfect Information." *Journal of Economic Theory* 27: 253–79.

Kristof, Nicholas D. 1989. "Organization Woes Slow China's Student Protesters." *New York Times,* 1 May, pp. 1, 7.

Laver, Michael. 1981. *The Politics of Private Desires.* New York: Penguin Books.

LeBon, Gustav. [1895] 1960. *The Crowd.* New York: Penguin Books.

Lelyveld, Joseph. 1985. *Move Your Shadow.* New York: Elisabeth Sifton Books.

Leuchtenburg, William E. 1958. *The Perils of Prosperity, 1914–32.* Chicago: University of Chicago Press.

Lewis, Anthony (and the *New York Times*). 1964. *Portrait of a Decade: The Second American Revolution.* New York: Random House.

Lewis, David. 1969. *Convention: A Philosophical Study.* Cambridge: Harvard University Press.

Lewis, David. 1970. *King: A Critical Biography.* New York: Praeger.

Little, Bradford. 1968. "Walk Leader Describes Albany's Police State." In *Nonviolent Direct Action,* ed. A. Paul Hare and Herbert H. Blumberg. Washington, D.C.: Corpus Books.

Luce, R. Duncan, and Howard Raiffa. 1957. *Games and Decisions.* New York: Wiley.

Luker, Kristin. 1984. *Abortion and the Politics of Motherhood.* Berkeley: University of California Press.

Mansbridge, Jane J. 1986. *Why We Lost the ERA.* Chicago: University of Chicago Press.

Margolis, Howard. 1982. *Selfishness, Altruism, and Rationality.* Cambridge: Cambridge University Press.

Marwell, Gerald, Pamela E. Oliver, and Ralph Prahl. 1988. "Social Networks and Collective Action: A Theory of the Critical Mass, III." *American Journal of Sociology* 94: 502–34.

Matthews, Donald, and James Prothro. 1966. *Negroes and the New Southern Politics.* New York: Harcourt, Brace & World.

Matusow, Allen J. 1984. *The Unraveling of America.* New York: Harper & Row.

McAdam, Doug. 1982. *Political Process and the Development of Black Insurgency 1930–1970.* Chicago: University of Chicago Press.

———. 1983. "Tactical Innovation and the Pace of Insurgency." *American Sociological Review* 48: 735–54.

———. 1986. "Recruitment to High-Risk Activism: The Case of Freedom Summer." *American Journal of Sociology* 92: 64–90.

———. 1988. "Social Movements." In *Handbook of Sociology,* ed. Neil J. Smelser, 695–737. Beverly Hills: Sage.

McCarthy, John D., and Mayer Zald. 1976. "Resource Mobilization and Social Movements: A Partial Theory." *American Journal of Sociology* 82: 1212–41.

McNall, Scott G. 1988. *The Road to Rebellion.* Chicago: University of Chicago Press.

McPhee, William. 1966. "When Culture Becomes a Business." In *Sociological Theories in Progress,* vol. 1, ed. Joseph Berger, Morris Zelditch, Jr., and Bo Anderson. Boston: Houghton Mifflin.

Mehta, Ved. 1976. *Mahatma Gandhi and His Apostles.* New York: Penguin Books.

Meier, August. 1970. "Who Are the 'True Believers'?—A Tentative Typology of the Motivation of Civil Rights Activists." In *Protest, Reform, and Revolt,* ed. Joseph R. Gusfield. New York: Wiley.

Meier, August, and Elliott Rudwick. 1969. "The Boycott Movement Against Jim Crow Streetcars in the South, 1900–1906." *Journal of American History* 55: 756–75.

———. 1975. *CORE: A Study in the Civil Rights Movement 1942–1968.* Urbana: University of Illinois Press.

Miller, William R. 1968. *Martin Luther King. Jr.: His Life, Martyrdom, and Meaning for the World.* New York: Avon.

Moore, Barrington. 1978. *Injustice: The Social Bases of Obedience and Revolt.* New York: M. E. Sharpe.

Morris, Aldon. 1981. "Black Southern Student Sit-In Movement: An Analysis of Internal Organization." *American Sociological Review* 46: 744–67.

———. 1984. *The Origin of the Civil Rights Movement.* New York: Free Press.

Morris, Charles R. 1984. *A Time of Passion: America 1960–1980.* New York: Harper & Row.

Nelkin, Dorothy, and Michael Pollak. 1981. *The Atom Besieged.* Cambridge: MIT Press.

Newfield, Jack. 1966. *A Prophetic Minority.* New York: Signet.

Newsweek. 1963. "The Negro in America." 29 July, pp. 15–36.

Norrell, Robert J. 1985. *Reaping the Whirlwind.* New York: Vintage Books.

Oates, Stephen B. 1982. *Let the Trumpet Sound: The Life of Martin Luther King, Jr.* New York: Harper & Row.

Oberschall, Anthony. 1973. *Social Conflict and Social Movements.* Englewood Cliffs, N.J.: Prentice-Hall.

———. 1978a. "The Decline of the 1960s Social Movements." *Research in Social Movements, Conflicts, and Change* 1: 257–89.

———. 1978b. "Theories of Social Conflict." *Annual Review of Sociology* 4: 291–315.

———. 1980. "Loosely Structured Collective Conflict: A Theory and an Application." *Research in Social Movements, Conflicts, and Change* 3: 45–68.

———. 1989. "The 1960 Sit-Ins: Protest Diffusion and Movement Take-Off." *Research in Social Movements, Conflicts, and Change* 11: 31–53.

Oliver, Pamela, Gerald Marwell, and Ruy Teixeira. 1985. "A Theory of the Critical Mass. I. Interdependence, Group Heterogeneity, and the Production of Collective Action." *American Journal of Sociology* 91: 522–56.

Olson, Mancur, Jr. [1965] 1971. *The Logic of Collective Action.* Cambridge: Harvard University Press. Reprinted with a new app., 1971.

Parfit, Derek. 1986. "Prudence, Morality, and Prisoner's Dilemma." In *Rational Choice,* ed. Jon Elster, 34–59. New York: New York University Press.

Piven, Frances F., and Richard A. Cloward. 1977. *Poor People's Movements: How They Succeed, Why Some Fail.* New York: Vintage Books.

Popkin, Samuel. 1979. *The Rational Peasant.* Berkeley: University of California Press.

———. 1988. "Political Entrepreneurs and Peasant Movements in Vietnam." In *Rationality and Revolution,* ed. Michael Taylor, 9–61. Cambridge: Cambridge University Press.

Quarles, Benjamin. 1969. *Black Abolitionists.* Oxford: Oxford University Press.

Raines, Howell. 1977. *My Soul is Rested.* New York: G. P. Putnam's Sons.

Rapoport, Anatol. 1970. *N-Person Game Theory.* Ann Arbor: University of Michigan Press.

Rapoport, Anatol, and Albert M. Chammah. 1970. *Prisoner's Dilemma.* Ann Arbor: University of Michigan Press.

Rosenstone, Robert A. 1975. *Romantic Revolutionary: A Biography of John Reed.* New York: Vintage Books.

Schattschneider, E. E. 1960. *The Semi-Sovereign People.* New York: Holt, Rinehart and Winston.

Schechter, Betty. 1963. *The Peaceable Revolution.* Boston: Houghton Mifflin.

Schelling, Thomas C. 1960. *The Strategy of Conflict.* Cambridge: Oxford University Press.

————. 1966. *Arms and Influence*. New Haven: Yale University Press.

————. 1973. "Hockey Helmets, Concealed Weapons, and Daylight Savings." *Journal of Conflict Resolution* 17: 381–428.

————. 1978. *Micromotives and Macrobehavior*. New York: W. W. Norton.

————. 1980. "The Intimate Contest for Self-Command." *The Public Interest* 60: 94–118.

Schlesinger, Arthur, Jr. 1965. *A Thousand Days: John F. Kennedy in the White House*. Boston: Houghton Mifflin.

Schmemann, Serge. 1989. "Deja Vu in Prague." *New York Times*, 28 November, p.6.

Schofield, N. 1985. "Anarchy, Altruism and Cooperation: A Review." *Social Choice and Welfare* 2: 207–19.

Scitovsky, Tibor. 1976. *The Joyless Economy*. New York: Oxford University Press.

Scott, James C. 1985. *Weapons of the Weak: Everyday Forms of Peasant Resistance*. New Haven: Yale University Press.

Scriven, Michael. 1966. *Primary Philosophy*. New York: McGraw-Hill.

Sen, Amartya K. 1967. "Isolation, Assurance, and the Social Rate of Discount." *Quarterly Journal of Economics* 80: 112–24.

————. 1973. "Behavior and the Concept of Preference." *Economica* 40: 241–59.

————. 1974. "Choice, Orderings, and Morality." In *Practical Reason*, ed. Stephan Korner, 54–67. Oxford: Basil Blackwell.

————. 1977. "Rational Fools: A Critique of the Behavioral Foundations of Economic Theory." *Philosophy and Public Affairs* 6: 317–44.

Sexton, Joe. 1990. "What Do You Expect From the Son of a Legend? Brett Hull Delivers." *New York Times*, 8 January, p. 35.

Sitkoff, Harvard. 1978. *A New Deal for Blacks*. New York: Oxford University Press.

————. 1981. *The Struggle for Black Equality: 1954–1980*. New York: Hill and Wang.

Smelser, Neil. 1962. *Theory of Collective Behavior*. New York: Free Press.

Song, Y., and T. Yarbrough. 1978. "Tax Ethics and Taxpayer Attitudes: A Survey." *Public Administration Review* 38: 442–51.

Stark, Rodney. 1972. *Police Riots*. Belmont, CA: Focus Books.

Steinbeck, John. 1936. *In Dubious Battle*. New York: Penguin Books.

Sundquist, James L. 1968. *Politics and Policy*. Washington, D.C.: Brookings Institution.

Taylor, D. Garth. 1986. *Public Opinion and Collective Action*. Chicago: University of Chicago Press.

Taylor, Michael. 1976. *Anarchy and Cooperation*. London: Wiley.

————. 1982. *Community, Anarchy, and Liberty*. Cambridge: Cambridge University Press.

————. 1987. *The Possibility of Cooperation.* Cambridge: Cambridge University Press.

————. 1988. "Rationality and Revolutionary Collective Action." In *Rationality and Revolution,* ed. Michael Taylor, 63–97. Cambridge: Cambridge University Press.

Taylor, Michael, and Hugh Ward. 1982. "Chicken, Whales, and Lumpy Goods: Alternative Models of Public Goods Provision." *Political Studies* 30: 350–70.

Thomas, George B., and Ross L. Finney. 1979. *Calculus and Analytic Geometry.* 5th edition. Reading, MA: Addison-Wesley.

Thornton, J. Mills, III. 1980. "Challenge and Response in the Montgomery Bus Boycott of 1955–56." *Alabama Review* 33: 163–235.

Toner, Robin. 1989. "Right to Abortion Draws Thousands to Capital Rally." *New York Times,* 10 April, pp. 1, 8.

Tullock, Gordon. 1971. "The Paradox of Revolution." *Public Choice* 11: 89–99.

Turner, Ralph H. 1981. "Collective Behavior and Resource Mobilization as Approaches to Social Movements: Issues and Continuities." *Research in Social Movements, Conflicts, and Change* 4: 1–24.

Twain, Mark. 1985. *Adventures of Huckleberry Finn.* Berkeley: University of California Press.

Ullmann-Margalit, Edna. 1977. *The Emergence of Norms.* Oxford: Oxford University Press.

White, James W. 1988. "Rational Rioters: Leaders, Followers, and Popular Protest in Early Modern Japan." *Politics and Society* 16: 35–69.

White, John. 1985. *Black Leadership in America 1895–1968.* New York: Longman Group Limited.

Wilkins, Roy (with Tom Mathews). 1982. *Standing Fast: The Autobiography of Roy Wilkins.* New York: Viking.

Williams, Juan. 1987. *Eyes on the Prize.* New York: Viking.

Wilson, James Q. 1973. *Political Organizations.* New York: Basic Books.

Wolff, Miles. 1970. *Lunch at the Five and Ten.* New York: Stein & Day.

Woodward, C. Vann. 1967. "What Happened to the Civil Rights Movement?" *Harper's,* January, pp. 29–37.

————. 1974. *The Strange Career of Jim Crow.* 3d edition. Oxford: Oxford University Press.

Wright, George C. 1982. "Desegregation of Public Accommodations in Louisville." In *Southern Businessmen and Desegregation,* ed. Elizabeth Jacoway and David R. Colburn, 191–210. Baton Rouge: Louisiana State University Press.

WuDunn, Shirley. 1989. "A Million Chinese March, Adding Pressure for Change: Resolute Student Protesters Are Now the Pride of Beijing." *New York Times,* 18 May, pp. 1, 6.

Ya'ari, Ehud. 1989. "Israel's Prison Academies." Translated by Ina Friedman. *The Atlantic,* October, pp. 22, 24, 26–27, 30.

Zurcher, Louis A., and David A. Snow. 1981. "Collective Behavior: Social Movements." In *Social Psychology: Sociological Perspectives,* ed. Morris Rosenberg and Ralph H. Turner, 447–82. New York: Basic Books.

Index